Redemptive Hybridism in Post-Postmodern Writing

Redemptive Hybridism in Post-Postmodern Writing

Tasha Haines

BLOOMSBURY ACADEMIC
NEW YORK • LONDON • OXFORD • NEW DELHI • SYDNEY

BLOOMSBURY ACADEMIC
Bloomsbury Publishing Inc, 1385 Broadway, New York, NY 10018, USA
Bloomsbury Publishing Plc, 50 Bedford Square, London, WC1B 3DP, UK
Bloomsbury Publishing Ireland, 29 Earlsfort Terrace, Dublin 2, D02 AY28, Ireland

BLOOMSBURY, BLOOMSBURY ACADEMIC and the Diana logo are
trademarks of Bloomsbury Publishing Plc

First published in the United States of America 2023
This paperback edition published 2025

Copyright © Tasha Haines, 2023

Cover design: Eleanor Rose
Cover Image by Tasha Haines.

All rights reserved. No part of this publication may be: i) reproduced or transmitted in any form, electronic or mechanical, including photocopying, recording or by means of any information storage or retrieval system without prior permission in writing from the publishers; or ii) used or reproduced in any way for the training, development or operation of artificial intelligence (AI) technologies, including generative AI technologies. The rights holders expressly reserve this publication from the text and data mining exception as per Article 4(3) of the Digital Single Market Directive (EU) 2019/790.

Bloomsbury Publishing Inc does not have any control over, or responsibility for, any third-party websites referred to or in this book. All internet addresses given in this book were correct at the time of going to press. The author and publisher regret any inconvenience caused if addresses have changed or sites have ceased to exist, but can accept no responsibility for any such changes.

Library of Congress Cataloging-in-Publication Data

A catalogue record for this book is available from the Library of Congress.

ISBN: HB: 978-1-5013-9450-8
PB: 978-1-5013-9454-6
ePDF: 978-1-5013-9452-2
eBook: 978-1-5013-9451-5

Typeset by Integra Software Services Pvt. Ltd.

For product safety related questions contact productsafety@bloomsbury.com.

To find out more about our authors and books visit www.bloomsbury.com
and sign up for our newsletters.

For Kelvin and Maisie, with boundless gratitude and love.

With heart-felt thanks to Marion May Campbell, each inspirational writer here, and the team at Bloomsbury Academic.

Contents

Preface	ix
List of Abbreviations	x
Introduction: The Enemy Within	1
Taking enemies in	1
This multivariant plot	5
The vitality of difference	7
A lineage of wariness and influence	9
The terrible postmodern party	14

Part 1   Features of Redemptive Hybridism

1	The Redemptive Textual Body	23
	Etymologically speaking	23
	Umbilical connection, author to text	29
	The Word made flesh	37
2	The Hybrid Middle	45
	Pushing out towards ends	45
	Sarraute as middle	47
	Parataxis and the middle	54
	Time and unfinishedness	58
3	Family Traits of Fragmentation	65
	The fragmented mind	67
	Constraint, minimalism, and the caveat	70
	Vestibule and fringe	73
	Ethics, alterity, and the reader	76
	The ethical, the moral, and the difference	78
	High, low, high, low, it's off to blend we go . . .	82

Part 2 Figures of Redemptive Hybridism

4 Woolf's Atom; the Image of Hybridity — 91
Begin with the atom, Virginia Woolf — 91
Saturation in Woolf and Wallace — 94
Mrs Dalloway as fertile ground — 96
Inter-genre Woolf — 101
It ends where it begins, with the atom — 105

5 Finding a Name for Possibility — 109
Postmodernism, feminism, and agency — 109
Finding names and building frames — 112
Call me[a]taxy: some recent pre-fixes — 119

6 *The Pale King*'s Constellation; Factoids, Ghosts, and Boredom — 123
Tell the truth, David Foster Wallace — 123
Everyday ghosts, souls, and phantoms — 132
Ambiguity and contradiction in *The Pale King* — 137
Boredom: between crisis and epiphany — 140

A Conclusion, of Sorts: This Is Not the End — 147

References — 155
Index — 162

Preface

During the twenty-first century, there is an increase in—even a mainstreaming of—genre collapse and collaboration by which we might move closer to others and ourselves.

Simultaneity and contradiction produce some of the everyday signifiers of *ourselves* as hybridizing in this post-postmodern era where truth and lies or high and low blur as they always have done; the difference is that now you can buy hybrid texts at airport kiosks. Previously, in the long and broad postmodern paradigm, hybrid methodologies made histories contingent, they gaslit memory and deconstructed truth. But the vast possibilities of hybrid forms and hybridizing practice are more urgent than ever before (which of course no one can prove); they are *redemptive* apropos of possibility, and a unifying celebration of difference.

While there had always been *hybridity* (a generic word needing application) and hybrid forms (less generic), the world now fits inside our smart phone; that ubiquitous hybridizing mode for the consumption of mashed-up 'facts' from where there is perpetual access to brutal anthropogenic matters—to suffering, beauty, inspiration, and mind-numbing vacuity all side-by-side. The frequency of access we now have to 'content' plays into our prejudices, inciting all manner of responses as we see ourselves reflected back in curated and globally disseminated moments which attract or do not attract the 'likes' that tell us we are loved. But there is also now great access to communities beyond geographical and other constraints. There is an art of fragments and fragmentation which reflects the fracture of lives riddled with simultaneities. There is a turn towards illuminating the spaces-between; the liminal, the uncertain, the ever-changing, and the connective tissue—the in-betweens that resist categorization and simple genre distinction—not throwing structure away but investing it with wider parameters.

So, here I am in long-form communication with you via a standard modality of sequential words politely interrupted by paratextual devices at times, for emphasis or digression and to engage spaces of possibility in recognition of the fact that nothing ever really dies, it simply crosses over, hybridly and redemptively.

****

Abbreviations

BotDRF	*Blood on the Dining Room Floor*, Gertrude Stein
BtA	*Between the Acts*, Virginia Woolf
D&G	Deleuze and Guattari
Diary	*A Writer's Diary*, Virginia Woolf
MD	*Mrs Dalloway*, Virginia Woolf
TPK	*The Pale King*, David Foster Wallace
TtL	*To the Lighthouse*, Virginia Woolf
TW	*The Waves*, Virginia Woolf

Introduction: The Enemy Within

The hybrid is drawn to a magnetic line of truth, redemptively.

Taking enemies in

Here, I mark out the 'battlefield'...

New names are suggested for a *post*-postmodern era by those who claim that progress needs a framework like a container to fill,[1] but *I* am not marking-out exclusive territory, I am identifying the hybridizing features of a heuristically representative framing of the literary modernisms continuum where housed *enemies* (Hassan 1987) become collaboratively constructive. Importantly, without the orientation supplied by the addition of a word that stands for a force of repair and unification, hybridism lacks direction or art. This is where *redemptive* comes in with its suggestive scope and for the productive friction it makes with postmodernism's wariness for metanarratives (Lyotard) as well as for the possibility it invokes along the modernisms continuum.

To be 'post' is to hold on to the past while transforming it. 'Post' is a defining caveat at the front of a chain of characters that do not claim entirely new territory; the construction embodies the past and the present. In this project, I propose that the fragmentation and deconstruction that made truth contingent and therefore impossible according to mainstream postmodernism, may now speak (write) in a redemptively hybridizing voice—one authorially reflective of lived experience while framing ideas with and within the modernisms' philosophical positionings towards extensions of textuality.

---

[1] Linda Hutcheon called for a new name for the paradigm after postmodernism ([1989] 2002, p. 181).

Redemptive Hybridism encapsulates the specific textual manoeuvres of an era of practice *post* impossibility on a continuum of modernisms. Importantly, it pushes this Work towards the speculative while retaining certain academic strategies. This Work is non-fictional and it is art and testimony in so far as reflexively, it is me, a multitude like you, and *we* are sceptical about the systems that form us while we acknowledge their inevitable complicity. So, here I am in discussion with you about us, in the creative non-fictional language of an auto-form which will always be susceptible to accusations of naivety[2] or unfinishedness, those hallmarks of humanness which feature whether we like it or not. I will discuss this and show it metonymically.

Ihab Hassan's work is significant, especially at the beginning of my own, in so far as his characterizes the in-between of genre and the problem of striving for a reasonable and productive postmodernity. With Hassan I address the subsumption of *a* postmodernity as well as antidotes (to it). In *The Dismemberment of Orpheus: Toward a Postmodern Literature* (1971), he was one of the first to use the term *postmodernism* progressively. Subsequently, his *Paracriticisms: Seven Speculations of the Times* (1975) is a work of creative idealism forging *para-critical* territory for (not against) postmodernism, but as it turns out also beyond that.

Throughout my Work, I refer to Hassan's notion of the 'hosted enemy'. Interestingly, his use of masculine pronouns becomes differently illustrative of 'the enemy' in texts so otherwise connective. Hassan's address to *he* about *him* forms a barrier to access until this comes to exemplify the work of the 'enemy' which he later discusses in relation to the modernisms in his essay *Towards a Concept of Postmodernism* (1987). "The word postmodernism […] evokes what it wishes to surpass or suppress, modernism itself. The term thus contains its enemy within" (Hassan 1987, p. 3). 'Containment of the enemy' is a succinct image of the enemy-containment inside *post*-postmodernism. Of course, the idea that there are subsummations rather than paradigm deaths or cessations is not unique to Hassan, and the irony of my casting Hassan's extraordinary work as an 'enemy' (apropos of pronoun use) is an addition to the complexity, in-built conflict, and the 'rhizomatic' nature of continuums, the modernisms, and human nature.

---

[2] Someone once told me in a booming voice: "Naivety is a strategy!" And while I don't agree that 'not knowing' is quite so deliberate, that is of course on a continuum. Naivety makes an unstable narration—not as a pre-empting of failure, but as an unwitting declaration that subjectivity is always worked on by forces outside our control.

Another pivotal work of theory is *A Thousand Plateaus: Capitalism and Schizophrenia* ([1980] 2014). This is volume two, after their *Anti Oedipus: Capitalism and Schizophrenia* of 1972. Rooted (and rhizomed) in poststructuralism, collaborators Gilles Deleuze and Félix Guattari (D&G)[3] also make a masculine address when presenting their critique of arborescence[4] and their rhizomatic schema of interconnected concepts. But theirs is insidious because it puts the woman and girl at the centre (of all becomings) and builds a theory or suite of ideas around and through her because of *what* not *who* she is. "…all becomings begin with and pass through becoming-woman. It is the key to all the other becomings" (D&G 2014, p. 277). As I will discuss in later chapters, the female (attribute or person) has been variously formed in her absence. Like many of my examples, the use of Deleuze and Guattari's work tends to be aphoristic in so far as I amass fragments that take on re-purposed veracity and tension in the new context. This fragmentation (plus connective writing) contributes to a testimonial quality, bringing *redemptively* hybrid features to this Work.

The Deleuzoguattarian telling of histories from across the fields of psychoanalytic theory, philosophy, and theories of art and literature, capitalizes on a predominantly masculine point of view which contrasts usefully and thornily with 'becoming-woman.'[5] But the opportunity to use the Deleuzian "tool box" (Massumi, more shortly) of concepts and to bring it forward, hybridly into a new setting is a tempting synchronicity and deeply beneficial to redemptive philosophy apropos of the intertextual, the metafictional, and other possibilities for re-making in texts.

---

[3] At times of high use and repetition, I refer to Deleuze and Guattari as D&G, because this is more concise and also because I believe they would not mind being treated meme-ishly.
[4] Arborescence is the vertical, tree-like, hierarchical system, as opposed to the rhizomatic network. About a dominant arborescence they write: "It is odd how the tree has dominated Western reality and all of Western thought, from botany to biology and anatomy, but also gnosiology, theology, ontology, all of philosophy…" (D&G 2014, p. 18).
[5] 'Becoming-molecular' is central to Deleuzoguattarian theory (D&G 2014, pp. 248–276). "Becoming-woman or the molecular woman is the girl herself" (p. 276). Becoming-woman in D&G is a necessary pathway even for non-women. They claim that "[the girl] never ceases to roam upon a body without organs. She is an abstract line, or a line of flight." (pp. 276–277). While this is steeped in psychoanalytic theory, its language is problematic for what it does to the girl, here a trope: "[girls] slip in everywhere, between orders, acts, ages, sexes; they produce *n* molecular sexes on the line of flight in relation to the dualism machines they cross right through" (p. 277). Like a molecular hijack. In *Can the Subaltern Speak* ([1985] 2010) Gayatri Spivak takes issue with Deleuze on becoming-woman.

Dense with images that show the character of categorical and expansive moments and the relation of thought to these as well as to movements and continuities, Deleuzoguattarian theory provides an opportunity to consider 'wrestling with the enemy' or taking it in. The concepts in *A Thousand Plateaus* act interdependently while along lines or networks, bringing 'enemies' which they call "disparate elements" (p. 343) into the unifying "cosmic machine" (p. 344). Such a machinistic cosmology *could* be considered a master-discourse or at least a master *network* exemplifying univocal 'difference in unity' (the becoming-other of difference, or its levelling) and a patriarchal blending-in of the Other[6] (the woman or subjugated person) inside a neatly articulated net or trap—a problematic smoothing out of difference. Nevertheless, in *A Thousand Plateaus* there are points of access for women or other non-men regarding stand-alone ideas. Brian Massumi, translator of *A Thousand Plateaus,* points out the rationale for the titular *plateau*. He suggests that in D&G, "…a plateau is reached when circumstances combine to bring an activity to a pitch of intensity that is not automatically dissipated in a climax" (Massumi, in D&G 2014, p. xiv). This sustained intensity is creative, it recalls their *becoming* and makes a multi-linearity or rhizomatic image of a type of possibility.

The reference to *becoming* via "atoms of womanhood" (D&G 2014, p. 276) in Virginia Woolf, has great symbiosis in my project where Woolf's hybridizing is examined and explored concurrent with David Foster Wallace's, with support from and deviation into various other writers of hybrid forms and theory. Massumi suggests that Deleuzoguattarianism is generously hybridizing for the journey:

> You can take a concept that is particularly to your liking and jump with it to its next appearance […] the reader is invited to lift a dynamism out of the book entirely, and incarnate it in a foreign medium, whether it be painting or politics. […] Deleuze's own image for a concept is not a brick but a 'tool box.'[7] (Massumi, in D&G 2014, pp. xiv–xv)

In its breadth of potential application, Deleuze and Guattari's hybridly imagistic work exemplifies the rhizomatic movements it describes. There is beauty in

---

[6] In this project, the *Other* with an uppercase O is the esteemed autonomous Other-self, whose difference is brought into relation with, for example, my own.

[7] In his citation for "tool box," Massumi points to Deleuze and Foucault in conversation: "A theory is exactly like a box of tools. It has nothing to do with the signifier. It must be useful. It must function. And not for itself. If no one uses it, beginning with the theoretician himself (who then ceases to be a theoretician), then the theory is worthless or the moment is inappropriate" (Deleuze, in Foucault [1972] 1977, 'Intellectuals and Power', p. 208).

the unlikelihood of any exact epistemology as their work moves across various terrains of theory and practice. 'Entry' is also gained for the reader who suspends any need for linearity while assuming appreciation, acceptance of, and self-binding (Hale 2007) to the multifaceted text.

This multivariant plot

A conception of the broad and *deathless* modernisms continuum[8] necessitates specific examples from a representative sampling or framing, hence the bookending duo of (many specific works by) Virginia Woolf and (*The Pale King*, *TPK*, [2011] 2012 in particular, by) David Foster Wallace. Woolf features for her ideal of atomic saturation and exemplifications of that, and Wallace for a particular and exemplary unfinishedness in *TPK*. Also contributing to this work are Nathalie Sarraute with her *tropisms* (poetic affects), Edouard Levé for his poetic parataxis, Maggie Nelson's lived-hybridity and autotheory[9] as a pragmatic new form, and many others including various hybrid non-fiction writers and work. Each is a multitude of intertext and connection beyond their pages and into mine; none identifies with a closed phase on the modernisms continuum, nevertheless, I place them in comparisons and draw on them for traits and possibilities. It is a fine matrix in acknowledgement of complexity, but also of the outside-over there; the unknown and its articulation and formation of 'what is' and 'what is not' (I point here to Kant on the *Sublime* and Foucault on formative *absences*). I curate textual theories, writers, and modalities of practice to show how categorization is problematized, abandoned, or hybridizing in response to the heterogeneity of experience.

The compound Redemptive Hybridism is a 'room' I place in a post-postmodern 'house' within the 'neighbourhood' of the modernisms continuum—a trajectory that lends a visual sensibility to the abstract ideas connected with the recurring notion of 'containment within'. There is a hybridizing circularity to the

---

[8] 'Modernisms continuum' features modernisms plural (no apostrophe, not possessive), it includes modernism, postmodernism, and post-postmodernism.
[9] Publications (other than M. Nelson) that use the term 'autotheory' particularly in relation to women's practice from 2011–2018: https://en.wiktionary.org/wiki/autotheory.

schema whereby the context around any individual/particular moment or writer is broadened to incorporate even the invisible space between visible moments or pieces of evidence, which are viewed in new conjunctions. For example, Woolf is viewed adjacent to and compared with Wallace; an unlikely pairing but a useful one because of the crow-bar effect that the presence of unlikelihood has on discourse and the relation of that to possibility. I compare Woolf and Wallace with respect to era, gender, their hybridizing of literary pre-occupations and contrasts in practice, and because both are neurodiverse,[10] which makes the author–reader and author–text partnership urgent or intense. I also juxtapose them for their occurrence in time along the modernisms continuum, bookending a broad and connective span.

There are spaces of intense feeling, movement, or pause, for example: the day of a life in Woolf, or the life of a text in Wallace; spaces which are collective via inter-genre thickenings at the 'found' or 'given' crossovers, or via any errors that leave a trace, and by moments of unfinishedness. Each component contributes singularly-and-collectively to the testimonial properties that are observable and potentially nameable as Redemptive Hybridity[11] in a post-postmodern context.

Importantly, manoeuvres of Redemptive Hybridity are located *across* the modernisms, not timebound. My investigation of Woolf's hybridity and my developing understanding of what her work offers this discourse, assists with defining the scope of the space inside my landscaping pegs which make a mutable frame inside the territory. Woolf and Wallace may seem antithetical to each other but when viewed in contrast and complicity they form a dialogic that instates an esprit de corps replete with saturations and intensities that speak of the diverse textures of the modernisms. The possibility that heralds *post-post*-modernity's *something new*, becomes hybridizing in its containment of co-existent and/or synchronous modalities and genres which are receptive to and affective of each other.

---

[10] It is well-known and broadly written that both Woolf and Wallace suffered with severe depression. The notion of a dual mind or one that oscillates between states of wellness and other movements, underpins the metonymic aspect in this work and any exemplifications I make—and the awe I feel for each writer. There are at least anecdotal links between mental distress and what is called genius in art and writing. Importantly, mental unwellness (while needing support and recovery) does NOT need redeeming any more than anything else might. Rather, the genius produced by a diverse mind might have 'redemptive powers' offering a reader insight and connection to an-Other. I assert that the author and their work are inseparable because even after the umbilical cord (Bakhtin) is cut, there is no getting away from DNA.

[11] I use variations on the two words: 'redemptive hybridity', e.g., redemptively hybrid, redemptive hybridizing, hybridly redemptive, redemptively hybridizing, redemptive hybridism.

I am wary of a potentially brittle communication when employing the technical semaphore of in-text citations and footnotes, but I am also aware of the practical necessity of this and intrigued about the texture of its contrasts where, for example, authoriality and academic writing intersect. The paratextuality in this Work performs a minor version of Wallace's anguish-and-the-IRS,[12] in *The Pale King*.[13] Footnotes speak in a different accent and at a different volume. They create a textual dialogic, poetic texture, and give additional information.

The vitality of difference

The air around a modernist's protagonist is thick with ideas, and thickened air becomes a protagonist; a 'space' between (ideas, moments, objects, happenings, memories). This calls to mind Deleuzian *différence* insofar as the space is haecceitical (of 'it-ness'). 'It' *is*, in and of 'it-self' pure difference; liminalizing, and hybridizing in its becoming as it collapses oppositions. Deleuze writes: "Difference appears only as a *reflexive concept*. In effect, difference allows the passage from similar neighbouring species to the identity of a genus which subsumes them" ([1968] 1994, p. 34). Thus, Deleuze sets up a challenge to unity in difference (the preserving of distinct voices and moments) in favour of difference in unity which turns differences into textures inside a new assemblage. This is encapsulated in D&G's approach to becoming: "Becoming is a verb with a consistency all its own; it does not reduce to, or lead back to, 'appearing,' 'being,' 'equaling,' or 'producing'" (D&G 2014, p. 239). Everything is becoming. Deleuzoguattarian difference renders null any affectation in favour of always becoming (p. 258).

The unfinished *TPK*, is a case of both/and regarding difference in unity *and* unity in difference. Wallace does not switch between contradictory beliefs or simultaneous oppositions but shows the formulation of options, ideas, and rehearsals (of finished parts) that make a schema-in-formation (an unfinished unity) where textual inclusions that may conflict (the differences) forcefully load unity with its bristling character. Any 'difference in unity' is becoming-redemptive this way while any 'unity in difference' appears to guard its distinct moments, even if unity is 'only' a goal or something distant through the viewfinder.

---

[12] The IRS is the Internal Revenue Service in the USA.

[13] Also, on the important subject of en and em dashes: these are bridges. One requires a jump, a pause, a jump; the other is a smooth and easy crossing. Ellipses are stepping stones … / …

The space between is where difference is activated as it either retains its borders or floods beyond them. There is not one true model; *différence* is hybrid and hybridizing, and therefore also unifying and disunifying.

The reflexivity of difference (in Deleuze) would be problematic in Wallace who while flattening characters as he possesses them, also strives for a sincereist's visibility via an almost self-punitive effort towards genuineness and ingenuity. Wallace's agenda of visibility must heed the expanding presence of predecessors (after Hassan) and the haecceitical expansion of the borders which postmodernism rehearsed, in order to reconcile present-future possibilities with the past.

Passing trains, and ectoplasm

If for example, one looks Kafkaesque into the rushing while remaining motionless in the moment, like the arrow caught in a series of 'almost infinite'[14] moments as it moves through space,[15] the space-between becomes 'one' of seemingly-infinite time and possibility because it is outside the flow of perceived elements. It is a space implicitly negative of form while charged with form's energy. If the train stops, however, everything is different, and glitteringly so.

A surface-narrative depiction of 'train passing' (in Kafka) for example, would miss the opportunity to explicate, particularly in the (void or) negative space between narrative spaces, those background machinations and ontological cues, those moments of 'fully' inhabited experience: "Everything that happens to us, happens precisely now", writes Gabriel Josipovici (2010, p. 84). While this conceives of time as a suite of micro-experiences, in hybridizing as I frame it, the 'now' is never detached from its context. For example, once it has been said, thought, or written it is no longer 'now' but 'then', and all that remains under consideration is a framed section of context, in extension of the moment 'now'.

Woolf's 'saturated atom'[16] expands into the now, to seize time, perceive it with haecceitical intensity, and/or to take off on a 'line of flight' (Deleuze). Not only does Woolf imbue the space between characters, moments, feelings, observations, etc., with a charge or force—a distinction, but she breaks down the elements of 'now' to their smallest component in a staged unfolding of

---

[14] 'Almost infinite' would relate to 'ultra-finitism', a concept Wittgenstein upheld by his finitism. From Wikipedia, retrieved 12 February 2019, https://en.wikipedia.org/wiki/Ultrafinitism.
[15] See Chapter Two for more on Kafka's train-rushing-space, and Zeno's arrow.
[16] From Woolf's *A Writer's Diary 1918–1941* ([1953] 2014, np). More on this in Chapter One.

essence and of (re)writing essence. There is harmonious slippage between consciousnesses, where all characters remain intrinsically connected while representative of their unique traits and motivations. One character redeems another via the lines of continuity between them, and the overarching suggestion in Woolf is that characters interact to create a sustainable multi-force, even if the act is unbeknownst to them. For example, when one character dies the vacuum is filled either by another or by the ectoplasm of the lost one's absence.

In *To the Lighthouse* (*TtL*, Woolf [1927] 1994), Lily suffers acutely the loss of Mrs Ramsay, but she also floods into the vacant 'Mrs Ramsay space', taking up some of it while also setting up a psychic shrine made of memory and physical trace:

> In the midst of chaos there was shape; this eternal passing and flowing (she looked at the clouds going and the leaves shaking) was struck into stability. Life stand still here, Mrs Ramsay said. 'Mrs Ramsay! Mrs Ramsay!' she repeated. She owed this revelation to her. (Lily, p. 152)

Woolf's schematic approach to characters and their being archetypal yet mutable in flow-over to others, is more restorative but also more text-bound than Wallace's in *TPK*, where a character might be absent, but ghosted and present; trapped and forever 'now', infecting memories and becoming an unspeakable force of inaccessible knowledge.

In *To the Lighthouse* Mrs Ramsay lives in her absence via Lily Briscoe's re-telling and embodiment of her. This is a manoeuvre of mutual redemptivity – fleshing Lily but not the author so much. By comparison, *TPK* jangles with (unfinished) characters that live impressionistically in contrasts and anecdotes that conjoin with the author, even becoming him.

A lineage of wariness and influence

In his introduction to Lyotard's *The Postmodern Condition: A Report on Knowledge* ([1979] 1984), Fredric Jameson suggests that when high modernist grandeur becomes too élitist and hierarchical, the antidote involves a (postmodern) commitment to surfaces and illusions (Jameson, in Lyotard 1984, p. xviii). But as postmodernism undermines the high-modern ivory tower, it gradually builds its own high place—one even more difficult to scale because of its diffusion into the mainstream, and all of the blurred and contingent edges. This makes postmodern élitism insidious, forging a greater distinction between itself and its predecessor (the enemy within). On the other hand, postmodernism forms a *simultaneous* élitism with high modernism; none of which any group or person may partake in without first abdicating their particularizing affiliations or 'reality' (Lyotard 1984, pp. 76–79). Lyotard writes the following about moving towards a kind of nihilism but more particularly, towards the (postmodern) sublime:

> Modernity, in whatever age it appears, cannot exist without a shattering of belief and without discovery of the 'lack of reality' of reality, together with the invention of other realities.
>
> What does this 'lack of reality' signify if one tries to free it from a narrowly historicized interpretation? The phrase is of course akin to what Nietzsche calls nihilism. But I see a much earlier modulation of Nietzschean perspectivism in the Kantian theme of the sublime. I think in particular that it is in the aesthetic of the sublime that modern art (including literature) finds its impetus and the logic of avant-gardes finds its axioms. (p. 77)

For Lyotard, Modernism and Postmodernism are not consecutive but are borne out in the 'sublime' modelled after Kant whose sublime includes: "...*limitlessness*, yet with a superadded thought of its totality" (Kant [1790] 1952, p. 495); or that which is "absolutely great" (p. 497). Lyotard's sublime includes the turning away from high modernism (and realism) while taking modernism in, less as an 'enemy' (Hassan) and more as something unfinished: "A work can become modern only if it is first postmodern. Postmodernism thus understood is not modernism at its end but in the nascent state, and this state is constant" (Lyotard 1984, p. 79). Postmodernity's representative gestures become 'sublime' in their packing contradiction and failure into a frame while denying the possibility of totalizations and even distinctions. This formulation has a contestable impact on groups that wish to retain agency and difference rather than giving these over to be flattened beneath the paint of contingency and relativity.

Jameson claims that Lyotard's anti-master-narrative becomes self-refuting (Jameson, in Lyotard 1984, p. xi) and that a solution might be:

> ...to posit, not the disappearance of the great master-narratives, but their passage underground as it were, their continuing but now *unconscious* effectivity as a way of 'thinking about' and acting in our current situation. (p. xii)

The "passage underground" (ibid.) is where the modernisms intermingle and throw off limiting categorizations while retaining definitive difference. But does not master-narrative's 'passage underground' also become a contradiction that undermines postmodernism and loosens up space for the 'something new'? Lyotard defines a circuitry into which breaks and new circuits can be made, but for how long can language games and semantics defer from the permanent and ubiquitous features of the circuit itself? Lyotard suggests that life and its particularities ('reality') exists at points and in relations. But what about the beyond of subjective points?

As a counter-mapping that effectively updates Lyotard's 'sublime contradiction' Jameson describes the movement across the modernisms as both trajectorial *and* of immanence. His is not so much a movement underground, as a process of gain via subsummation and subsequence, entailing the shedding of unworkable ideology and the retention of productive ideas, depending on the requirement for particularity. He says this about a trajectorial but also recursive model of influence and impact:

> …besides being a realist, Flaubert also turned into a modernist when Joyce learned him by heart, then unexpectedly turned into something like a postmodernist in the hands of Nathalie Sarraute. (Jameson 1991, pp. 302–303)

Flaubert → Joyce → Sarraute → is a living lineage because writers are their texts and continuums are likewise hybridizing due to the gathering-in and overlapping that occurs. For Jameson, this is a re-writing or re-contextualization of enshrined writers through different or new lenses which update, personalize, or even commodify texts. This is important for the reading of my own project where an artistic lens does not show *truth* as much as it forms true connections among sampled texts and authorial interests. In relation to *A Thousand Plateaus*, Massumi writes:

> The question is not: is it true? But: does it work? What new thoughts does it make it possible to think? What new emotions does it make possible to feel? What new sensations and perceptions does it open in the body? (Massumi, in D&G 2014, p. xv)

Texts become maps of a lineage in conjunction with their being inscribed with the thumbprint of their author. "…the Romantic Self becomes the Modernist Ego becomes the Postmodernist empty Subject" says Hassan in interview with Cioffi (Cioffi 1999 p. 359). 'Taking in' is also 'keeping close' in recognition that opposition can be a constructive force.

The phases of the modernisms continuum are not *only* linearly arrayed but are known in traits that pop up un-bound by time. "Modernism does not suddenly cease so that Postmodernism may begin: they now *coexist*" (Hassan 1975, p. 47). And processes are hybridizing; whether practitioners view the past as the enemy or not, it is inherent in the trajectory and any simultaneities. For example: romanticism → modernism → postmodernism → post-postmodernism, and notwithstanding the realisms and more speculative movements. Each phase or genre is a refusal as well as an embrace; each intercepts the other (and even jumps over) as Hassan argues (pp. 46–47), no phase stands alone unaffected.

According to Hassan, the Continental Theory brought recently into America "…ignores its own insecurity and changes nothing" (pp. xiv–xv). He claims that the literary criticism of Barthes, Foucault, Derrida, Deleuze, and others "…leaves 'texts' behind, wanders brilliantly through language, and vanishes finally into consciousness" (p. 140). This is the risk of univocity if its difference and agency are disenfranchised.

Emancipation, disenfranchisement, agency, categorization, and subjectivity are among the various issues for feminism. In Chapter Five I will examine some of the arguments from Linda J. Nicholson's *Feminism/Postmodernism* (1990), a curated collection of diverse and sometimes conflicting opinions and beliefs about the relationship between feminism and postmodernism, which explores the question 'what is feminism'? These arguments are important in so far as redemptive hybridity operates in contested spaces, in articulation of possibility and because the *post*-postmodern advances practices and theories that move beyond 'or in opposition to' certain core theories of the status quo.

It will suffice here as an example of feminism as a high-stakes ideology of ideologies to refer to two differing perspectives on Michel Foucault from Nicholson's book.[17] Firstly, according to Nancy Hartsock's essay 'Foucault on Power: A Theory for Women?' (1990), Foucault sits "…in opposition to modernity, he calls for a history that is parodic, dissociative, and satirical […] Foucault is attempting to oppose the establishment of the relations of the colonizer to the colonized" (p. 165). Hartsock suggests that rather than decry the power relation: colonizer vs colonized, or oppressor vs oppressed, Foucault toys or plays, not finding it necessary to concede that he is a member of the group 'colonizer'. For Hartsock, this becomes a satirization of lived realities,

---

[17] Foucault is a post-structural/postmodern Continental Philosopher and theorist whose work threads through mid-late twentieth and now twenty-first century theories of art and text.

and problematic where emancipation or reparation are embodied necessities. Hartsock describes Foucault's negation of the subject thus:

> Foucault's is a world in which things move, rather than people, a world in which subjects become obliterated or, rather, recreated as passive objects, a world in which passivity or refusal represent the only possible choices. (p. 167)

The Foucauldian suite of ideas is counterproductive to Hartsock's conception of a movement of women and to 'being a woman'. By way of a contrast, Judith Butler's essay 'Gender Trouble, Feminist Theory, and Psychoanalytic Discourse' (1990) concurs with Foucault's idea of 'inscription' as outlined in his *Discipline and Punish* (1977) whereby notions like the law, sexuality, and the soul configure bodies that reveal and are formed by absences. For example, in relation to the soul, Foucault writes: "…its primary mode of signification is through its very absence, its potent invisibility" (cited in Butler 1990, p. 335). In Foucault, the soul "…exists, it has a reality, it is produced permanently around, on, within, the body" (ibid.). Butler shows that Foucault's analogy of the soul is similar to her own on:

> …gender as the disciplinary production of the figures of gender fantasy through the play of presence and absence in the body's surface, the construction of the gendered body through a series of exclusions and denials, signifying absences. (Ibid.)[18]

Butler and Foucault share a conception of the transitory and absent as formative, an idea which is difficult to dispute; however, their understanding that identity traits and preferences are erasable inscriptions is as problematic for some feminists as their notion of what I am calling 'shared subjectivity' (Butler prefers the "category of women" which is a *sharing* kind of formulation, rather than 'women'; p. 325).[19] Shared subjectivity is the notion that all subjects are becoming-other (even the word 'subject' fails where becoming-multiple flourishes) but a more utilitarian view of subjectivity is required for emancipatory purposes. For a feminist like Hartsock, Butler's 'inscribing' or 'fluidity' negates the power in/and/of the subjectivity required by women and feminists in order to *be* or to *act*. She writes:

> We need to develop our understanding of difference by creating a situation in which hitherto marginalized groups can name themselves, speak for

---

[18] This is similar to D&G's concept: "Body Without Organs, the anorganism of the body" (D&G 2014, p. 276).

[19] I go out on a limb here in a fascinating area of theory where I must tread carefully.

themselves, and participate in defining the terms of interaction, a situation in which we can construct an understanding of the world that is sensitive to difference. (Hartsock 1990, p. 158)

Butler writes: "When the category [of women] is understood as representing a set of values or dispositions, it becomes normative in character and, hence, exclusionary in principle" (1990, p. 325). So, in conjunction with Hartsock, we have a picture of the movement in different directions within the broad 'family' of *feminism*. The collection of essays (edited by Nicholson) brings awareness and balance to the difficulty, advantage, and even necessity of feminism as a multiplicity of views making a network of possibilities despite conflict over *difference*.

According to Deleuze: "A single voice raises the clamour of being" (1994, p. 35). It is difficult after immersion in 'all this'[20] not to read *that* univocity as male-centric, or at least as the male speaking *for* the female or another. However, constituent clamorous components need not lose distinction in univocity.[21] *Unity in difference* ensures component distinctions, and retains the subjectivities necessary for redemptively hybridizing articulations of the veracity of difference within a polyvocal whole.

The terrible postmodern party

In 1993, when a late and tenacious postmodernism clung on in North American culture (as in other settings), David Foster Wallace was tired of what he perceived to be happening around him postmodernly. The following quote, from an interview by Larry McCaffery that year, is pivotal to the paradigm shift

---

[20] Strident-looking books by last-century men surround me as towers that loom importantly but dangerously; these are adjacent to books by women that appear more like stairways.

[21] 'Univocity' is invoked in reference to the Deleuzian concept after Duns Scotus (1265–1308) and Spinoza (1632–1677). Deleuze's univocity is 'difference in being', which is univocal because of the equivocity of the multiplicity of difference. It is a cyclic model that 'feeds' the primacy of difference while instating the functionality of multiplicity as a model, for example, of the universe, instead of unity (Deleuze 1994, pp. 34–36). To be representational in Deleuze denies the force of being and truncates its vibratory rhizomatic becoming, moving close to a 'black hole'. Here is another way of framing it: Deleuze's univocity of being is a singular multiplicity of becoming or perpetual differentiation; the multiple 'with one' or 'in one voice'. References to univocity are scattered throughout *Difference and Repetition* (pp. 34–42, p. 66, pp. 303–304). Deleuzian univocity is certainly hybridizing, but the *hole* in it may be at its flattening of difference; if difference is always and only becoming in univocity, does it lose that which makes difference (the different) what it is?

Wallace begins to signify. This excerpt is succinct on what Wallace believes and feels about the late postmodern environment he finds himself in:

> It's not a perfect analogy, but the sense I get of my generation of writers and intellectuals or whatever is that it's 3:00 a.m. and the couch has several burn-holes and somebody's thrown up in the umbrella stand and we're wishing the revel would end. The postmodern founders' patricidal work was great, but patricide produces orphans, and no amount of revelry can make up for the fact that writers my age have been literary orphans throughout our formative years. We're kind of wishing some parents would come back. And of course we're uneasy about the fact that we wish they'd come back—I mean, what's wrong with us? Are we total pussies? Is there something about authority and limits we actually *need*? And then the uneasiest feeling of all, as we start gradually to realize that parents in fact aren't ever coming back—which means we're going to have to be the parents. (Wallace, in McCaffery [1993] 2012, p. 52)

The analogy of a waning party of postmodern 'children' expresses Wallace's antipathy towards the ego-ism of postmodernism, and his readiness for something new (which may also be old). Being "the parents" (ibid.) means being the changemaking restorers of order. The postmodern "patricide" and subsequent deconstruction of institutions like academia, religion, and science, makes intellectual, emotional, spiritual, and artistic "orphans" of us.

In *The Condition of Postmodernity* ([1990] 1994), David Harvey analyses the postmodernity of the twentieth century, showing it to be characterized by various intersections but all within a prevailing capitalism. Neo-liberal capitalism is on the rise at the time of Harvey's book and postmodernism is floundering in failure. Where capitalism and postmodernity converge, value and price are synonymous and the individual is lost amongst a rampant commodification that claims to empower them while taking their money. In the twenty-first century, we see the logical conclusion of a system of commodification that has paid little attention to ethics and morality; this is everywhere endemic to the fervent neoliberalism of Internet-based capitalism.

While neoliberalism and postmodernism are contextually different—politics and economics vs art and culture—they perform something similar as they intersect. Value is deemed relative to popularity and desire (relative to the particular marketplace or audience) to the extent that emotions and privacy become commodities, and personal choices are data-mined, overridden, or rendered irrelevant to the economic or power-holder's agenda at which time no one has place or significance beyond their economic or social value to others.

Harvey discusses the possibilities for what might be emergent since internationalism and "economic nationalism" (1994, p. 358) have impacted on disillusionment in economics and culture at large since approximately 1992. He suggests that theorists and cultural practitioners are reverting (referring to the mid-1990s), variously, to ethics, romanticism, and realism, and that "…postmodernity is undergoing a subtle evolution, perhaps reaching a point of self-dissolution into something different. But what?" (ibid).

> …there is a renewal of historical materialism and of the Enlightenment project. Through the first we can begin to understand postmodernity as an historical–geographical condition. On that critical basis it becomes possible to launch a counter-attack of narrative against the image, of ethics against aesthetics, of a project of Becoming rather than Being, and to search for unity within difference. (p. 359)

Harvey implies that one modality might redeem another, and while the placement of the word "renewal" seems agreeable, the idea that postmodernity is a "historical–geographical condition" seems inadequate. Jameson's paradigm absorption, Hassan's containment of enemies, and Lyotard's postmodern preceding the modern (Lyotard 1984) place postmodernism *then* but also *now* (even with that awkward but helpful '*post*-post…') and in so far as it is *now*, postmodernity is thoroughly caveated by the simultaneous working-in of ideologies and methods that in the days of its patricidal and deicidal tendencies, it might have precluded.

Stephen Metcalf's article 'Neoliberalism, the Idea that Swallowed the World', in *The Guardian* (2017), outlines the predicament, explaining that neoliberalism contrives even the power to commodify emotions. "All is algorithm" says Metcalf, referring to an Internet-based society in which every 'private' Internet search is ranked by number of clicks or hits, supplying a currency of personalized topics to which advertising is subsequently ascribed. Metcalf suggests that because our personal data can be harvested, it has market value, therefore for the neoliberal practitioner the process is morally irreprehensible.

The commodification of the personal in the postmodern and neoliberal frame, fuels the anger expressed by Wallace in the 1993 McCaffery interview. It is why he asks, rhetorically: "Is there something about authority and limits we actually need?" Even as a placeholding term, 'post-postmodernity' contextualizes postmodernity (inside itself) and constructs the necessary 'moving beyond'. The 'post-post' chain while cumbersome, is caveating and in turn, it inserts possibility.

Sincerity in Wallace

"What my problem is is the way it seems that we as individual citizens have adopted a corporate attitude. That our ultimate obligation is towards ourselves" (*TPK*, p. 137). Despite admonishing himself and others, Wallace becomes a hero for a kind of aspirational rigor (post-postmodernly). What he seeks is a kind of virginity or the first-ness of things, repeatedly, a remembering and re-enactment of a state of innocence:

> [Wallace's style is an] uncomfortable but sincere realism for a world that was no longer real. Making the head throb heart-like had the potential to become a literary movement. Different names were bruited for it, from the New Sincerity to Post-postmodernism. (D.T. Max [2012] 2013, p. 231)

This brings to mind Woolf's search for the *saturated atom*. While I cannot find any evidence that Wallace believed he was producing "for" a world (Max, above)—that self-as-human-being again—his chagrin with the tide and times of late postmodernity and capitalism certainly resonates with many readers.

Wallace traverses a sincerity that is quite un-ironic while also involving irony because he cannot unknow his influences (the taking in of his postmodern forbears). In a 2006 radio interview by Michael Silverblatt, the two discuss Wallace's 'Consider the Lobster' ([2004] 2014b). Silverblatt confesses to being surprised at the moral stance Wallace enacts in what Silverblatt calls a "post-moral" world, to which Wallace counters, after a tumble-weedy pause, that he does not know what is meant by post-moral. It comes across (in words, voice, and tone) that Wallace sincerely yearns for the world to *not be* post-moral, but with a simultaneous yearning for commentators and critics to not wrap things up in phrases that sign-off or exclude, especially at a time of flux and possibility. In this interview, Wallace says several times that he is providing a "service" to the readers of *Gourmet* magazine who could not be at the festival and who might be interested in a thorough interpretation of the experience and a rigorous consideration of the life and death of a lobster. And there it is, Wallace's (apparently quite unironic) sincerity and, according to what I hear in the interview, a certain sense of Wallace embodying the lobster, perpetually on the brink of being boiled alive.

'Consider the Lobster', is replete with acronyms, encyclopaedic facts, and lengthy footnotes (like *TPK*). If the intention is to provide a service, as Wallace says, then he comes across as somewhat unfiltered and naïve given the mandate to also entertain. It is as though when faced with the juncture of rampant consumerism and tragedy, he becomes entirely and guilelessly 'honest' (visible) and devoid of irony:

> However stuporous a lobster is from the trip home, for instance, it tends to come alarmingly to life when placed in boiling water. If you're tilting it from a container into the steaming kettle, the lobster will sometimes try to cling to the container's sides or even to hook its claws over the kettle's rim like a person trying to keep from going over the edge of a roof [...] The lobster, in other words, behaves very much as you or I would behave if we were plunged into boiling water. (Wallace 2014b, p. 930)

Sincerity signifies a shift in attitude from an irony-based filtering of experience to a more altruistic filtration. A sincere realism for example, can be extricated from a work such as Wallace's essay 'E Unibus Pluram: Television and U.S. Fiction' ([1990] 2014a). This work astutely, though indirectly, performs a sincerity that Wallace invests with a meaning concerning truth-seeking, responsibility, and authenticity at the intersection between postmodernism and what becomes post-postmodernism.

"Sincerity is a congruence of avowal and actual feeling" (Trilling, in Adam Kelly 2010, p. 132). Kelly writes: "Trilling closely associates the cultural trumping of sincerity by authenticity with the intense but non-confessional exploration of the self characteristic of literary modernism" (ibid.). Referring to Trilling (1972), Kelly shows that the modernist texts cannot be judged according to sincerity where they deal in "…persona rather than person" (ibid.). Simply put, sincerity is a return to the person. However, Kelly problematizes the return to the textual and authorial person of sincere intent and the poetics of that, suggesting that sincerity must work in tangent with authenticity to be affective because the predicament of the sincere-ist is that once sincerity is planned and conceived in texts it may be lost. Sincerity's self-conscious avoidance of affect makes it buy-in to that, becoming another device. Meanwhile, the congruence of persona and person is a hybridizing one.

Whether launched inadvertently by Wallace, or whether the time was just right, a 'sincerity movement' may be a pronounced trait of a collective chagrin with capitalism, neoliberalism, and postmodernism. "I'm talking about the individual US citizen's deep fear, the same basic fear that you and I have and that everybody has except nobody ever talks about it except existentialists in convoluted French prose" (*TPK*, p. 143).

Sincerity may be an intentionally reparative approach to practice and an endeavour to repair and resolve. But, as touched on in my brief outline of

Metamodernism in Chapter Five, the oscillations invoked by pursuing 'sincerity' without accretive action and conviction may result in a self which swings between grabbed handfuls of frayed ideological rope, ultimately not building anything other than a picture of doubt.

Sincerely single-entendre

Wallace's overarching agenda is to invigorate 'single-entendre writing' that does not seek to trick or have hidden meanings that denigrate the reader, as seen in this fragment from 'E Unibus Pluram':

> The next real literary 'rebels' [...] have the childish gall actually to endorse and instantiate single-entendre principles. [...] These anti-rebels would be outdated, of course, before they even started. Dead on the page. Too sincere. Clearly repressed. Backward, quaint, naïve, anachronistic. Maybe that'll be the point. Maybe that's why they'll be the next real rebels. Real rebels, as far as I can see, risk disapproval. The old postmodern insurgents risked the gasp and squeal: shock, disgust, outrage, censorship, accusations of socialism, anarchism, nihilism. Today's risks are different. The new rebels might be artists willing to risk the yawn, the rolled eyes, the cool smile, the nudged ribs, the parody of gifted ironists, the 'Oh how *banal*.' To risk accusations of sentimentality, melodrama. Of overcredulity. Of softness. (Wallace 2014a, p. 707)

Broadly speaking, the 'soft and sincere' single-entendre is an antidote to postmodernity's double-entendre, but it is not necessarily altruistic: the hybridizing that is endemic within its context and modalities of practice is complicated by a connection to everything that has gone before; it does not vanquish or deny any 'outgoing' regime or refuse to reside simultaneously with it.

In the McCaffery interview, Wallace reveals his 'single-entendre' intentions in what he identifies as a time of discontent and change. He is not pushing sincerity in the manner of a humanitarian prophet of change, but he is pushing *something* vociferously:

> Fiction's about what it is to be a fucking *human being*. If you operate, which most of us do, from the premise that there are things about the contemporary U.S. that make it distinctively hard to be a real human being, then maybe half of fiction's job is to dramatize what it is that makes it tough. The other half is to dramatize the fact that we still *are* human beings, now. [...] I just think that fiction that isn't exploring what it means to be human today isn't good art. (Wallace, in McCaffery [1993] 2012, p. 26)

These, Wallace's thoughts from more than a quarter of a century ago, reflect a time when postmodernity, passed its height, had 'hit the suburbs' while still prevailing in 'ivory tower' art schools and writing programmes. Artists and writers, along with audiences and readers, should be at liberty to make individual and distinct responses to the difficulty of 'being human'. But while the desire to be a part of the solution seems typical of an emergent post-postmodern interest in reflecting flesh-and-blood realities, the desire to play, and to explore hybrid multiplicity and abscond from particularizing explorations of "…what it means to be human" (ibid.) may also be relevant in post-postmodernity. We shall see.

The 'space between' judiciously or randomly juxtaposed and often discordant theorists/theories, and writers/writing becomes for the willing, an innervated space that gives form to the concepts: *hybrid* and *redemptive*. It is a post-postmodern space from which to examine what is shared in the moment. It is a space of possibility *and* impossibility where only literary/artistic, and hybrid-or-hybridizing enactments prevail, even fortified by internal strife.

Part One

Features of Redemptive Hybridism

1

The Redemptive Textual Body

The truth-value in a work of fiction might/could/would/ surpass non-fiction if taken heart-wise.

Etymologically speaking

Whether as the noun 'redemption', verb to 'redeem', or adjective 'redemptive/ redeeming', a moral overlay is implied. In conjunction with hybridism, the yearning-fulfilment complexity of *redemption* becomes *post*-postmodernly complex, developing into the image of 'room, in house, in neighbourhood.' Writing redemptively concerns the motivation that orientates the text and enables the activation that is its moving-beyond habitually closed forms and ideology. As a concept, redemptive hybridity and its hybridizing, is transformative, embodying depth of mystery and invoking an agnostic space of unknowing between the ports of knowledge and belief.

Pivotal to the redemptive hybrid is the problem and advantage of multiplicity. The process of redemptive hybridizing opens out beyond genre and any categorization, with an inclusivity that curates via amalgamations (of even contradictions) rather than via exclusions.

Etymologically, 'redemption' is seldom extricated far from its theistic function, otherwise why use a term which is so metaphysically suggestive? From the Greek of early biblical use, *redemption* is a hybrid of several words with varying meanings. In Hart (1997) the biblical Redemption is comprised of a complicity of Greek concepts: *Lutron* is Ransom, inside *Apolutrosis* it is 'ransomed from slavery', or it is deliverance (p. 194). Redemption as *apolutrosis* incorporates reconciliation and forgiveness (p. 190) as well as release, transformation, and "…change in the human condition" (p. 194). This also provides access to "atonement (*hilasterion*)" (p. 195). Redemption, says Hart, is the "…ongoing activity of the Holy Spirit" (p. 196), which gets interesting when brought adjacent to hybridizing and applied in

Wallace whose *The Pale King* is riddled with ghosts and God-author → human-character or text slippage, as I discuss in Chapter Six.

The sacrificial Christ becomes the 'vicarious victim' which enables a "vicarious redemption" [*our* apolutrosis] writes Joseph Lilly (1947, p. 257). The notion of vicarity feeds back into the matter of texts and hybridizing/taking in— and of power. And while redemption's 'ransom and deliverance' might sound like a *Western*, these are multiplicities recursively attached to the human being through the Christ Image, which is the embodiment of Being-itself (Tillich 1954). Meanwhile, modernism's *anti*-Christ image[1] shows a redemption that is powerful in negation-or-absence of a saviour. Like a shadow, this redemption goes just as far in reverse, as the human considers its vicarious heroes.

Harold Bloom claims that recognition has more currency than redemption in a literary context (2010, p. xv). He does not show recognition doing redemption's work though; rather, he suggests that redemption/'redemption'/*redemption* is irrelevant:

> Total self-recognition is anything but redemption, just as inaugural error is absolutely unlike original sin. The morality of literature evades good and evil. Shakespeare is not interested in saving you or in solving your problems. (p. xvi)

Alternatives to redemption, like recognition, restoration, or reprieve, might veer away from grand narratology, but in doing so might limit possibility. No replacement seems to carry the gravitas and imagistic scope of *redemption* whose big role sometimes gets forced into synonyms that become swollen and unwieldy with the load. Bloom's assertion that "literature evades good and evil" (ibid.) truncates literary scope by delimiting the idea of the metaphysical or supernatural in which 'evil' if not 'good' is located.[2] Literature frequently deals with 'good and evil' in so far as these plot the extent of possible actions for characters and innervate notions of risk and threat. Anecdotally, it seems that evil is a state of abjection that mystifies and incites fear. Evil is a manifestation of human undoing. In relation to this, if the bookends 'good–evil' are relevant in literature then 'redemption' is relevant for its metaphysical, non-empirical insinuation of more than reparation, that is, of transformation.

I will not steer this work off-course by swimming far out into the waters of theology or psychology (I will drown), suffice to say it is precisely the

---

[1] Some examples: Camus, *L'Etranger*; Kafka, *The Trial*; Beckett, *Waiting for Godot*; Joyce, *A Portrait of the Artist as a Young Man*.
[2] 'Evil', the broad etymology of: in Old English it meant 'bad'; then in Middle English, *moral* badness; retrieved 11 August 2020, https://www.etymonline.com/word/evil.

expansiveness and intensity of Redemption/redemption/'redemption'/*redemption*, its invocations and tense fit with modern thought that makes it evocatively replete with narrative tensions and possibility for today's cultural landscape. *Redemptive* may also be self-reckoning as it redeems its own problematic monologue when making a compound with *Hybridizing*.

Moving into the conceptual framework of a post-postmodern redemptive hybridity, I propose the possibility that redemption could be conceived of as encoded at the atomic core of hybridizing practice; the 'ransom and deliverance' from mental, emotional, physical, and textual blockages; from psycho-spiritual black holes and arborescent thinking (Deleuze & Guattari [1980] 2014). Intrinsic to this conceptualizing, is whether the *sub*-representational becomes representational via a redemptive urge despite us. The idea of the *sub*-representational connects throughout this project to Woolf's desire, as expressed in a diary entry, to 'saturate the atom': "The idea has come to me that what I want now to do is to saturate every atom. I mean to eliminate all waste, deadness, superfluity: to give the moment whole; whatever it includes" (*Diary*, Wednesday, 28 November 1928, np). Atomic saturation becomes a succinct yet problematic image of the Redemptive Hybrid's becoming. Succinct for reasons of possibility and dually problematic because of the impossibility (or at least the obscurity) of an atom being saturated, or a creative person achieving perfection.[3] However, what Woolf expresses, and what the redemptively hybridizing goal becomes, is the participant's full involvement with a process of saturating in all its intensity.

Perhaps the image only works in so far as metaphors carry concepts forward, and only in art, is *anything* possible. Possibility, and saturation by insight and feeling make a worthwhile stage to play on, while eventually, practices seek connections to more than themselves, which is where possibility meets evidence and art meets theory.

Even in Deleuze (and Guattari)

In his Translator's Foreword to *A Thousand Plateaus*, Massumi implies the presence of a certain redemptivity in that (co-authored) work. Meanwhile, Peter Hallward applies a specific redemptive cast to Deleuzian theory, showing

---

[3] If an atom, being a building block or interdependent component of a molecule *could* be saturated from the outside in, that atom would, presumably, collapse. But concepts and images work according to their context and take on new meanings. Perhaps there is a possibility of saturation from the inside out?

a generative multiplicity in Deleuze and suggesting that the pluralism makes a complex puzzle which can be solved in different ways. According to Hallward, the reader might be redeemed from responsibility and connection and move into self-sufficiency:

> Deleuze writes a redemptive philosophy. In conjunction with its mainly artistic allies, it is designed to save its readers from a situation contaminated by 'consciousness', 'representation', 'analogy', 'repression', 'lack', and 'the Other [*autrui*]'. Redemption from these things, according to Deleuze, provides immediate access to a very different kind of situation – a situation defined by its radical self-sufficiency, its literal, absolute, all-inclusive immanence to itself. In a whole variety of ways, Deleuze writes the passage from our *given*, contaminated situation, to the purer, more *primordial* situation. (1997, p. 6)

While the entire Deleuzoguattarian "tool box" (Massumi) is available for the use of its parts in moments, each tool remains tied to the next like a Swiss army knife. Writes Hallward: "Deleuze's redemptive philosophy always works from, within and toward the assumption of ontological univocity, the redemptive identity of the One and the multiple" (p. 8).

Redemptive haecceity

On one hand, Deleuze and Guattari might dispute a finding of redemptivity *in* their work. Redemption implies a tending-arborescence, which could be blackhole forming in their theory. On the other hand, the liberty invoked by their haecceity redeems striving, which connects to what Hallward suggests. And so, ultimately, redemption-and-D&G make a hybridizing tension that reflexively interrogates each component. I will explain…

Via the haecceity, according to Deleuzoguattarian theory, one might be "…present at the dawn of the world" (D&G 2014, p. 280).[4] And the haecceity is *not* redemptive, because it is the undiluted essence of the moment or thing, a vitality which subsumes or overrides totalizing concepts (like redemption). However, for the purpose of literature and art, the haecceity is the *force* of life expressed in luminous units that interconnect. In its infinitesimal and immeasurably pervasive attributes, the haecceity's expression of magical moments of aliveness and its disruptions make it a concept of advancement.

---

[4] "…at the dawn of the world" is quoted again (more fully) in Chapter Four.

The imagistic Scotist-Deleuzian notion could be considered a momentary redemption, but only if the subject-object relationship turns the subject *beyond* the point. The haecceity's 'thisness' or 'itness' individualizes and particularizes the person, idea, or thing, revealing difference, and difference can be understood—in the terms Deleuze lays out in *Difference and Repetition*—as a middle-ness. In *A Thousand Plateaus* the middle has momentum:

> The plane of consistency contains only haecceities, along intersecting lines. Forms and subjects are not of that world. [...] A haecceity has neither beginning nor end, origin nor destination; it is always in the middle. It is not made of points, only of lines. It is a rhizome. (p. 263)

Terry Eagleton suggests that the Deleuzoguattarian haecceity or haecceities (itness/es or thisness/es) derived from Duns Scotus' *Haeccitas*, can be well-exemplified in the work of Scotus devotee Gerard Manley Hopkins (Eagleton 2012, p. 2). For example, Hopkins's joyful embodiment of the falcon is haecceitical:

> I caught this morning morning's minion, king-
>   dom, of daylight's dauphin, dapple-dawn-drawn Falcon, in his riding
> Of the rolling level underneath him steady air, and striding
> High there, how he rung upon the rein of a wimpling wing
> In his ecstasy! then off, off forth on swing [...] ([1918] 1961, p. 32)[5]

Eagleton describes the Scotist *Haecceitas* thus:

> ...the excess of a thing over its concept or common nature – an irreducible specificity which can be grasped not by intellectual reflection on what an object is, but only by a direct apprehension of its luminous presence. (2012, p. 2)

Deleuze and Guattari write: "For you will yield nothing to haecceities unless you realize that that is what you are, and that you are nothing but that [...] You are longitude and latitude, a set of speeds and slownesses between unformed particles, a set of nonsubjectified affects" (2014, p. 262).[6] To be a set of coordinates renders-nonsensical redemption as transformative but not necessarily nonsensical as productively immanent in the haecceitical-molecular

---

[5] Interestingly, D.F. Wallace suggested G.M. Hopkins could be the "touchstone" for how to break literary rules by making new ones so that there are still rules. Hopkins, he says, "...made up his own set of formal constraints and then blew everyone's footwear off from inside them." (Wallace, in McCaffery [1993] 2012, pp. 51–52).
[6] Which is why they resist molar pack identities like 'we as women'.

life. "It is the entire assemblage in its individuated aggregate that is a haecceity" (ibid.).

The following from *The Pale King*'s 'Notes and Asides' (*TPK*, pp. 539–547), shows a haecceitical bliss unfolding – fictitiously – but after excruciating experience (boredom) and imagining. This ends up somewhere near Woolf's *atomic saturation* and begins to reveal a gesture of possibility in textual rhetoric that indicates something far more redemptively hopeful than vaguely transformative:

> It turns out that bliss—a second-by-second joy + gratitude at the gift of being alive, conscious—lies on the other side of crushing, crushing boredom. Pay close attention to the most tedious thing you can find (tax returns, televised golf), and, in waves, a boredom like you've never known will wash over you and just about kill you. Ride these out, and it's like stepping from black and white into color. Like water after days in the desert. Constant bliss in every atom. (*TPK*, p. 546).

In *TPK*, there is an undercurrent (with quick-sand features) of desire for redemption via boredom, but this quote is especially pertinent for its mention of: "Constant bliss in every atom." Both Woolf and Wallace work with extracting essences, and distillation; the redemptive by-pass of body/mind (di)stress, and the apotheosis of art. Both seem invested and investing in a seeded or encoded redemption—that is, the unseen, un-felt possibilities that underpin, via hope, throughout any 'second life' found in the production of literary art.

Reminiscent of Søren Kierkegaard's vividly feeling the lack of a conclusion in order to find one ([1872] 1955, p. 4)[7] is Wallace's 'facing what's dreadful' (below). Both imply the refusal of denial, which moves towards redemption:

> I strongly suspect that a big part of real art-fiction's job is to aggravate this sense of entrapment and loneliness and death in people, to move people to countenance it, since any possible human redemption requires us first to face what's dreadful, what we want to deny. (Wallace, in McCaffery 2012, p. 32)

While it is a dreary idea to give art-fiction a 'job', in a literary context to speak of redemption is not to speak of purism, another set of rules, it is to speak of possibility and expansion – even escape, of the writer and reader (or writer, interpreter, editor, and reader) as well as the space of overlap or collapse between them. Wallace's "what we want to deny" is enacted by the characters in *TPK*

---

[7] I mention this again later.

in expressions of abject pointlessness and boredom inside the all-pervasive capitalist machine that entraps them, and where redemption is possible only via submission to the mechanism of entrapment. This is reminiscent of Kafka's torture machine in *In the Penal Colony*, and certainly of Dostoyevsky's work on the noble criminal. Wallace was greatly enamoured with Dostoyevsky, calling him "…earnestly and unapologetically moral" (Max [2012] 2013, p. 209). In *TPK*, the corporate 'machine' uses bodies and minds to enable wealth creation and subjugation, offering redemption by succumbing. But back before the turn of this century, Wallace tells McCaffery that if we can "…identify with characters' pain, we might then also more easily conceive of others identifying with our own. This is nourishing, redemptive; we become less alone inside" (Wallace, in McCaffery 2012, p. 22). And while that might seem a bit beige, its redemptive sentiment precedes the building of his IRS hell-scape of control and boredom made worse by its interspersion with insights and digressions that open windows but slam them shut again. One might say Wallace takes to the brink the urge to 'identify', making us sweat for our redemption.

Umbilical connection, author to text

God is an image of omnipotent power, symbolizing the ultimate frontier of the objective. Typically, antithetical to the modernisms while performing as its important nemesis, God affords an image of possibility in this 'post-post' latter phase. Sometimes, the problem is in the name, ergo, 'Being-itself' (Tillich 1954) is more ontologically specific than 'God' and may represent a site of necessary movement towards the *Other* in becoming-complete along the hyphen. Meanwhile, the Christian image of a relationship between 'persons' requires the compound (three-part) 'God', which, with the human, configures the analogous possibilities for being-redeemed. It may seem grandiose, but what we cannot fully comprehend will always be grand while it orbits (or slips away from) the particular and the mundane. One's gaze at particulars (Eagleton 2012) goes stale after analysis leads the questioner beyond the frame.

The relational divine-human compound can be embodied in the author–text process and resulting (textual) objects. This is an analogy of a hybridizing which enables us to look into bracketed moments (particulars) and view there the atomic or ontological aspect of the composition while seeing, showing, or knowing a glimpse of the broader territory of Being-itself—which 'we' are tied to by virtue of the nature of things (cause and effect). This connection, according to the relational model I have just outlined, is discussed in Bakhtin who outlines a series of views on glossia (voices) in texts. Like Deleuze and Guattari's analogies, Mikhail Bakhtin's are valuable to this project because of their visual symbolism and interfolding concepts that orbit a core set of values. In his *Problems of Dostoyevsky's Poetics* ([1929] 2014), Bakhtin claims that a work of art or text should not be monologic;[8] the polyphony of life should be reflected in it and a dialogic approach is preferrable. According to Bakhtin, if the author (God-like) appears in the text they commit takeover acts that flatten and strip characters of their opportunity to gain an independent, or even a plausible, life:

> Self-consciousness, as the artistic dominant in the construction of the hero's image, is by itself sufficient to break down the monologic unity of an artistic world—but only on condition that the hero, as self-consciousness, is really represented and not merely expressed, that is, does not fuse with the author, does not become the mouthpiece for his voice; only on condition, consequently, that accents of the hero's self-consciousness are really objectified and that the work itself observes a distance between the hero and the author. If the umbilical cord uniting the hero to his creator is not cut, then what we have is not a work of art but a personal document. (Bakhtin 2014, p. 51)[9]

With no interchangeability between hero and creator in Bakhtin, the author's hero/ine (or God's human) lives in a different though dependent paradigm from their Creator. This is of course necessary for the creation of fictive and author-independent textual worlds, but what about worlds that are tending-real and auto-formed, and those textual worlds that configure the hybrid space between genres, between fiction and non-fiction, between truth and lies?

The monologic approach is mostly *not* present in Woolf, while mostly present (even if off site) in Wallace's *TPK*.[10] I use the caveat 'mostly' because that incites the fullness of these authors' hybridity as they push out from the middle of any bracket on the modernisms continuum to resist simple categorization while carving out a new category (each). Arguably, degrees of monologism are ever-present in later narratively authorial, auto-fictional, or auto-theoretical works such as those by Edouard Levé and Maggie Nelson et al. who muddle the distinction

---

[8] Monologism = single-thought or single-voice discourse. In Bakhtin this can cause a certain flattening of discourse and an arrest of possibility and potential.
[9] 'Heroines unite! Or at least multiply the possibilities of 'hero'....
[10] Monologism in *TPK* may be a background tendency upon which other modes of discourse play; always important but always interacting with the reader's job as maker of the discourse—as discussed further along in this chapter.

between hero and author in extension of poetic and hermeneutical possibility. In tending-monologic works like theirs, the necessary dialogism between the author and reader, like a collaboration, veers the work away from solipsism.

While Bakhtin's textual glossia—the text as a body of multiple voices around whom more voices speak—is necessary in a discussion about textual hybridity, according to Wayne C. Booth in his 'Introduction' to *Problems of Dostoyevsky's Poetics* (2014), the artist is tasked with a 'superior' textual practice, which provides grist for the mill in terms of hybridizing's high-low collaborations in which superiority becomes redundant. Booth writes that for Bakhtin:

> The artist's essential task [...is...] to achieve a view of the world superior to all other views; fiction of the right kind, pursuing the right tasks, is the best instrument of understanding that has ever been devised. It is indeed the only conceptual device we have that can do justice, by achieving a kind of objectivity quite different from that hailed by most western critics, to the essential, irreducible multi-centredness, or 'polyphony,' of human life. (Booth 2014, p. xx)

As classifications of value and hierarchy, 'superiority' and 'rightness' don't wholly characterize Bakhtin's work on multiplicity and his awareness of the "'irreducible multi-centredness, or 'polyphony,' of human life".

The text is the author in authorial practices as much as it is *not* that in practices where the author dons an invisibility cloak. Why can't the previously quoted "personal document" (Bakhtin 2014, p. 51) be a work of art? Why shouldn't God appear in his own text and the author in hers? The Creator's desire for engagement is intrinsic to the process of and reason for creation, and the "'polyphony' of human life" (ibid.) is exactly why superiority and hierarchy in textual or other practice are challenged.

Wallace in Wallace

For a 'visible' or 'umbilically-tied' author like Wallace,[11] the plot's terrain shifts between the text and the author while the author articulates it-and-themself via autobiography, autofiction,[12] auto-theory, ficto-theory, or another compound in

---

[11] I am always based in the latter/last phase in Wallace: *TPK*, which I set apart from his other works here, while of course that book is tied to everything that went before and everything simultaneous to it.

[12] Autofiction, coined in the 1970s by Serge Doubrovsky, is a term used in literary theory to refer to fictionalised autobiography. See: https://oxfordre.com/literature/search?btog=chap&f_0=keyword&q_0=autofiction (retrieved 12 May 2023). Dubrovsky's first autofictional work was his novel *Fils*, 1977 (from various sources).

the making which does-away with the simplistic binary of fiction and non-fiction. In a manner of speaking, the author and his/her/their 'seasons' becomes the plot, especially in textual spaces that are no longer demarcated by genre machinations.

Wallace makes his plot by undermining it; via setting us up to believe him and then admitting his lies via footnotes and 'main' textual asides that disclaim, claim, and re-claim what he has previously stated and will state again. For example: "All of this is true. This book is really true" (*TPK*, p. 67). Wallace puts himself on the line between the functions of the different parts of the text. As a 'visible' author, his plot is entangled with his self-insertions and their paradoxical denials and claims—their curated humanity—which arguably, becomes, reflexively, a plot. Wallace's visibility in the plot then, is a splendid exemplification of the art-life matrix, the instability of thought, feeling, and of hybridizing.

In relation to the movements of visibility and discourse in Wallace's fiction, David Hering, in his book *David Foster Wallace: Fiction and Form* ([2016] 2017), contends that Wallace employs a both/and approach:

> ...I simultaneously read monologism and dialogism in Wallace's fiction as occurring within an ongoing process of oscillation that is based around the continual risk of a master discourse engendered by the degree of Wallace's authorial presence. In this sense, the model I describe in Wallace's fiction is both dialogic and *dialectic*, as it continually presupposes a greater degree of dialogical engagement toward some (crucially undefined) future communicative end. (p. 7)

In my reading of *TPK*, any sense of a looming "master discourse" swerves into the space between fragments from where the text bursts forth as something in-between modes of discourse. No one knows whether the work that we know as *The Pale King* would have been overtly monologic had Wallace finished it, but its set-pieces and character studies embed the author and foreground character and language metafictionally. This undermines master discourse and monologism while dividing the reader's attention and bringing them significantly into the authorial equation. Hering's "(crucially undefined) future communicative end" (ibid.), expresses the prescience of *TPK*'s overarching legacy of unfinishedness.

TPK's editor, Michael Pietsch, provides evidence that the fragmentation may have been intended; an author note in Wallace's manuscript describes the novel as "...full of 'shifting POVs, structural fragmentation, willed incongruities'" (Pietsch, in *TPK*, p. vii). For me, it is the "willed incongruities" that best depict Wallace's intentionality for some of what has emerged as *The Pale King*.

Wallace works from the central author-self and proceeds to blur and sharpen that person (portal) and any claims to presence, as if hiding then jumping out, rather than being sometimes there and sometimes not (the oscillatory image). I agree with Hering that in *TPK*, Wallace employs dialogic and dialectic strategies, and it also seems that the centrality of the author in *TPK* causes the argumentation to be couched in and tempered by a borderline mix of confession and play, consequently handing to the reader the job of determining any discourse, as judge and finisher of the text.

While contributing to the dialectics of the work, the various David Wallaces and their other-possessions, perpetually swerve away from categorial or closed schemes; away from being outed as the true "David Wallace" (*TPK*, p. 66) while simultaneously and contradictorily claiming to be that "real author" (*TPK*, pp. 66–67). This is de-stabilizing, but also laden with extensive possibility for the reader's contribution to the narrative. Importantly, *TPK*'s various Wallaces refrain from a narrative overlay that forecasts an 'end'.

Once finished and sealed by publication, umbilical cords, while not severed are at least slackened. Meanwhile, the unfinished *TPK*—effectively a process in arrest—is inextricably tied to Wallace, and always strained, as if severance is forever passing through the author's mind. This makes that book a useful example of process and practice while the editor posthumously makes the manuscript something it would not have been, and carefully so, on behalf of Wallace and for the reader.

The manuscript notes referred to by Pietsch (previously) indicate that structure-wise, fragmentation is pivotal. Perhaps it is also pivotal to the plot/s. Pietsch confirms: "Nowhere in all these pages was there an outline or other indication of what order David intended for these chapters" (Pietsch, in *TPK*, pp. vi–vii). In McCaffery, we see that at the time of that much quoted interview, Wallace sought visibility, accountability, and redemption:

> But if a piece of fiction can allow us imaginatively to identify with characters' pain, we might then also more easily conceive of others identifying with our own. This is nourishing, redemptive; we become less alone inside. It might be just that simple. (Wallace, in McCaffery 2012, p. 22)

This indicates sincerity, and a camaraderie of readers into which the author is insinuated, especially if that author is also the narrator and/or his/her/ their characters. In his Wallace biography, *Every Love Story is a Ghost Story* ([2012] 2013), D.T. Max shows an excerpt from Wallace's correspondence to his editor Michael Pietsch about Mark Leyner, a "hidden" writer like an exhibitionist engaged in literary "tightrope-calisthenics" (all Wallace, in Max 2013, p. 172). Wallace tells Pietsch that he does not want to be like that. In extension of Bakhtin's umbilical image, to be (postmodernly) "hidden" is a conflation of the cord itself so that it is neither cut nor thriving. Meanwhile, Wallace's presence in *TPK* is a frequent distraction and a diversion from that book's fictionality, until the distance, distinction, and overlap between 'truth' (non-fiction) and 'lies' (fiction) *becomes* the Work. This is a thoroughgoing extension of the idea of *interruption* which Wallace explores so emphatically via much shapeshifting as author, and it is a deconstruction of the idea of *saturation* (in Woolf).

Throughout *TPK*, Wallace is present, whether hovering (like a ghost), as a fictional character, or via direct reader address within swathes of footnotes. One might argue that Wallace's prevalent-while-evasive appearance in the text conflicts with any sincerer aspirations to visibility. *TPK*'s multiplicities and duplicities throw into disarray the matters of genre, sincerity, truth, about which Wallace speaks opaquely in various interviews (notably here, in McCaffery [1993] 2012). Since the almost puritanical aspirations Wallace expressed in 1993, he seems to return to *some* of the hiddenness and game-like attributes typical to postmodernity—as if he must use the strategies of the cultural setting in which he grew up in order to challenge those strategies, grafting-on something to do with truth and visibility.

Arguably, the main challenge to *TPK*'s readers comes via Wallace's repeated contradictions of his previous claims to truth.[13] However, this is the logical conclusion of sincerity attached to public self-disclosure; it is the becoming of the problem by also becoming the solution.[14] The umbilical cord is not only unsevered in Wallace, it is on display in all its bloody glory. The *TPK* sees its author performing and visible in terms of his textual self-subjection, as *it* roams between various (literary/textual) urges, influences, and intentions.

The unfinishedness of *TPK*, allows us to see Wallace. But when we search him out in his visibility for a straight account of what's going on, it turns out

---

[13] "All of this is true. This book is really true" (*TPK*, p. 67). And/or: "…it is a mainly true and accurate partial record" (p. 69).

[14] My use of 'sincerity' incorporates its late currency or re-emergence post-postmodernly as an aesthetic/poetic sentiment becoming a style. However, I also often simply refer to the general meaning of the word.

that the book's frayed edges contribute to its becoming a valuable example of something post-postmodernly new—where high visibility can, simultaneously, be perpetual and/or repetitive absence.

Woolf in Woolf

Woolf is saturated in the atomic make up of each of her characters such as Clarissa Dalloway, or in recoil from characters like the doctors that enrage Septimus. For example, in the semi-autobiographical *To the Lighthouse*, the recognizable structural elements 'from life' are Woolf's canvas upon which to paint her artful untruths with a fluidity that would be meaningless without the various touchstones from life as background. That said, authorial visibility is anathema to Woolf – until *Between the Acts* (*BtA*, [1941] 2005), but even then, she only toys with it.

Woolf works with and against archetypes within fine-tuned plots like music scores where complex characters are built around traits, yet traits cross-over between characters as though ideas and other affects exist both in and beyond the person for the score as a whole. Woolf, and persons known to her are gathered in her textual characters but denied autonomy. "Vita should be Orlando, a young nobleman" (*Diary*, Tuesday, 18 September 1927, np), Woolf writes. But her Orlando is a multiplicity, running and flowing through time while time runs and flows through him/her/them. Woolf requires but also transcends plotted confines to live in minds and bodies as sensation while she 'saturates the atom' with all the intensity of that, not authorially but not without authoriality. This is her hybridizing.

Woolf commits Bakhtin's cord-cutting while simultaneously using her author-self as the page space and the in-between of plotted atomic moments— like a mother to the released text, severed but always present, she holds and extends the cord just enough that her fiction might fly. There is a mix of intuitive and (pre)meditated editorial labour, and always tension and plurality. She strives to keep the process visible or at least the *imprimatura* of first gestures alive. She writes: "Suppose one can keep the quality of a sketch in a finished and composed work? That is my endeavour" (*Diary*, Sunday, 7 September 1924, np). The "quality of a sketch" is a foretaste, albeit more surface, of Woolf's (previously given/cited) *saturated atom*. But on the value of polish, Woolf is more puritanical, as if formality is a necessary linked-arm-walk with the "proportion" (of Holmes and Bradshaw) in *Mrs Dalloway* (*MD*, [1925] 1973). Here, around the work on *MD*, Woolf tells her diary why "writing must be formal":

> What I was going to say was that I think writing must be formal. The art must be respected. This struck me reading some of my notes here, for if one lets the mind run loose it becomes egotistic; personal, which I detest. At the same time the irregular fire must be there; and perhaps to loose it one must begin by being chaotic, but not appear in public like that. (*Diary*, Tuesday, 18 November 1924, np)

'Formal with fire' expresses the expansive tension in Woolf. There is 'love with hate' of plot. *The Waves* (*TW*, [1931] 1998), for example, can be received as a patchwork of loosely plotted poetic fragments, while it is also certainly not that. To read *The Waves* is to be pulled into, and sluiced forward by, the language of sensation with arguably little overt plot. Nevertheless, its various sub-plotting connections flow back behind characters whose interrelationship and interdependence constitute a poetic narrative about being and becoming. This becomes so closely rendered that all the borders (edges of plot points, etc.,) are deeply internal to the 'flow of blood' Woolf wanted:

> What it wants is presumably unity; but it is I think rather good (I am talking to myself over the fire about *The Waves*). Suppose I could run all the scenes together more?—by rhythms chiefly. So as to avoid those cuts; so as to make the blood run like a torrent from end to end—I don't want the waste that the breaks give; I want to avoid chapters; that indeed is my achievement, if any, here: a saturated unchopped completeness; changes of scene, of mind, of person, done without spilling a drop. (*Diary*, Tuesday, 30 December 1930, np)

Images of fluidity are prevalent in Woolf; there is much mention in her diaries as in her fiction, of liquid terms like 'flow', 'flood', and 'saturation' in relation to intensity, continuity, and the interconnectedness of characters and ideas.

Plot then, may function as a kind of nemesis which Woolf provokes while working to override or interrupt with fluidities, and while fluidity is the goal there remains an emphasis on analogies and images. Woolf continues to wrestle with plot's crude function in *BtA*:

> Did the plot matter? She shifted and looked over her right shoulder. The plot was only there to beget emotion. There were only two emotions: love; and hate. There was no need to puzzle out the plot. [...]
>
> Don't bother about the plot: the plot's nothing. (p. 56)

The plot, says Woolf, begets emotion and is necessary as a conveyance of 'love and hate', a powerful duality that may usurp the plot and emerge in some other way. Woolf writes: "Surely it was time someone invented a new plot, or that the author came out from the bushes" (p. 134). It seems that Woolf might be approaching something closer to letting "the mind run loose" (recently quoted diary entry). A few weeks after finishing *BtA*, she writes:

> I think I shall write out some very singular books, if I live. I mean I think I'm about to embody at last the exact shapes my brain holds. What a long toil to reach this beginning—if *The Waves* is my first work in my own style! (*Diary*, Sunday, 8 March 1941, np).[15]

In Woolf, the umbilical cord (Bakhtin) is replaced with something more multiple than human tissue.

The Word made flesh

> Is not the secret task, for poet and critic alike, to participate
> in the magic process whereby the word is turned into flesh?
> (Hassan 1975, p. 4)

Here, and on the pages of *Paracriticisms*, from where the above quote is lifted, Hassan proposes that it is entirely reasonable for the critic to show 'feeling' in their text. I posit that genre distinctions blur and expand at the expression of authorial feeling. Stepping back to etymologies for a moment, 'fleshing' is not *only* 'making-physical' but is also loaded with the meaning signified by the powerfully loaded image of the transubstantiation of Christ as God's flesh; a becoming human-and-divine: "The Word became flesh and made his dwelling among us" (John 1:14). The word-as-flesh image has subsets: wine into blood, bread into flesh, blood and flesh into the Word (the Logos/the message), and the Word as bread, that is: "…man shall not live on bread alone, but on every word that comes from the mouth of God" (Matthew 4:4). And the Word of God is embodied as flesh. The biblical source image is not given as an abstract simile but as a physical reality (actual flesh) and necessity (real nourishment). The use

---

[15] Woolf died a few weeks after that 8 March diary entry, making the entry portentous, and an understanding of what soon takes place for Woolf, makes it seem extraordinarily alive.

of this image alone or in conjunctions, insinuates much more than becoming organic material.

The cycle: human to the divine and divine to the human,[16] engages the artist/creator for whom 'the word' (loaded now with that metaphysical and supernatural provenance) performs the divine or unlimited, the becoming-flesh or making-visible of the author in the Work and representing the embodied logos.[17] The word forms images that are fleshed by investment in the minds and bodies that form them. This fleshing, after self-revelation and/or embodiment of the divine/unlimited, signifies its hybridizing – in this case, of literary criticism – around the character and person of the author-creator whose word, work, or art is *also* fleshed in that state of immanent possibility, the unconscious state. This is given in Hassan as not an 'either/or' but as immanent to fleshing (which is also substantiation).

Dreaming of possibilities

In a performative monologue about the transformative creativity of sleep, Hassan's language and style is, as elsewhere, illustrative of the speculative nature of empirically-geared material (1975, pp. 151–153). His playful use of mediated intertext amounts to a making-empirical of conceptual or point-of-view-based 'knowledge' and its use of any state of mind. Hassan begins with a Dickens-like fragment: "Every age seems the best of times and the worst of times. Some ages engage in re-revolution; others re-cover rumors of some utopia or eden. But our intelligence remains rooted in the Human" (p. 151). The human, he goes on to say, sleeps for a large part of its life, forming dreams that "open on the future" (ibid.). The transformative potential of the unconscious is invoked. Hassan asks, rhetorically, "Does the transformation of man [and woman] renew itself continually in this struggle between waking and dreaming?" (ibid.). The problem becomes the perpetuity of 'sleep' in folded and folded relativities (of the postmodern kind) where unending deferrals *un-flesh* the word in counterproductive ways:

> We have no adequate, no truly contemporary, theory of change […] Currently, the dominant influences of Structuralism, Phenomenology, the New Linguistics,

---

[16] There is also earth into human at the making of the human, and the 'divine' embodied in the elements: fire, water, wind to manifest physical presence, in that biblical frame.

[17] Theology = the logos of theos. Greek, early Christian. Logos = the word, or message/discourse.

favor not change but codes, patterns, deep forms through which the mind, as Lévi-Strauss put it, 'imitates itself'; we move among crystals, mirrors and crystals. (p. 152)

The idea of a search for a new name or theory to give progress its trajectory, is reflected in Jacques Derrida's call for a new name for critical inventions that 'deform the limits' of literature (Derrida, in Derek Attridge [1989] 1992, p. 52) (see Chapter Five) as well as in Hutcheon's ([1989] 2002) call for a new name for a post-postmodern era. Meanwhile, Hassan's paracriticisms have the effect of supplying knowledge with testimonial veracity, and any 'coded' text is 're-fleshed' by its leaning on possibility to signify the empty space or the beginning of the missing theory of change as if an opportunity awaits.

"Literature is the keystone of the humanities; it stands, like Man, between Earth and Sky, severed from neither" (Hassan 1975, p. 138).[18] To be in reach of earth and sky and severed from neither, is the figure of *modern* liberty, without the option of displacement or hiding. It is an embodiment of certain possibility; the human condition expressed in context rather than in unmoored concepts. Meanwhile, the fleshed man-word reaches nothing in that mode. Hassan shows that in William Burroughs, post-word, there is only ailing flesh. The word has been shoved in a bag and thrown off a bridge so that it can no longer corrupt because, as Burroughs identifies in *The Ticket that Exploded* (1962):

> The word is now a virus. . . . The word may once have been a healthy neural cell. It is now a parasitic organism that invades and damages the central nervous system. Modern man has lost the option of silence. (Burroughs, in Hassan 1975, p. 140).

Burroughs' anger, says Hassan, is towards a deceptive and controlling "Old Consciousness" which is articulated by the Word (ibid.). The loss of the option of silence, is the dependency—drug-like—on the perpetuity of words. Hassan shows that in Burroughs, the word (and language) is fleshed by its constant articulation of the body from which it emanates and the bodies to which it speaks. An insufficiency of word/s keeps the body conscious, present, and limited. "It's time we thought about leaving the body behind" says Burroughs

---

[18] I like to redeem (*launder*) the masculinization of people as 'man' by imagining 'woman' in texts. It's not easy when they talk past you while you read their book. I do realize that for some, neither 'woman' nor 'man' is an adequate option, I only hope there may at least be a sense of restorative balance where both of those are spoken to. And there is possibility in the space between or beyond.

(ibid.) in an expression of a desire to escape the confines of the body and its words. Post-Burroughs, in the twenty-first century, the Internet becomes a viral hell of anthropogenic white noise where the new (or failed) silence is comprised of incessant electrical/mechanical activity; a 'silence' made noisier by a perpetual cacophony of words. Even our deletions leave digital marks, becoming inscriptions upon a defaced silence.

Unlike Burroughs who proposes a solution to the viral word via negation of the body, Wallace leaves his (figurative) blood on the page, re-iterating the body-mind as a hybridizing site of possibility. He testifies to the condition or paradigm in which he finds himself and brings *everything*: the world and his self-consciousness into his writing, in a grand multi-fleshing of the multi-word, as both an expression of anxiety and an attempt at constructing something new that matters.

Leaping forward, I assert that simultaneous with Wallace's becoming fed-up with invisibility and insincerity (of author), there is a groundswell of refusal by women and feminists to ridicule the consciousness required for the ongoing work of emancipation. Some might say theirs is a puritanical sincerity falling on one side of an ideological divide, but any point-of-view is populated by presences *and* absences; any 'ism' is ideology, and life is steeped in side-taking—which, I might add, is not a closure of options for hybridity. The practitioner of hybrid forms pokes holes in ideology with sharp implements of possibility.

In her book *Nothing Mat(t)ers* (1992) Somer Brodribb writes about a masculine and tyrannical postmodernism:

> It is my contention that postmodernism is a masculine ideology based on a notion of consciousness as hostile, and an epistemology of negation which is one of separation, discontinuity and dismemberment. Narcissistic and romantic, these *idéalogues* (late Enlightenment nominalists) imitate divine process. They are engaged in the process of disengagement. As such, it is not possible to reclaim or rehabilitate postmodernism for feminist uses. (pp. 19–20)

After this vehement summary of postmodernism's allegedly injurious effect on women, Brodribb goes on to link postmodernism with male violence and the death of women (p. 20), and while I understand this place on the feminism spectrum, I also see that the practice and appreciation of hybridism instates possibility and alternate ways of leveraging and dealing with (certainly not forgetting) subjugation and past wrongs. My project's often-mentioned 'taking in' of enemies configures restoration and progress. For example, a swelling and space-filling of redemptive women's practice, rather than its encampment at the margins.

Many years since Brodribb's book there *might* be no more need to "rehabilitate postmodernism for feminist uses" (ibid.) because postmodernism is now the background not the foreground of contemporary practice.[19]

Hybridizing practices and hybridity may be gamelike; there is no doubt that contemporary hybrid forms have the advantage of the postmodern predilection for play, mutability, and the exploration of transience in matters of reality and truth. This might help a feminist practice apropos of a thickening of possibilities, while it poses a problem for the building of anything that will not crumble (the fleshed and the sentient body loses veracity). The postmodern practitioner re-invents or re-starts the game each moment, and fleshed things become residual, making an interesting problem in relation to the whereabouts of substance.

The innervated body of the book

> A book has neither object nor subject; it is made of variously formed matters, and very different dates and speeds. To attribute the book to a subject is to overlook this working of matters, and the exteriority of their relations. It is to fabricate a beneficent God to explain geological movements. (D&G 2014, p. 3)

Deleuze and Guattari side-step the form or subject that the writer might instate or 'flesh', while their "variously formed matters" *is* a fleshing of sorts. They assert that one cannot know everything about a book; not even the writer can know it by each of its uncountable lines of flight. They suggest that the book has a post-author life with therefore an unmediated power to speak, heteroglossically.

> The ideal for a book would be to lay everything out on a plane of exteriority [...] on a single page, the same sheet: lived events, historical determinations, concepts, individuals, groups, social formations. (p. 9)

I have had this thought myself; that the problem is that there is any form at all. The form is an arborescent truncation of broadening or free-flowing thought; it can be a brutal constraint. However, a form is also the only way to present a thing or idea to ourselves or anyone else. Even a thought is a form, if splitting

---

[19] I discuss Feminism further in Chapter Five.

hairs. We exteriorialize into a form in order to see, edit, accept, or reject what we have done/thought/made.

Deleuzoguattarian theory can be used to extrapolate an image of a borderless and genre non-specific "book" of openings-out (possibility), insinuating a hybridizing of the former "tripartite" divisions of: the world, the book, and the author. A conception of the "assemblage" is the way around the form as a constraint:

> There is no longer a tripartite division between a field of reality (the world) and a field of representation (the book) and a field of subjectivity (the author). Rather, an assemblage establishes connections between certain multiplicities drawn from each of these orders, so that a book has no sequel nor the world as its object nor one or several authors as its subject. (p. 23)

This presents an ideological possibility for borderlessness despite the form (of the book). It is dependent upon the author's-and-reader's uptake of, and belief in the non-subjective attributes of the long-and-pageless concept.

Word as spirit

During and after the body, is the spirit as part of the trifold image of the threefold: Spirit in Soul in Body, which mirrors the three-part nature of the God in biblical imagery. Threes are also reflected in this project's conception of the modernisms continuum and its variable guises; room in house in neighbourhood. While the Word-as-flesh is an image of transubstantiality, the Word as spirit is an image of extra-corporeal possibility: "The spirit gives life; the flesh counts for nothing. The words I have spoken to you—they are full of the spirit and life" (John 6:63). This is no Burroughs-esque chagrin with the body, but a figuration of amalgamated parts rendering a multi-part collaboration. Matters of extra-corporeality and word as spirit, are relevant among the writers I discuss, and for the character of post-postmodernity in so far as it is discussed in reaction to postmodernism—*becoming* in difference to it and because of it. And the spirit is in relation to the soul in which it is housed.

The afterlife (spirit life) of fiction and its *becoming*, post-authorially, is an important site of redemptive hybridity; the textual 'afterlife' may be redemptive in so far as its becoming-other is legacy-making in lieu of anything left unsaid. After all, we fear what we might *not* leave behind.

Chaos and floating parts while I stitch

"'We will each write a ghost story,' said Lord Byron," recounts Mary W. Shelley in her Introduction to *Frankenstein; or the Modern Prometheus* ([1818] 1968, p. 261). Shelley recalls that after many days bereft of ideas for this group game, she decided that the implements of story and change must be already available: "Invention, it must be humbly admitted, does not consist in creating out of void, but out of chaos" she writes (p. 262). Also, "Invention consists in the capacity of seizing on the capabilities of a subject; and in the power of moulding and fashioning ideas suggested to it" (ibid.). Conversations with Byron and PB Shelley ensued in which they discussed Darwin "…who preserved a piece of vermicelli in a glass case till by some extraordinary means it began to move with voluntary motion" (p. 263). Together they mused: "…perhaps the component parts of a creature might be manufactured, brought together, and endued with vital warmth" (ibid.). Then, after dreams and visions in which the ideas came and insinuated themselves to Shelley, Dr Frankenstein and his 'Adam' were imbued with "vital" and terrifying warmth.

Shelley suggests that her story is about the created terrifying the creator (pp. 262–263), an effective analogy of the process for writers and artists in so far as what is created takes on a life of its own with the potential power to out-wit its creator. The hybrid 'life out of chaos' that Shelley writes, is redemptive (for a moment) of chaos, which it orders, but is perhaps unredemptive when out of chaos a creature is formed which *monstors* its creator. However, redemption might look different in the short versus the long term. Interestingly, the biblical image of creation is out of void: "Now the earth was formless and empty…" (Genesis 1:2–3). Creation out of chaos is apparently the *human* endeavour.

If one constructs a hybrid in a rustic laboratory from looted parts, the *hybrid* is obvious while the *redemptive* concerns the functionality and manner of the 'connective tissue' or bond between creator and created. It is not necessary to think of this in *umbilical* terms (there is nothing that closely resembles an umbilical cord in processes of thought or super-nature) but it is necessary to think of the process as a conduit of constructive possibility, which *might* need a moral overlay to make sense… but I will suspend that in its subjectivity for now.

While the connection between the previous writer and the next is a stretch, it is also not that, because I have done it. The link forged here, makes a temporary assemblage which in turn makes space for particular inter-paradigmatic relations between the Gothic Romantic and the contemporary interdisciplinary poetic. This may be spurious as well as selectively specific, as I place the *stitched* aspect of monster body parts from an easy-to-read and plot-driven text (Shelley) alongside the *unstitched* of (an) ephemeral textual object/s (Anne Carson's *Float*) in a balanced and oppositional pairing which contributes an image to this project.

Carson does not stitch a Gothic horror; she does not stitch her *Float* (2016) at all: it 'floats' within its clear plastic case; twenty-two loose but almost *unquotably* tight pieces assembled or not assembled by the reader whom Carson enables to makes their own ever-changing poetic 'creature' or apprehension of a fragment as described by Carson in an interview with Kate Kellaway:

> *Float* is a transparent slipcase containing 22 chapbooks to be read on 'shuffle'. They were mostly originally performance pieces—composed and performed individually and often with other people—so the collection is just that, a collection, not an organic whole, not intended to be read in any particular order, not designed to flow from beginning to end visually and conceptually (as previous books were). (Carson, in Kellaway 2016, np)

Float is variously hybrid: when cased-up it is 'one' collection of parts, a hybrid thing; and when 'opened' or spread out, it is not fixed in a singular formation but always separate pieces where the reader makes their hybridizing movement of shared editorship as they select the order of the parts. Of course any reading can be like this, but the reading required by *Float* is explicitly physical in so far as its parts are literally movable. Meanwhile, *Frankenstein* uses the epistolary form to convey its narrative in fixed pieces that portray a literally hybrid subject.

I have no greater excuse to abut Shelley and Carson than the connection of 'stitching'—a monster, versus an unstitched book of floating parts. The resulting possibilities that form synaptic connections come out in typed words, like a community of disparate yet overlapping ideas.

2

The Hybrid Middle

Perfection is un-redemptive in its symmetrical and arborescent maze of hard surfaces.

Pushing out towards ends

A middle-ness is posited (Deleuze & Guattari [1980] 2014, p. 25), a seeing-from-all-sides kind of transparency for an assemblage, which is, in this case, a book in connection with the 'outside', which may include various incarnations of 'reader', and even the table or shelf the book sits on. They raise another clarion call: "…overthrow ontology, do-away with foundations, nullify endings and beginnings […] The middle is by no means an average; on the contrary, it is where things pick up speed" (ibid.). The middle is the place of intensity, of *becoming*.

To 'verb' the hybrid enables that noun to act or move, to hybridize. *Hybridizing* is the process that shows the character and extent of unfinishedness. The *becoming* of post-postmodernism (of anything) is unfinished and so, conceptually, is located at the 'middle'. In post-postmodernity there is a generative value on spaces between[1] (middles) where creative gestures enact the breaks, bridges, interruptions, overlaps, and pauses between merging or emulsifying components—preserving simultaneous differences, univocally. This is a space of non-linearity, conceptually rich in possibility, which can be exemplified by the bringing together of Woolf and Wallace as this project's 'middle', as if they

---

[1] The 'space between' as I refer to it is a liminal space between objects/concepts that connects or links/bridges, creating relations between objects. It is variously the negative space (the aesthetic or physical space between positive items being visually or physically apprehended); or it is a break in time or 'dead space' between moments of apprehension (boredom may reside in the space between); or it is the overlapping area of two or more concepts or objects, which are thickened in the overlap. The space between has its own particular, mysterious and layered credibility. The impossible might be possible in between.

are collaborators while also *not* that – in some ways sharing only the category of 'writer'.

My work joins with others to push out towards ends of resistance while being and becoming a work-in-progress where the middle has nothing to do with an economic or social hierarchy, nor a political position between the left and right, or non-committal. Structures of conformity or the mainstream do come to mind though when thinking about 'the middle'.

The Pale King also comes to mind as an apotheosis of unfinishedness, which is of course middling (not reaching either end or any boundary marker). It works with tropes of a middling conformist mainstream; while its unfinishedness, posthumousness, and metafictional status as an important literary object or moment exemplifies the Work's post-author busy-ness and the in-betweening of genre.

The 'middle' in Woolf is the possibility of atomic saturation, which is pertinent for her characters who speak and move in textual forms created by and for them.

To *become* is to be en route or *during* the 'journey'. It could be said that *becoming* in Deleuze and Guattari, moves and takes-in; repairs and segues – not without problems for difference, but with analogous possibilities. "All becomings are molecular" write D&G (2014, p. 275), but this is not a takeover of the molar entity—i.e. men become animals or women by proximity, as in molecular goings-out in desire or dreams, not by imitation but by a "…microfemininity, in other words, that produce in us a molecular woman" (ibid.). This makes way for possibilities apropos of becoming-hybrid. Here is a useful example of *becoming* but also of the previously footnoted 'molecular hijack', in the Deleuzoguattarian invocation of Woolf and becoming-woman:

> [Virginia Woolf] was appalled at the idea of writing 'as a woman.' Rather, writing should produce a becoming-woman as atoms of womanhood capable of crossing and impregnating an entire social field, and of contaminating men, of sweeping them up in that becoming. (p. 276)

Becoming concerns "molecular collectivities, haecceities" (p. 275). "You do not become a barking molar dog, but by barking, if it is done with enough feeling, with enough necessity and composition, you emit a molecular dog" (ibid.).[2]

---

[2] I can only report what interests me in relation to my subject, and faithfully represent the source. As I said in my Introduction, Deleuze and Guattari have given us permission to play with their concepts (Massumi, in D&G 2014, pp. xiv-xv). Each intense embodiment forms a molecular bond between subject and object. Where does that leave us other than flowing over in each moment to butterflies and slices of honey-dripping crusty bread? I would emit molecular espresso.

The molar is the species-specific entity which is "…trapped in its molar form" (ibid.). Molarities can become other entities molecularly, like Ahab becoming-Whale in order to adequately meet his foe. In Deleuze and Guattari becoming-woman is the molecular/psychic/conceptual gateway for all other human becomings, whether *her* molecular fragments are embodied or *she* is given in textual and artistic gestures (pp. 275–276).

The value to my project of this *becoming* is the intensity it brings to the writer of texts who explores their own becoming/s and those of their subjects, like Woolf does. The Deleuzoguattarian image of "…becoming-woman as atoms of womanhood" (p. 276) concerns expansiveness, intensity, and importantly commitment from the atom out (and in), even if some of the description is difficult where 'impregnating' and 'contaminating' are given a shared purpose. The matters of becoming which I invoke are re-purposed for textual-art-making. These now work towards the hybridizing Self-Other self, a dialogical author-as-character—and other examples of unity in difference.

"A line of becoming has only a middle" write Deleuze and Guattari (p. 293). It is difficult to talk of the middle without also discussing ends (the middle is a measure of space and position, equidistant between ends). The concept enriches the present, the *being* at the hybridizing middle.

Sarraute as middle

Elliptical reading

Nathalie Sarraute (1900–1999) writer, Russian-French Jew, lawyer, activist, etc., provides a century-spanning golden thread to the aspect of survey and is an exemplar of multiplicity and continuity. Sarraute's *tropistic* work-and-life spans a twentieth century which includes two world wars, wide-reaching anti-Semitism in Europe, women's suffrage, the protests of 1968, and more. Woolf (and Proust) had a formative influence on Sarraute's writing (Project Gutenberg 2020). Her spacious and cerebral engagement with semantics and language suggests a direction Woolf might have taken had her agenda not been to express the *élan vital* (Bergson 1907)[3] and the becoming-saturated of her textual atom

---

[3] The concept of *élan vital* in Bergson, is the vital impulse of life in relation to a creative rather than a mechanistic evolution. See Bergson 1907, *Creative Evolution*, mentioned at: https://www.britannica.com/biography/Henri-Bergson#ref202559, retrieved 28 August 2020.

(the diary entry of 1928). Woolf's diary shows that Proust had an enormous influence on *her* too. Synchronicities elaborate the continuum. Sarraute's work exemplifies an invisible turn or perhaps a pivot between modernism and postmodernism—the subsummation, the always was/is, the collapse of linearity and the retention of the particular in favour of the advantage of difference. Hers are multiple contributions: an eloquent becoming-the-page-space, the measured suggestiveness around and of her ellipses, dissolving characters who leave a powerful tonal effect more than flesh and blood, and the collapse of presupposed forms for the novel.[4]

Sarraute exemplifies haecceitical 'middle-ness'. Her text moves despite, but intrinsic to the narrator—it moves according to a nominal scheme designed to engage with the question: how might the novel grow from within? But Sarraute's is not a catalogue of mix-and-match options (which is marginally truer of Levé and certainly of Wallace's *TPK*). Sarraute, performing more like Woolf, crafts a highly-tuned mechanism of middle-ness that was born in the middle and does away with ends—or, using another image, causes 'ends' to breathe lung-like, becoming fibrous roots. Ends are insinuated, but ends are living, whether intertextually, metafictionally, or auto-fictionally beyond any 'ending' words. In some cases, such as in *The Golden Fruits* ([1963] 1965), Sarraute writes 'the middle' in a hybridizing manner by using a form that strings fragments together while maintaining a theme of 'the middle-ness of writing' and of fiction as an overarching force or impetus. The publisher's note written by John Calder on the back cover of *The Golden Fruits* (1965) participates by explaining something about Sarraute's ploy:

> [*The Golden Fruits*] has neither characters nor plot. Its central figure is, in fact, a novel entitled The Golden Fruits, its subject the reactions that this novel and its reception provoke among those who either like or dislike it.

There are acts and scenes in paragraphs and tracts that stand alone, except that they also need to be played against other fragments that interact in the page

---

[4] Wallace's homophonic play apropos Dr. 'Merrill Errol Lehrl' (*TPK*, p. 6) turns in its triplicate incarnations of the sound 'erl', to the homophonic and paratactical sequencing employed by Sarraute: "Hérault, héraut, héros, aire, haut, erre haut, R.O.," in rhythm with the sound of the wheels, rolling across the flat white plains in *Between Life and Death* ([1968] 1969, p. 16). This enacts the rhythmic possibilities of language which may or may not be made to intersect on a continuum, but which does in the mind of this reader. The intertext connecting Sarraute with Wallace here contextualizes and hybridizes time and person, producing a ghost to haunt the text.

as a score; all of which Sarraute has wittingly constructed in the manner that pearls on a string make sense together. The following example is comprised of the end of one fragment, the whole of a second, and the beginning of a third, seen here with the important spaces between; those demarcations of white space that act as pause, frame, paratextual moment of becoming-other (that is, enabling a reading-and-blending between the lines), or becoming a 'large white pearl' on the aforementioned string:

> Well, you know, as for me, I must admit that I myself like The Golden Fruits very much.
>
> There. I am a fool. I am a fool: they should look. One second more and I'm going to display before them the secret sign I bear, the indelible mark that they themselves engraved, and shame and slight embarrassment are going to make them avert their eyes.
>
> As for me, I like The Golden Fruits . . . (Sarraute 1965, pp. 120–121)

The book is constructed, and then again in its absence by its critics, but also and importantly by enactments of the elliptical sensations of reading. The reader/critic becomes *writer* in their responses, because of the book and *its* writer: "I am displaced, deported . . . everything is wavering . . . I am cast away into a corner" (p. 122).

In Sarraute, possibility, perpetuity, and luminosity are virtualities in the mind of the reader. Jean-Paul Sartre, in his preface to Sarraute's *Portrait of a Man Unknown* ([1958] 1959), writes that this book is "…an anti-novel that reads like a detective story" (p. viii). This summary is also true of Gertrude Stein's *Blood on the Dining Room Floor* (*BotDRF*, [1948] 2004; see Chapter Three). Sartre identifies a preoccupation with authenticity and inauthenticity in Sarraute's *Portrait*, where any 'heart' value is in the space of doubt or concern at the observation of "inauthenticity rising":

> Nathalie Sarraute shows us the wall of inauthenticity rising on every side. But what is behind this wall? As it happens, there's nothing, or rather almost nothing. Vague attempts to flee something whose lurking presence we sense dimly. Authenticity, that is, the real connection with others, with oneself and with death, is suggested at every turn, although remaining invisible. We feel it because we flee it. (Sartre, in Sarraute 1959, p. xi)

Given the context of the 1950s, the above statement and indeed Sarraute's novel, indicate something (or Sartre's "almost nothing") that weaves through postmodernity and 'out the other side' into a *post*-postmodernity—that is, the tussle between inauthenticity and authenticity and the writer's capacity to deal with either. Sarraute's work shows that the writer is almost bound to deal in *inauthenticity* because the written word is not in the business of constructing singularities.

As exemplified in the broad context around and through a post-postmodern paradigm, categories and binary oppositions begin to collapse after close study, while the middle, the change itself, the point of slippage and difference is the vitality (caveated only by the need to sometimes amplify difference). This is what is being explored in Sarraute, as signified on the surface (in the text) by her reflexivity, parody, and serial ellipses. Her middle-ness is redemptive of the bridge between the authentic and the inauthentic.

Tropism in particular

A tropism is a reaction-to, and evidence of an agent of change. Tropisms are characterized via the affective agent and its effect. The space between agent and object is articulated and there is dependency and pattern in the movement. Just as the flower is changed by the sun, the reader is changed by the writer via the text. And while agents of change may be invisible, they are known by their impressions and effects.[5] Sarraute's work is tropistic of writing itself and of the desire to write. She says the following about her work in the Foreword to *Tropisms* ([1939] 2015):

> These movements seemed to me to be veritable dramatic actions, hiding beneath the most commonplace conversations, the most everyday gestures, and constantly emerging up to the surface of the appearances that both conceal and reveal them. (pp. vi–vii)

Tropisms are the "living substance" of all Sarraute's books (p. viii). Sarraute's 'both/and' of authoriality and non, of visibility and non, is preoccupied with tempo, page-space, voice-work, and a Woolfian-Deleuzian 'it-ness'. In the following example, *he* observes *her* and while she is "mild and flat, quite smooth" she is also "threatening". For example, she says "yes" four times, and her 'eyes

---

[5] The unprovable work of God is proved by its impressions (Tillich 1954, p. 35).

bulge'. Tension is created by the contradictions and the sense that the reader sees only the tip of the iceberg while sensing the whole iceberg; this reveals the tropistic force that stirs the 'disquiet', as exemplified in *Tropisms*:

> She was sitting crouched on a corner of the chair, squirming, her neck outstretched, her eyes bulging: 'Yes, yes, yes, yes,' she said, and she confirmed each part of the sentence with a jerk of her head. She was frightening, mild and flat, quite smooth, and only her eyes were bulging. There was something distressing, disquieting about her and her mildness was threatening. (p. 21)

The interactivity between the human and their environment in Sarraute reveals the 'dramatic action rising up'. It is a sketch of a moment, a fragment, the tropism observed in its turning. Sarraute's human (writer, narrator, reader) has fallen into language where they become redefined as inextricable from words and meanings.

Woolf too performs tropisms that gather a scene in all its materiality of character and place, in a systematic swirl of interdependence. An impression is given of (a) force at work, one constructed in the text and agential of a character's tropisms. For example, in the following scene depicting Clarissa Dalloway's preparations for her party, the language and the sentiment reveal Clarissa's 'turn' to the idea of an audience, of impending thrill, of her self-sabotaging mind; But the text is finished, the turn complete in so far as there is nothing for the reader to add, and arguably, there are a finite number of interpretations to be made in the modernist sense of highly organized forms:

> What a lark! What a plunge! For so it had always seemed to her when, with a little squeak of the hinges, which she could hear now, she had burst open the French windows and plunged at Bourton into the open air. How fresh, how calm, stiller than this of course, the air was in the early morning; like the flap of a wave; kiss of a wave; chill and sharp and yet (for a girl of eighteen as she then was) solemn, feeling as she did, standing there at the open window, that something awful was about to happen. (*MD*, p. 5)

Something is being set up or developed across a series of transactions. There is cause and effect for Woolf's tropistic characters. There is a sense in her schematics that it couldn't be written any other way; that each character is themselves but also interdependent with others, and performing non-negotiable manoeuvres. For example: in *The Waves*, Percy dies, and the others are changed; in, *To the*

Lighthouse, Mrs Ramsay dies and the others are changed; in *Mrs Dalloway*, Septimus dies and the others are changed. There are nameable and lamentable causes and effects.

Unlike Sarraute, Woolf does not explore the moment detached from a moral context, nor detached from a relatively traditional approach to formatting the text. Characters remain novelistic steppingstones in Woolf, where multi-scene texts rhizomatically weave characters, spatial moments, and intuitions together, and all is surrounded and framed by the context with acute attention to resonance and reciprocity in the text and inevitably also with the reader.

Woolf's characters resonate as parts of a smooth textural narrative. Her characters are flattened by their being used as illustrative moments while simultaneously fleshed-out as part of that textural humanizing.

In Sarraute, ellipses—as well as commas, tiny sentences, and poetic play in general, make poetry of narrative threads and draw attention, metafictionally, to the possibilities of language. As a recurrent device, ellipses fray the very situation of writing and reading. They move *beyond* the story, tasking the reader with guessing either what's missing, or where the ellipses may lead. Of course, ellipses may also indicate incomplete-ness in their opening out to unknown or imagined possibilities. Sarraute's ellipses make rhetorical gestures towards the reader, and recursively into the text; they are placeholding marks that instate the quiet expanse of possibility...

According to Hassan, *The Golden Fruits* is "...a novel about a novel which cancels itself in the very act of reading" (1975, p. 12). He points out that in this book, Sarraute uses a "non-telic" form (ibid.),[6] incorporating ambiguity and blurring the representation of time and the effects of action. The non-telic form is frayed-edged but not necessarily unfinished.

In Sarraute's *Here* ([1995] 1997), twenty tropistic fragments lightly glean elements from her previous works and re-boot it all as elliptically as ever, making a hybrid of present thought and past tropisms—of 'action that emerges' where her ellipses create a hybrid space-between, which signifies the blending of one idea into another. Such a space resists closure and suggests the space between 'solids' and moments or acts, by disrupting the sentence and/or making it ambiguous. The repetitive nominative 'it' in *Here*, for example, becomes a

---

[6] 'Non-telic' form is an open-ended form. According to Hassan, W. Burroughs does this too.

blank-slate pronoun around and in which anything the writer chooses to press on or encompass may interact.

The detached 'it' allows for *its* potential as defined by *its* inputs and influences—all listed paratactically and in a caveat-like mode—not as a list with no internal coherence, but rather, haiku-like; building an image or impression. In this case, the impression is of a dialogue that seems 'real' while Sarraute's dialogic fragments remain ambiguous as they open-out hermeneutically in *Here*:

> 'Whatever side you look at it from, it holds its own, doesn't it?' 'Yes, yes. . . .' There is no danger for it here. . . Not the shadow of a menace. . . the laws of hospitality, so respected here, protect it. . . (Sarraute 1997, p. 33)

It turns out that the dialogic aspect of this fragment becomes interior monologue (and monologizing) further on. The reader then questions that preceding dialogue because 'it' (*the text*, we now see) collapses subject and object in an abstraction of both, and a reification of the written word ('it'). Sarraute's 'it' resonates in its accreting borderless-ness, with the "I AM" (of God), and *it* establishes a subliminal hybridity, a *tropistic* move (of language) away from expectation and preconception towards the light of the autonomous Other— which in Sarraute's case, is within the rhizomatic matrix of textual and spatial possibility. The force is the necessity (of language) to reshape and re-configure textual spaces:

> . . . They are still at home here. They are at home everywhere. . . Everywhere, their words have complete mastery. . . they alight with perfect liberty. . . there?. . . yes, even there. . . and they remain fixed there forever, they stick fast. . .'Admirable'. . .'Amazing'. . .'A gem. . . A real marvel'. . . (1997, pp. 34–35)

While it is motion rather than stasis in Sarraute, her elliptical spaces run out abstractly (with a fluidity like Woolf's, only, in a different language) making a very different kind of rhythm to the wash and overlap in Woolf; Sarraute's is more surface, staccato, the steps and the dance, the intellectual score . . .

Woolf's *The Waves* features strong characters or types that are 'fleshed' while flowing over into Others and archetypes. There are concrete images weighty enough to make narrative stepping stones but light enough to be carried on a vast *surge* of time:

> Up here my eyes are green leaves, unseeing. I am a boy in
> grey flannels with a belt fastened by a brass snake up here. Down
> there my eyes are the lidless eyes of a stone figure in a desert by
> the Nile. I see women passing with red pitchers to the river; I

see camels swaying and men in turbans. I hear tramplings, tremblings, stirrings round me. (*TW*, p. 7)

There is up and down and interrelationship between life/death and unborn/undead, in Woolf. In Sarraute it is more planar: there is the invisible narrator-character plus glimpses of temporary voices and minds in dialogue, plus words—their stand-alone shape and meanings—marks, and page-space that equally construct impressions. In Sarraute, the space between fragments, and the reader's mind-and-body opens a zone of hybridizing action for the tropism; a making-hybrid of intellects, intuitions, and time; and the reader blends their own experience and knowledge with the writing being received.

In line with Sarraute, Deleuze and Guattari suggest a reduction of "…oneself to an abstract line, a trait, in order to find one's zone of indiscernibility with other traits, and in this way enter the haecceity and impersonality of the creator" (D&G 2014, p. 280). And while 'reduction' is an arborescent concept, it is difficult to account for life only in rhizomatic terms. There is for example, Woolf's *arborescent* hybridizing from atom through writer and writing to reader, and there are Sarraute's *rhizomatic* elliptical traces . . .

While *not* conceiving of process and practice in terms of the redemptive hybrid (a unifying expansion that seeks *the* magnetic line of truth), the Deleuzoguattarian point of view makes a conceptually unusual foil to it. The root-process of their rhizomatic ideal is a process of seeking the golden thread that insinuates a broader or longer view, while not *necessarily* plotting (pre-empting or scripting) along the way.

Parataxis and the middle

In Wallace

Various treatments in Wallace's *The Pale King* present as spikes of connectivity within the modernisms continuum, and the use of parataxis is one of these. The asyndeton or stripping out of connective tissue, a feature of parataxis, instates leaps around the syntactical scheme and enhances *TPK*'s disjunctive approach to time and form in emphasis of a conjunctive space-between.

The few pages of §25 are set in double columns. Here, parataxis builds a mechanistic rhythm that makes more than an image of workers at their desks:

> 'Irrelevant' Chris Fogle turns a page. Howard Cardwell turns a page. Ken Wax turns a page. Matt Redgate turns a page. 'Groovy' Bruce Channing attaches a form to a file. Ann Williams turns a page. Anand Singh turns two pages at once by mistake and turns one back which makes a slightly different sound. David Cusk turns a page. (*TPK*, p. 310)

The rhythm is interrupted occasionally by jazzy surprises, like the 'devils' in the next quote, providing a metafictional reminder that the text is also a game, dance, poem, list, a cathartic thing:

> Rosellen Brown turns a page. Ken Wax turns a page. Devils are actually angels. Elpidia Carter and Harriet Candelaria reach up to their Cart-In boxes at exactly the same time. (p. 312)

Like a parody of the 'begat'-ting in the bible, the parataxis marks time, fills space, provides a musical interlude, a check-list, and illustrates the mechanistic nature of the IRS in becoming a redemptive machine of (repetitive) production in or from stuckness. What results is a profound sense of everything that *is*, laid out as a mediated assemblage, that is, order disrupted in orderly fashion by the illusion of free thought. Wallace shows us that the space-between the parts of IRS procedure are bursting with what has been repressed. And the realizations gained by the reader hybridize them with the author, the author's characters and agenda/s, until the art object/book is truly public and thereby malleable.

It follows, that Wallace's *TPK* can be conceived of as all 'middle', being an unfinished and posthumously published 'best-guess' compilation by its editor Michael Pietsch. It is not ordered as it might have been had Wallace finished it, and this gives it its middle-ness.

TPK's grandly specious and pastoral opening 'scene' is magnificent while incongruous with the rest of the book. I half-waited for a breathing space like that to return, meanwhile, matters incidentally unresolved or unfinished provide a view to the author whose process becomes a significant aspect of the story. It is its connection to other texts during the writing, such as to the stories in Wallace's collection *Oblivion* ([2004] 2005) for example, written in overlap with *TPK*, which blur its *actual* beginning and emphasize its 'middle-ness'.

As an admirer of Wittgenstein, Wallace establishes an approach to textual 'middle-ness' partly via repetitions, and by his view of language as a vehicle for a kind of honesty. According to Heaton and Groves ([1994] 2005), Wittgenstein's seminal text, *Tractatus Logico-Philosophicus* (1921) is "…an initiation, drawing a limit to the expression of thoughts by expressing what can be said as clearly as possible. 'The more the nail has been hit on the head – the greater will be its value'" (Heaton & Groves 2005, p. 29).

Max writes that the Wittgensteinian value of repetition and emphasis resonates with Wallace. In Max's words, Wittgenstein claims: "…you can with certainty know nothing outside of yourself" ([2012] 2013, p. 44). This frightened but intrigued Wallace, suggests Max, as it signified: "The loss of the whole external world" (Wallace, in Max 2013, p. 44). Wittgenstein eventually gives language a more "communal" and game-like framing (p. 45), which also interested Wallace who seemed to harbour an interest in both that original nail-hitting clarity and an appreciation for games. This comes together in *TPK* as an ambiguous authorial visibility seen in its repeated ironic and/or overly-mediated claims of truth and (other) authorial interruptions all confounded by the unfinishedness of the text.

'Hitting the nail on the head' (re Wittgenstein, in Heaton & Groves 2005) is a glorification of 'correct' perception, or at least perception's shared aspect, while repetition (of hammer blows) provides an opportunity for Wallace to be emphatic—even if emphatically ambiguous.

"…there is no beginning or end to the *Tractatus*. We start in the middle" (Heaton & Groves 2005, p. 30). No one can definitely say where *TPK* 'starts'[7] and while its 'beginning' looks like a beginning, it soon becomes tentacles and streamers/snakes and ladders, in terms of form.

In others

Levé's *Autoportrait* ([2005] 2012) is middling too; there are no formal hierarchies or obvious reason to the sequencing; it is a curated list of fragments whose sequencing offers meaning by virtue of the effect of juxtapositions and subsequent relationships:

> I have trouble believing that France will go to war in my lifetime. I like to say thank you. I cannot perceive the delay in mirrors. I don't like narrative movies any more than I like the novel. 'I do not like the novel' doesn't mean I do not like literature, 'I don't like narrative movies' doesn't mean I don't like movies.

---

[7] See Pietsch's Editor's Note in *TPK*, pp. v–x. And there are author notes and early drafts at the Harry Ransom Center archive that reveal a lineage of work towards the *TPK*, as discussed in Hering (2017).

> Art that unfolds over time gives me less pleasure than art that stops it. The second time I walk the same route, I pay less attention to the view and walk faster. (Levé 2012, p. 26)

By framing this de-contextualized fragment from Levé's book inside *this* page space, I interrupt the parataxis with a view from the middle. Like this, a readerly intervention becomes authorial and also collaborative, bringing me into the text and making it move beyond itself—a hybridizing manoeuvre reflective or repetitious of what Levé is doing with the material of his life, which is curating 'endless' fragments with the advantageous union of chance and constraint, leaving writer and reader in the middle without ends.

Ben Lerner's *Leaving the Atocha Station* ([2011] 2013) is an example of a veering-auto-fictional novella-length work that never leaves the 'middle' of insinuation regarding in particular, slippages of truth. Perhaps more consciously and resolvedly 'middling' than *TPK*, Lerner's book incorporates pictorial illustrations that read as map-like or *like* journal entries made in real places, alongside other meta-fictional triggers that seem truthful while also unbelievable due to the overt *sense* of fictionality and play in the text. Lerner's work incorporates post-postmodern sincerity with authorial visibility while beating postmodernism at its own game precisely because of the extant *sense* that any authorial visibility and sincerity might be language-and-word games, the commodification of sincerity. In *Leaving the Atocha Station*, Lerner writes: "Love for *that other thing*, the sound-absorbent screen, life's white machine, shadows massing in the middle distance, although that's not even close, the texture of et cetera itself" (2013, p. 16). "…the texture of et cetera" brings to mind Sarraute's *Here* with its prolific ellipses which demonstrate that texture, and also Jameson's observation about paradigms and writers 'becoming' each other across time, place, and gender (Jameson 1991, in my Introduction).

And what there is-now-was, is only ever partially retrievable by the 'it' (of Sarraute's *Here*) being taken in by the present in the manner that the modernisms are a continuum that 'takes in' its parts. And while the 'now' is post-postmodern (regardless of any other name), it incorporates the modern and the postmodern, becoming a complex hybrid fabric of options and influence whereby the post-postmodern, and even post, post that, is created by perpetual tropistic movement from the perpetual middle.

Time and unfinishedness

> The huge black clock hand is still at rest but is on the point of making its once-a-minute gesture; that resistant jolt will set a whole world in motion. The clock face will slowly turn away, full of despair, contempt, and boredom, as one by one the iron pillars will start walking past, bearing away the vault of the station. (Nabokov [1928] 1968, *King Queen Knave*, p. 1)

The bored clock/train imagery in Nabokov recalls the moment of train passing in Kafka's one-sentence diary entry of 1910: "The onlookers go rigid when the train goes past" (Kafka, in Josipovici 2010, p. 159). Both show the effects on perception of time and movement. The question wrought by the image of boredom in the Nabokov example is: what is actually moving? Is anything moving? There are moments, like Zeno's paradox of the arrow, where perpetual movement is also stillness at any particular point of apprehension (Huggett 2019).

Boredom's obliteration of one perspective in the creation of another, becomes a collapse of sorts, but also an expression of timelessness, that is, the sudden perception of a moment of difference, which characterizes an epiphany.

As though it were boredom's nemesis, the "irreducible specificity" (Eagleton 2012, p. 2) of the Deleuzoguattarian haecceity, is another de-limiting of time. In literary terms, regardless of era or cultural paradigm, the value: 'timelessness', which is simultaneously *all* time and being *without* time, is informed by continuity. Timelessness is engagement with the space between, and it is a showing (such as the moment the train passes) of what lies beneath the surface or adjacent to it in an alternate view.

Via the textual presence of clocks, time in *TPK* becomes an ever-present menace (a picture of boredom) *or* a reprieve (a picture of release), and Wallace's images of airlessness show the effect on oxygen, space, and people of *too much* time passing. The tedium experienced by the character, as thematized in the text, becomes reader tedium; it is contributed to by textual congestion plus a hovering or a tending-to-hover-y[8] micro-managing author. Wallace curates his

---

[8] 'Hovering' because the author walks around amidst his characters, or 'hover-y' because he floats above them. The terms are somewhat interchangeable while semantically distinct. And whether hovering or hover-y, Wallace is ghostly, and/or alive in his characters. Wallace refers to the ghost in his fiction; however, while I acknowledge that the ghost is a smudged character that blends entities in *TPK*, I assert that it has less veracity as a poetic device than does the 'hovering' author, with the ambiguous *and* neurotic micro-managerial detail inferred by that.

story elements to reveal partial layers, like parts of time; hours breaking into minutes, breaking into seconds, and on down to something like the Woolfian atomic saturation:

> He [Lane Dean] imagined that the clock's second hand possessed awareness and knew that it was a second hand and that its job was to go around and around inside a circle of numbers forever at the same slow unvarying machinelike rate. (*TPK*, p. 381)

It is the éclat[9] of the transcendent; the middle of the whirring clock 'tick-tocked' white noise of the office, the base guttural of the mental/physical distress that is shown to be located sideways along a continuum of character and life; and then there is past, present, and future in collapse within the perpetual and claustrophobic now of the IRS.

Clocks are implements of torture in *TPK*, and yet Wallace's bored-and-tortured characters are co-dependent in the textual space-time, which becomes bigger than they are. It is similar but different in Woolf where characters attach to story in ways that make them non-negotiable to and necessary for the making of the text that is steeped, like Wallace's, in textual mutability.

Clocks have a character in-between abject menace and beating heart in Woolf's *Mrs Dalloway*. "Shredding and slicing, dividing and subdividing, the clocks of Harley Street nibbled at the June day" (*MD*, p. 113). Time shown on clocks is the metronome geared by Sir William's "proportion" (pp. 110–113), the normalcy of which becomes the innervating rhythm, the making-mad of sensitized types (Septimus and Clarissa); the life that goes on beyond one's will but simultaneously, because of it. Time is the ultimate hybridizer in so far as individual memory, as well as the corporate memory of the history-makers, merges and recounts events and objects according to the conditions in which the thinker remembers. Time is a perpetual pressure in *Mrs Dalloway*, blending and forcing free-floating minds to conform—or more pertinently, to alight at the 'right time' and inhabit a body, preferably their own, yet, to be always aware of when the mind soared and mingled with the mind of another. Time is hybridizing in Woolf, and *redemptive* in the flood beyond the self into empowering re-connections.

---

[9] "The éclat means the sudden, extraordinary idea or innovation that brings you to the notice of those at high levels" (*TPK*, p. 528).

Constrained time

In Levé's writing too, time floods, with a momentum made of the tension the reader experiences in the presence of the constrained and Oulipo-esque poetics while they search for conjunctions in the space between abutted stand-alone sentences. In Levé, moments are disconnected one from the other across paratactical phrases and images, making textualized 'life' into a suite of fragments divorced from any connective tissue other than what the reader surmises and provides, and with a sense of the kind of time that grows things. But fragments become starting points in Levé; even a luminous catalogue of moments that avoid normative cohesion. Fragments allow a multiplicity of methods for traversing or collapsing the time-space between them, as seen here in *Autoportrait*:

> International news, even dramatic news, leaves me pretty much indifferent, I feel guilty about that. I do not remember the first time I saw a character die in a movie or a book, but I remember the first time I saw a dead man, more precisely, I saw a man's leg sticking out of the trunk of a black car on the boulevard Berthier, I remember this detail: he was missing a shoe, and his sock was purple. My feet are always hot, sandals would help, but they're too ugly. (Levé 2012, p. 50)

Pertinent here too, is Levé's *Suicide* ([2008] 2017), a hybrid novella and his final work, articulating the time and space of a life. It is arguably the author's own suicide note,[10] and takes on a rarefied aspect in terms of the privileged information it gives the reader who mines for treasures and information (similar to the experience of reading *TPK*), while knowing in advance that the end of the book signifies the end of the author, which makes the reading an unnerving but privileged experience. The time-tide in *Suicide* is different from that of *TPK*, while the reader's anxiety *where will this lead?* Or, *what am I witnessing?* is similarly present:

> You used to want only to perform acts that would resonate for a long time, gestures that, though completed in a few minutes, would leave vestiges to persist and continue to be seen. Your interest in painting depended upon this suspension of time in matter: the brief time of its realization is succeeded by the long life of the painting. (Levé 2017, p. 66)

---

[10] Levé completed *Suicide* and gave it to his editor ten days before taking his own life in 2007 at the age of 42 (Steyn, Afterword in Levé 2017, p. 119). *Quiet moment again, of deeply felt compassion.*

Time is a gift the reader gives each text in expectation. Perhaps the writer requires the reader's understanding, or perhaps something more narcissistic than that—immortality perhaps, as per Levé's author-character's hope for immortalization in "the long life of the painting" (ibid.). Either way, time can only be *written* or re-made according to its writer's ability to embody time and then to invest their sense of it in the body and mind of the reader. Something is certainly given across the 'time' that Levé deconstructs, and this might be the reader's production of images, aromas, textures, and absences. We hear his confession and absolve him—precisely because of our activation of the liminal space which lends such paratactical work its connectivities.

Behold, a long day given briefly in Woolf where paratactical beats work apropos of Jacob Flanders in *Jacob's Room* (Woolf [1922] 1989), to compress time and pass it quickly. Woolf shows Jacob's character in the character-specific rhythms of *his* time, and by all that his rushing life takes in:

> About half-past nine Jacob left the house, his door slamming, other doors slamming, buying his paper, mounting his omnibus, or, weather permitting, walking his road as other people do. Head bent down, a desk, a telephone, books bound in green leather, electric light....'Fresh coals, sir?'... 'Your tea, sir.' ...Talk about football, the Hotspurs, the Harlequins; six-thirty *Star* brought in by the office boy; the rooks of Gray's Inn passing overhead; branches in the fog thin and brittle; and through the roar of traffic now and again a voice shouting: 'Verdict – verdict – winner – winner', while letters accumulate in a basket, Jacob signs them, and each evening finds him, as he takes his coat down, with some muscle of the brain new stretched. (pp. 86–87)

In relatively few words, we see Jacob's entire day as a kind of train window-smear-scape, showing us that he gobbles or is gobbled by time, making his writer run after him.

Unfinished since 1872

In *On Authority and Revelation: The Book on Adler* ([1872] 1955) Kierkegaard writes: "To find the conclusion it is necessary first of all to observe that it is lacking and then in turn to feel quite vividly the lack of it" (p. 4). This suggests that feeling a 'lack of conclusion' is necessarily embodied—whether the feeling is heavy or light—for the process of summarizing that to which the conclusion comes. To be innervated (motivated) by a lack-of-conclusion, moves differently across the modernisms. It also articulates the character of the modernisms if we view that as a continuum; from an existential and modernist space, to a postmodern one where *lack* is a motif usurped by the shifting sands of agency and identity, and on into a post-postmodernity where we re-invigorate self-other unity in appreciation of the kind of difference that is redemptive. 'We' do not do this by fixing fractures and combining fragments, but by observing and holding difference in adequate frames. In a post-postmodernity we 'vividly feel the lack of a conclusion' (again, the/our unfinishedness) and this brings urgency and hope, engaging with the possibilities I articulate as redemptive hybridism.

Unfinishedness in Wallace

The reader may find unfinishedness where the author did not intend it. Unfinishedness may be present in and beyond each (or any) text. It may reflect the mind of the reader and their preferences. For many writers, imperfect preliminary drafts are the bulk of their work, representing stages, phases, and changes.

When Wallace died on 12 September 2008, he left the *TPK* manuscript as an unfinished collection of fragments, notes, and instructions. He had been writing the book around and between other collections of stories and essays in the years since *Infinite Jest* was published in 1996. The process of bringing *TPK* together involved working with bags and piles of material to carefully reveal the Work. (Pietsch's Editor's Note, in *TPK*, pp. v–x). As the *TPK*'s editor, Michael Pietsch demonstrates the extent to which he, and then also the reader of *TPK* are given privileged access to Wallace's drafting process. He says: "David was a perfectionist of the highest order, and there is no question that *The Pale King* would be vastly different had he survived to finish it" (p. ix). "But an unfinished novel is what we have, and how can we not look?" (p. x).[11]

In its unfinishedness, *TPK* reveals the fascinating internal workings of a literary process, and because of posthumous completion, the process is a reified one. The "how can we not look" (ibid.), enacts the voyeurism of the Work's reader. There can be no easy assignation of closed and value-forming statements for

---

[11] While not a prerequisite for selection re the writers I have chosen, the tragic death of some becomes emblematic; creating an imperative regarding the impetus of the authorial, of redemption, and of literary legacies that stand in their writer's stead, giving them an echoing voice because of and despite unfinishedness.

an unfinished work of this magnitude—in every sense of 'magnitude'. However, Wallace left his manuscript with instructions, and so, unfinished-ness becomes a part of this work's particular finished-ness: a testament to the post-author life of a book and to editorial commitment.

In 2021, McNally Editions published the *The Pale King*'s 'Chris Fogle' chapter (§22, *TPK*, pp. 154–252) as a finished novella titled *Something to Do with Paying Attention*. Sarah McNally suggests in her preface that the novella sits fully formed inside *TPK*, now extracted because it is "…not just a complete story, but the best complete example we have of Wallace's late style" (McNally, in Wallace 2021, p. xi). It is certainly interesting to see the chapter presented as a stand-alone work, a manageable sample of the magnitude and intensity of *TPK* perhaps. While I am unsure about mining other people's unfinished works for finished fragments, reading *TPK*'s §22 as a novella certainly provides a moment of sharp focus. Switching to a conception of Wallace's last work as a small novella instead of an enormous bundle provokes the matter of authorial visibility and editorial involvement again. The complexity further invigorates *TPK*'s hybridity.

Unfinishedness raises questions, but it is not necessary for the reader to bring these to their reading. Unfinishedness is intrinsic to the text, it is part of *TPK*'s back story, while as a 'finished' and 'collaborative' work, it is something new; a hybrid of form, theme, strategy, intention, and genre; blending as it does memoir, anecdote, short story, journalism, essay, and the long-form maximal novel (Max 2013, p. 60).[12]

Unfinishedness in Woolf

Woolf's *Between the Acts* ([1941] 2005) is/was arguably unfinished at the time of her death. Leonard Woolf writes on the un-numbered page after the Foreword in *BtA* that at the time of Virginia Woolf's death: "She would not, I believe, have made any large or material alterations in it, though she would have made a good many small corrections or revisions before passing the final proofs". Like any posthumously published work, this one is scrutinizingly final; the book we might look to for hints about what happened or what might have happened, just as we look to *The Pale King* apropos of Wallace. The view of an arrested process is what interests me about unfinishedness, and any glimpse of the author it might

---

[12] As a writer, Wallace was a "folder-in and includer, a maximalist, someone who wanted to capture the *everything* of America" (Max 2013, p. 60).

provide. Hybridity is made particularly explicit in an unfinished yet published work. Where the post-author collaboration rears up, the reader reads the text not only as a literary artefact but also as a parting gift or a memento, whether that was intended by the author or not.

"On 27th March 1941, Woolf wrote to her publisher, John Lehmann" telling him that *Between the Acts* was "too silly and trivial" to publish in its current form and that she would look at revising it for publication later in the year. The next day she drowned herself (both quotes: Clark 2016, np). There are loose parallels here with Wallace. The reader *might* consider the death of the writer as they read a work that was left unfinished when the writer died, but it is the frayed-edged and porous *unfinishedness* itself—regardless of how it came to be, which gives special access for the reader to enter the text as well as the author's process. "'But we have other lives, I think, I hope,' she murmured. 'We live in others, Mr.… We live in things'" (*BtA,* Mrs Swithin, p. 43). 'Living in others' concerns unfinishedness's hybridizing value, and perhaps also its redemptivity.

3
Family Traits of Fragmentation

I discuss Fragmentation throughout this work from 'Woolf to Wallace'. It is suggestive of a multiplicity of the kind that constructs a unity in difference inherent to the appearance, concepts, and even the ethics of hybrid forms.[1]

Eagleton invokes the theory of 'family resemblance' from Wittgenstein's *Philosophical Investigations* (1953; in Eagleton 2012, pp. 20–22). I paraphrase: in relation for example to games, there is connection one to the other by virtue that each is a game while no two games have the same rules or objectives. The category of games is the 'family' within which individual games might resemble each other a lot or a little via any common attributes, or may not share any attributes at all while sharing the category of 'game'. The same goes for family members in families: there may be little resemblance, but the *fact* of the family remains. This can also be applied to literature, art, and philosophy where specific genre distinctions like 'memoir', 'painting', or 'postmodernism' may be comprised of vastly different members engaged in vastly different practices while working within the same 'family'. Categorization can be both problematic and advantageous.[2]

In relation to *Philosophical Investigations,* Wallace says "One of the things that makes Wittgenstein a real artist to me is that he realized that no conclusion could be more horrible than solipsism" (Wallace, in McCaffery [1993] 2012, p. 44). This foregrounds Wallace's own efforts later in *The Pale King* specifically in the area of authorial visibility as a mode of honesty, one which carefully avoids solipsism, unless the navel-gazing subject is the writing itself. Wallace lauds the Wittgensteinian value that language is a "...function of relationships

---

[1] Again, my work is metonymical, reflecting its subject and the author (I).
[2] Redemptive Hybridism liberates from and to categories in recognition of the inevitability and value of family resemblance and of the veracity of self-determination (despite categories)—that is, the veracity of the movement outside of category to explore that space of enquiry in case there is something valuable there. Wherever you stand on the possibility of loosing or losing family resemblance, the hybridizing of family/category with what you see through your viewfinder will make its progress.

between persons" and is "dependent on human community" (ibid.). It leads not to solipsism but towards connections. However, this leads ultimately to the postmodern belief that there is nothing outside language—a source of anxiety in Wallace who suggests that Wittgenstein unwittingly pushed his theory towards a "postmodern trap" of his own making (p. 45). "[Wittgenstein] died right on the edge of explicitly treating reality as linguistic instead of ontological. This eliminated solipsism, but not the horror. Because we're still stuck" (ibid.). Years later, towards *The Pale King*, Wallace attempts to write a way out of the trapped-ness of category.

In the preface of *Family Resemblance: An Anthology and Exploration of 8 Hybrid Literary Genres* (2015) edited by Marcela Sulak and Jacqueline Kolosov, Sulak brings in the central concept: "A family resemblance defines a particular genre, and for this reason, genre can be viewed as an affiliation, rather than a fixed point of identification" (Sulak 2015, p. xi). According to Sulak, genre is a loosely defining term which indicates shared traits within the 'family' (ibid.).[3] Even in a discussion about hybridity there is a genre-family and families within families, like unpacking Russian Dolls of affinity and affiliation. Meanwhile, perhaps it is also possible to look at it as a network of continuous change which needs genres less.

According to Maggie Nelson in *Family Resemblance*, her *Bluets* shows the "fragment as fetish, as catastrophe, as leftover, as sample or citation, as memory, and so on" (2015a, p. 142). For Nelson, *Bluets* exemplifies the "notion of collecting" (ibid.), and of collage, like Joseph Cornell's textural diorama work, she says. She uses words like "distillation", "disintegration", "aphorisms" and "abandoned" apropos of textual pieces in relation to the hybridizing manner by which her work eventuates (pp. 142–143). Nelson 'hits-on-head' the nail of (what I call) the redemptive hybrid's connection to possibility, where she writes: "…the mind will always work overtime to put disparate things together" (p. 144).

It seems that in relation to the effect of fragmentation in art and text, the more work the reader does in receipt of disparate parts and the more they

---

[3] I do not know that there always needs to be a family, genre, or category (except for strength in numbers). In my work with hybrid forms, it is categorization and those form-filling identifications with only one or the other, which truncates liberty. Sometimes family (genre) affiliation is stated so that the audience knows how to look at what they see – something is implicated here about trust in one's own ability to see and feel.

participate and commit ('bind' to the text, after Hale 2007), the more possibility they engage and the more they might gain.

The fragmented mind

> In hybrid forms, fragments are smoothed together, spaced apart (valuing absence and distance), or joined by visible connections.

Hybridity is associated with the dislocated "subjective 'I'" (Sulak 2015, p. xvi). It also creates new subjectivities and the liberation of form. But here, I am discussing the fragmented or fractured person as it is reflected in forms that exemplify, repair, and (tentatively in this context) perhaps also *redeem* the subject. The process of creative hybridizing might augur the re-integration of the fragmented mind after trauma and after problems associated with neurodiversity. Deleuze and Guattari write "…the unconscious itself [is] fundamentally a crowd" (2014, p. 29), one baying for harmony while also capable of simultaneity. The unconscious is a noun, a unity; a thing partial to categorization, blame, judgment and the authoring of identity formations. Be careful about the crowd you're in, and regularly disperse the one gathering in your head…

Multi-genre writer Susanne Paola Antonetta has two surnames; an official one Paola, and a pen name Antonetta. This becomes an image of her being in a sense *dual*. In *Family Resemblance*, Paola Antonetta writes *creatively* about the science of a bipolar brain like her own (2015, p. 21) and the relation of that to both inside and outside worlds. According to Paola Antonetta, the 'dark/light' duality of matter and energy reflects the divided brain. Embodying the bipolar duality as well as any other multiplicities common to us all or not, Paola Antonetta points out the deficit we share in knowledge of our world; that which points to possibility:

> Two unknown pieces of the universe exist, dark matter and dark energy. Dark energy's a quantum force and constitutes about two-thirds of the cosmos: dark matter, which we cannot see or uncover, about 25 percent. We have not the dimmest idea of 90 percent of our world. (p. 20).

I get the sense, in apprehension of images textual and otherwise, that despite the spectrum of suffering and also in support of difference, we might get ahead of any nemesis *it* when we saturate the atom (after Woolf) and dive into that unknown "90 percent" (ibid.).

Writers with experience of mental illness and neurodiversity, such as some I discuss in this work, might have an inclination to produce hybrid forms due to what could be described as 'fractured seeing', and the seeking of refuge in activities that reflect and help process a lived experience of fracture. They might push a more concerted effort into processing experience, and in ways that differ from those of someone with no experience of neurodiversity. As Joy Ladin writes in *Family Resemblance*, "…trauma interferes with the ongoing process of self-narration" (2015, p. 101). It collapses time and disintegrates memory. Ladin refers to an explicitly Jewish experience apropos of historical atrocities, invoking "…a hybrid God who presides over incomprehensible murder and equally incomprehensible deliverance" (p. 104). This response to God invokes the divergent relationship that the hybrid three-part self (body, mind, spirit) has with the Western canon's three-part God (father, son, and holy ghost). It also suggests and encapsulates the simultaneity of love and hate and the complexity of the broad hybrid space in-between. What is produced for example, by neurodiverse genius might redeem us all as it goes boldly into the unknown "90 percent" (Paola Antonetta) on our behalf.

Writing on modernist melancholia, Sanja Bahun refers to "the modernists'" use of the fragment as a "function of dislocation" and "a marker of the loss of 'totality'" but also as a liberator of the subject "from the shackles of 'totality'" (all 2014, p. 46). The "…modernist understanding of the mind as divided against itself" (p. 47) gets interesting when the authorial subject wishes to use the art/text as the form through which to re-integrate their fractured parts for presentation to the world as a collection of combined fragments—even nearing a restored and 'totalising' object. In 1908 Woolf sought a "…whole made of shivering fragments" (Woolf, in Bahun 2014, p. 46). In her diary, Woolf writes: "The only way I keep afloat is by working. […] Directly I stop working I feel that I am sinking down, down. And as usual I feel that if I sink further I shall reach the truth" (*Diary*, Sunday, 23 June 1929, np). Thankfully, we are the beneficiaries of Woolf's sinking into truth.

According to Bahun, melancholia is significantly agential in the modernist author/artist's collapse of exterior into interior space (2014, p. 55). This is a hybridizing manoeuvre without calling it that. As a watched (read) or felt condition it opens up to darker and/or reflective spaces. In relation to this Bahun writes: "…*Mrs Dalloway*, shuttles between the outer and the inner so as to integrate all the impressions and movements of the configured historical-social space" (ibid.). Clarissa Dalloway's oscillatory mental state is reflected in the timbre, diction, and structure of that book. Her mental fragmentation is assisted by the union of characters in parallel, and the floating sense in Clarissa that she becomes and is becoming more but also less, fading at any moment as she feels everything and 'goes through it all' (*MD*, p. 203), disembodied then embodied again because of the fragmentary nature of mental unwellness, her particular kind of melancholy.

Bahun writes: "The modernist chronotype is vitally shaped by the interplay of two basic aspects of space—presence and absence" (2014, p. 55). Premised on the absence of an object symptomatically felt as present, melancholia foregrounds the relationship of presence and absence (paraphrase, ibid.). The yearned for, the desired, the remembered, and the habitual are like the patient's experience of phantom pain in a missing limb, or a broken heart.

The hybrid might be utilitarian (a patchwork or minor repair), or almost imperceptible (ghost writing). But when we go into the hybrid's component fragments and consider context and re-contextualization and then move into the space between 'marble-picked' pieces (see Levé, upcoming) and engage there with the field of possibilities, it is then that something meaningful begins. *There is the seed of redemptivity, a picture of unfolding possibility.*

Levé's strategy works in reflection on the non-linearity and subjectivity of memory and knowledge and how these are 'best' articulated via hybrid forms—and mainly via form's *hybridizing* across suite, series, or page and into the author's self, who is not invisible but smeared/scattered/threaded across their pages—which in Levé, are a genre-defying suicide note, a meditation, a poem, a list, a lifeline, a love letter—into the unknown-beyond; the beyond of textual expression and of life, in a manner whose delicate brutality makes categorization less relevant.

Writers/artists/readers/viewers acquire and reify fragments—those non-linearly arranged pieces that may be framed by white space and pop out as bright shards, or threads, or phrases of wholes that *are* wholes on their own if observed beyond narrative. Surrounded by space, does the fragment become an artefact or cultural emblem?[4] The hybrid form may be most hybridizing when

---

[4] The 'artefact' is reified in Victorian Kitsch as well as by other cultures and ideologies for which re-contextualized mementos become surrogates. E.g. Catholic iconography may be viewed as a figure of God; Mexican folk art depicts the continuum of life; and collectors of anything anywhere build Frankenstein's monster/s from disparate parts.

its particulars are dwelt on, and even if these are not distinct and separate, the dwelling-on is meaning-making.

Constraint, minimalism, and the caveat

Constraint and minimalism

Via the influence of Oulipo[5] "especially Georges Perec" writes Jan Steyn in the Afterword of Levé's *Suicide* ([2008] 2017, p. 121), Levé summarizes his commitment to the fragmented nature of memory. Oulipo is a 'little hybridizing' in so far as it curates non-linear fragments like his:

> [t]o portray your life in order would be absurd: I remember you at random. My brain resurrects you through stochastic details, like picking marbles out of a bag. (Levé, ibid.)

According to Steyn, Levé's 'marble-picked' approach is present in all his writing (ibid.). Constraint and brevity tend to sharpen foci and make emphases; even where maximal wordage is deployed, these might be attended to in the work's constituent fragments.[6] Considering Levé's penchant for combining the minimal with the effusive (the effect of gathering clusters of sentences) and the fact that *Suicide* is posthumously published, it is easy to read it as autobiographical. "Your taste for abbreviation meant that instead of finishing the works you undertook, you finished yourself" (Levé, 2017, p. 41). Everything discussed and to be discussed in relation to authorial visibility is there: the text-as-author-as-text is terribly absolute in Levé's example of hybridity.[7]

---

[5] 'Oulipo' is "an acronym for Ouvroir de Littérature Potentielle (Workshop for Potential Literature), a group of writers and mathematicians formed in France in 1960 by poet Raymond Queneau and mathematician François Le Lionnais. Unlike the Dada and Surrealist movements, Oulipo rejects spontaneous chance and the subconscious as sources of literary creativity. Instead, the group emphasizes systematic, self-restricting means of making texts. For example, the technique known as n + 7 replaces every noun in an existing text with the noun that follows seven entries after it in the dictionary". (Poetry Foundation 2020, https://www.poetryfoundation.org/learn/glossary-terms/oulipo).

[6] In relation to Wallace, maximal wordage may apply in a book like his *Infinite Jest* more than in *TPK* for which any intentionality has less certitude and force due to unfinishedness. But Wallace too was influenced by Oulipo (Burn 2012, p. xiii).

[7] As I muse on a work like *Suicide*, which hovers at the brink (of death), I find a redemptive vitality in that space between 'before' and 'after'. It is a space of imminence, anxiety, and possibility (*what will happen?*). *Brink* texts seem very alive (Woolf, Wallace, Levé et al.) as the reader goes in search of the troubled author; rummaging for understanding; willfully treating fiction (one genre) as if it is tending-autobiographical (another genre)—almost as if something might be done to change what happens. This is where the post-author life of the text comes in, and *post*-author—even the living ones—the text expands or contracts depending on how it is read and by whom.

Wallace, who might appear to leave nothing out of his largest books, suggests that minimalism for its own sake is empty and fraudulent: "...it eschews not only self-reference but any narrative personality at all" (Wallace, in McCaffery [1993] 2012, p. 45). Wallace says that Raymond Carver, "...the inventor of modern U.S. minimalism" is a true "artist" (p. 46) who uses minimalism only where it suits the story and not where a story requires expansion. Meanwhile, the post-Carver "crank-turners" (ibid. and used repeatedly throughout the interview) engage in mimicry to the neglect of integrity. Because of his appreciation of an artistry and innovation that applies to his own view of what is right and good, Wallace boldly claims that (crank-turning) minimalism and metafiction are "...both so extreme they end up empty" (p. 45).

But of course, minimalism is everywhere in literary practice, and endemic in poetry, even the process of editing is one which keeps minimalist processes in mind to distil and refine. Daniel Grassian writes that the minimalist writers of the 1970s and 80s like Carver, are responsible for 'resuscitating' the short story (Grassian 2003, p. 11). And short stories are on the spectrum from flash fiction to novellas—each form working with ideas of constraint, brevity, and distillation.

The caveat

In Wallace, the caveat is exemplified in relation to his authoriality, risk-taking, and claims and counterclaims to truth. His footnotes are extraordinarily caveating. In relation to the space it opens, the caveat invokes words of non-committal, adjustment, and attenuating movements triggered by ill-ease or by the need for fortification or justification.

The 'space between' characters, subjects, moments, strategies, images, affects, etc., is a frame for particulars and their caveating work. The space between, or even the negative space (in terms of positive/negative in the visual sense), changes what it frames or abuts, being caveating in various incarnations and shapes and becoming a space of mystery where contradiction and fiction might reside even in meta-nonfictions. These spaces are, effectively, univocal multiplicities (particulars *becoming* hybrids) and relative truths that univocalize process to enact the hybridity of any writing and art.

The caveat is akin to a leak that challenges and extends the concept in question and all of its components. And like a stain on a previously unblemished cloth, the caveat imbues certainty with doubt. The caveating off-shoot is a line of flight (Deleuze & Guattari 2014); a hybridizing manoeuvere extending territory via the process of 'gathering in' and 'taking with'. The line (defining territory) is drawn wider because as the caveat adjusts (the concept) it expands it. This can be demonstrated by Samuel Beckett's explicit and contradictory caveating from the last lines of *The Unnameable* ([1952] 1966, p. 418): "I can't go on, I'll go on." On that same page (and beyond) the paratactical sequencing makes an exploration of truth, lies, objectivity, subjectivity, and the possibilities for texts. There is a mostly metonymous approach to the caveat, whereby everything is adjusted by what surrounds it—as if the text is arguing among its parts:

> …perhaps I'm at the door, that would surprise me, perhaps it's I, perhaps somewhere or other it was I, I can depart, all this time I've journeyed without knowing it, it's I now at the door, what door, what's a door doing here. (Ibid.)

Beckett uses the caveat as a primary textual concept, presenting the contradiction of simultaneous belief and doubt, assertion and negation. Textual caveats extend, dilute, and liberate particular concepts from the 'risk' of fixity while indicating authorial uncertainty.

Extending the operation of the caveat, is the concept of 'sideshadow' (sideshadowing) coined by Gary Saul Morson (1993), to contest or dispel the idea of inevitability in a text. Sideshadowing identifies a text's inference of sub- or-alter plots and/or alternate outcomes, possibilities, and ideas. Sideshadowing works against closure or fixity in texts, putting the textual material in 'the middle' of (implied or actual) *other* texts or occurrences and/or simultaneous ones. While it may have a linear historical, intertextual component, sideshadowing also has an autobiographical/testimonial, and unreliable one. It relates alluringly (and hybridly) to the idea that footnotes and other paratextuality make lines of flight. This is useful in the practice of autotheory, which can be complex in relation to genre-crossover.

A caveating tendency articulates the pervasive nature of the *between* of co-existent oppositions. The caveat is the shadow revealing extra-dimensionality, it is the uncertain or provocative space between certainties (lending dimension to these). It is infused with possibility; it opens a chink and lets in the light which illuminates the complexity of *being*. The caveat enshrines doubt and distils or unmasks truths amongst tending-murky materials.

Vestibule and fringe

Notes, citations, authorial inserts and amplifications, scene-setting quotes, and headings are more than peripheral detail in the hands of the redemptive hybridist. Paratextual material can be character and (sub)plot or caveating to the 'main' text while contributing to a *whole* text in essential ways. In Gérard Genette's *Introduction to the Paratext* ([1987] 1991), he asserts that paratextual material makes a "threshold", "vestibule", or "fringe" to the 'main' text, but also a frame for it; affecting how 'main' text is read. Genette writes:

> ...the paratext is for us the means by which a text makes a book of itself and proposes itself as such to its readers, and more generally to the public. Rather than with a limit or a sealed frontier, we are dealing in this case with a *threshold*, or—the term Borges used about a preface—with a 'vestibule' which offers to anyone and everyone the possibility either of entering or of turning back [...] or as Philippe Lejeune said, 'The fringe of the printed text which, in reality, controls the whole reading.' (p. 261)

Genette's borrowed terms, "vestibule" and "fringe" indicate a zone of transaction. That is, a transaction between parts of a whole text, as well as between writer/s, editor/s, and reader/s, where ideas cohere.

In *TPK*, Wallace elevates the paratext (including 'peri' and 'post' texts) to open up possibilities. The 'coherent' space between paratext and other/main text is vital and alive with the reader's work as they chase Wallace around the page, across font size shifts and in-text references that point like clues on a treasure map. And then there are the footnotes, the astounding scale of which, contributes in *TPK* to the construction of spaces within spaces. The footnotes are in a dialogic relationship with the 'main' text and in a visually immediate manner that endnotes can't emulate as the reader flicks back and forth, interrupting their reading. *TPK*'s footnotes could be considered to be main text in alternate view, while also being 'alter' to the 'main' text. Matthew Gilbert writes that Wallace's use of footnotes "...has inspired many comparisons to computer hypertext" (Gilbert [1997] 2012, p. 78). This is ironic considering the footnote came first and hypertext could be compared to it. Certainly, both are about ease of access and layers of information. Gilbert also writes that Wallace: "...likens footnotes to vaudevillian call-and-response" (ibid.). The back-and-forth on the same page allows for Wallace's "call-and-response" more than any cumbersome movement between main text and back of the book ever could.

The nature of the interaction between parts of the page is pertinent for what it suggests about textual hierarchies. However, occasionally, the reader of *TPK* has a sense of being hoodwinked; where swathes of footnotes make the work seem excessively and gratuitously large, and/or the non-linear process of reading becomes tedious. That Work's maximal material seems forcefully authorial, revealing a/his/their squeamishness about any 'cutting out', as much as it reveals a preference for making the creative process visible. In *TPK*, the formatting and other decisions are inextricable from the editoriality of the work which makes among other things a tribute to Wallace in his absence—making him present.

Following, is an example of authorial meaning-making; a footnote from *TPK* that interprets the David Foster Wallace author-character's pluralistic role as well as the pluralism of the role of the text:

> (Now you can probably see why this occasional 'author' appositive thing is sometimes necessary; it turned out that there were two separate David Wallaces posted at the Midwest REC, of whom the one who ended up accused of impersonation was guess who.) (*TPK*, Footnote #7, p. 414)

Without direct engagement with the reader as 'you' as we have it throughout *TPK*, the pushmepullyou of authorial truth and lies would be minimized.

Foretext is the material written prior, which may or may not be directly included in the published version but which has contributed to it and been subsumed in it. While most authors produce preliminary drafts and notes, the foretextual process is immanently visible in *TPK* by virtue of that Work's unfinishedness. In reference to *TPK*, Hering writes, "…the foretext is also the text" ([2016] 2017, p. 12). Yes, the foretext is all we have.

As Pietsch has written (shown in Chapter One), no one can ever really know what Wallace intended (Pietsch, in *TPK*, pp. vi–vii). *TPK*'s unfinishedness offers an insight into the liminality of practice, and to an extent, it collapses the hierarchy of finishedness over unfinishedness.

From his work among the Wallace archives at the Harry Ransom Center, Hering identifies three broad formative stages or phases of Wallace's work on *TPK*: "1997–2001, 2001–2005, and 2005–2007" (Hering 2017, p. 12). This contributes to the idea that *TPK* in its multiplicity and across its long development, might have been *anything*, or something else (as any text-information might). A broad base of foretext leading to unfinishedness shows that *TPK* will forever be a work-in-progress. Its published unfinishedness (not withstanding Michael Pietsch's outstanding achievement as editor) is key to *TPK*'s exemplary hybridizing in which the reader's uncertainty about context, content, and what Wallace intended, may cause them to read with a particular (even voyeuristic) care. *TPK*'s fragmentary formatting requires a tacit agreement from the reader to suspend *everything* and read on, even if they find themself tangled in the 'fringe' (Lejeune, in Genette 1991).

Genette ends his explication of textual manoeuvres with a small burst of authoriality. This amplification of momentary lapse reveals his presence in what is predominantly a non-fictional text, becoming a fortuitous exemplification of the textuality he discusses:

> The *pragmatic* status of a paratextual element is defined by the characteristics of its communicatory instance or situation: nature of the addresser, of the addressee, degree of authority and responsibility of the first, illocutionary force of his message, and probably some others which have escaped me. (Genette 1991, p. 266)

Where he writes "…and probably some others which have escaped me", Genette inserts himself in a caveating role. This brings to mind Deleuze and Guattari's many self-caveating inclusions, for example: "Wherever we used the word 'memories' in the preceding pages, we were wrong to do so; we meant to say 'becoming,' we were saying becoming" (D&G 2014, p. 294). Of course, it also brings to mind Wallace's plethora of addresses-to-reader from main text or footnotes in *TPK* where he contradicts what he previously wrote, conflates fact with factoid,[8] or adds a caveat to incite doubt and/or possibility. These examples perform collapses of expectation and of the boundaries between author-narrator and reader. Like Wallace's authorial intrusions, Genette's knowledge 'escaping' from the mind of the writer of an otherwise academic text, illuminates the author's presence in the work along with the presence of unfinished thought or of thought on a continuum. The examples also reveal the edificial nature of academic writing or indeed of any writing, and exemplifies non-fictions, like fictions, as never entirely reliable.

In *TPK*, Wallace formulates a realism that arrives (by virtue of its re-investiture of paratext and even of the author himself) at a maximizing of textual

---

[8] "Factoid", is a semi-truth. It is used by Wallace, notably here in *TPK*, and also by Norman Mailer in 1973. Discussed further in Chapter Six.

possibility. For example, the text encompasses the office in which it is created, the pages it is printed on, and the sense of over-flow caused by unfinishedness. Wallace contests truth-and-art in ways that give the reader cause to suspend their assumptions: "I am about art here, not simple reproduction" (*TPK*, p. 259). It is a reminder that truth can be simultaneously asserted and contested. The claim: "All of this is true. This book is really true" (p. 67) works in conjunction with truth becoming truer after adaptation. Footnote # 2 on page 67 re-frames the 'main' text's exhortation while effectively meta-fictionalizing the whole via slippage between true/false or, main text/para-text. A circularity of the parts of the text results: "…what I really mean is that everything that surrounds this Foreword is essentially true". This is a metafictionalizing jab at academic foot-or-end-noting and a wonderfully rhetorical exposé of textual rules as raw material to be broken or exposed.

Where paratextual and/or extradiegetic material is involved in a de-classification of what might otherwise be hierarchically arranged parts, there arises a non-hierarchical scheme and plenty of *tabula rasa* possibility. But whether this also indicates broad-spectrum innocuity (an anti-redemption per se) and the flaccid glorification of chance, remains to be seen. A close study of *TPK* in Chapter Six develops this further.

Ethics, alterity, and the reader

> I guess a big part of serious fiction's purpose is to give the reader, who like all of us is sort of marooned in her own skull, to give her imaginative access to other selves. (Wallace, in McCaffery [1993] 2012, pp. 21–22)

Redemptive manoeuvres and aspirations in or of textual and other creative practices most likely also reflexively redeem the socio-cultural context into which they are written or made, implicating the Other and our othering in what we produce. Whatever Redemptive Hybridity and any other post-postmodern bracketing of practice does, it is certainly going to be ethically particular and challenged in its transactions and relations.

In her essay *Fiction as Restriction: Self-Binding in New Ethical Theories of the Novel* (2007), Dorothy J. Hale makes a case for the novel as *the* arch literary form in terms of its unique possibilities for transformation and embodiment via the reader's ethical 'self-binding' to an experience of alterity.[9] Hale discusses a contract of willingness (the 'binding') that novel readers enter; this is a 'putting off' or suspension of judgement; it is an agreement to be changed or challenged. It is an act also of trust. In Hale, the 'Other' emerges for the reader, in the specific relationship with the novel they are submitting to. The novel's author is among the possible others that Hale calls "agents":

> This agent is the social Other that is produced by two related readerly acts: the act of self-subordination that enables the apprehension of alterity; and a prior act that makes self-subordination itself possible—the will to believe in the possibility of alterity. (2007, p. 189)

With the reader's "self-subordination" and "the will to believe in the possibility of alterity", their submission to the novel becomes:

> ...a necessary condition [[10]] for the social achievement of diversity, a training in the honoring of Otherness, which is the defining ethical property of the novel—and is also what makes literary study, and novel reading in particular, a crucial pre-condition for positive social change. (Ibid.)

Hale makes much of social alterity as raison d'être of a new ethical impetus in fiction (particularly the novel). She asks: "Can novel reading be theorized as helping to promote ethical emotions that would lead to the recognition of alterity [...] outside of novels?" (p. 190). I would add to the question: will "honoring social difference" (ibid.) only be geared by novels and not poetry, non-fiction, or new forms? What stops other genres from inciting a generative awareness of the Other? The answer Hale gives and the reason she privileges the novel's power in this area is because it requires a significant (sustained) self-binding. However, it is possible that just because a form is long or densely narrative, it is not ethically superior, nor does the reader's self-binding always result in a constructive engagement with the idea of alterity and the novel's Other/s. Hale's formulation works in relation to the aspect of duration of exposure (to the Other found in or through the novel) but needs caveating in terms of the power of some

---

[9] Alterity and Otherness may be interchangeable, except Alterity is a name, a refinement of Otherness.
[10] The "necessary condition" mentioned by Hale here, is according to the theorists she is discussing: Butler, Spivak, Huffer, Harpham, Hillis Miller—each of whose work (she asserts) ties back to Booth 1961 on ethics in literature; in which Booth names Henry James as an exemplar of the ethical in practice, as do Hillis Miller and Butler, at least.

short works, poetry, and other textual distillations which cannot be placed in a hierarchy of Other-awareness and ethicality based solely on matters of form and duration. Redemptively hybrid texts pre-conceive no limitations or rankings of genre and form. In broad but specifically constructive and heterogenous scope, redemptively hybrid texts definitively push manoeuvres towards an ethical uptake of matters particular to the Other, but also matters particular to the self in relation to the Other via a multiplicity of modalities and genres. In Hale, the unverifiability of the subject's ethicality is itself an a priori ethicality:

> ...what distinguishes this new theory of ethical choice from an older theory of the autonomous liberal subject is the self-consciously unverifiable status of the alterity that the ethical subject seeks to produce—an unverifiability that retains the post-structuralist's skepticism about knowledge as a tool of hegemony while bestowing upon epistemological uncertainty a positive ethical content. (2007, p. 190)

To be epistemologically uncertain is to be unfinished, agnostic, perhaps ethically wavering, but to be unfinished is not *necessarily* to be uncertain. Unfinishedness may, in relation to ethics, be a hybrid position of choice and one progressively broad in reach and definition, having little to do with claims of superiority or hierarchy (of genre, philosophy, theory, or anything) and more to do with process and seeking. Modalities of redemptive hybridity make a cautious approach to "knowledge as a tool of hegemony" (ibid.), while also seeking and building knowledge.

The ethical, the moral, and the difference

"God becomes an invisible, vanishing point, an impotent thought, and his power is to be found only in the ethical, which fills all existence" writes Kierkegaard in *Fear and Trembling* ([1843] 2005, p. 80). So, what is "the ethical, which fills all existence"? In the long dawn of the modernisms, doubt is institutionalized, underpinning thereafter a humanist ethics, perhaps even, as Hale discusses (2007, p. 190), an ethical unverifiability running counter to unethical assumptions. The 'unverifiable' is also the possible, so, can theory and practice remain 'fixed' at unverifiability while there is an undeniable urge to resolve, to know, and to verify, at least speculatively?

Meanwhile, God remains indicative of a (*the*) structure to work with, against, or both (agnostically). And whether the ethical is considered to be commensurate with God's power or not (Kierkegaard), it is inarguably an aspect of the human condition and everywhere relevant and innervating in our texts. Morality, however, is not the same as ethicality…

In his essay, 'Narrative Ethics' ([2013] 2014), at the *Living Handbook of Narratology* online, James Phelan uses the term 'moral' in conjunction with ethics, making a distinction. "Narrative ethics" is a container or frame for "moral values", which attach to stories:

> Narrative ethics explores the intersections between the domain of stories and storytelling and that of moral values. Narrative ethics regards moral values as an integral part of stories and storytelling because narratives themselves implicitly or explicitly ask the question, 'How should one think, judge, and act—as author, narrator, character, or audience—for the greater good?' (Phelan 2014)

And similarly, Hale writes that we, "…abstract from our experience to generalize about ethical values, to make moral judgements" (2007, p. 201). There may be a case for looking beyond the self via the alterity we engage when making, giving, and receiving art and texts, to ensure that any morality distilled from and informing ethical choices does not become inert. Can ethics be derived from and inform moral judgements if the self is *the* source and filter of that knowledge and belief? Visible in our texts or not, we are each an unreliable narrator of our own story, which is where an investment in alterity may be synchronously advantageous, if always effected by an internal script. Hale points out that according to Henry James, the novel "…emerges from the ethical value of voluntary self-binding" (ibid.). And from the novel genre's "inherent unboundedness" (p. 202). Making a case for the literary work as a moral investment, Eagleton too gives Henry James credit among other nineteenth-century novelists, for helping to "…shift the meaning of the term 'morality' from a matter of codes and norms to a question of values and qualities" (Eagleton 2012, p. 59). And into the twentieth century:

> …the literary had become the very paradigm of morality for a post religious world. In its fine-grained sensitivity to nuances of human conduct, its strenuous discriminations of value, its reflections on the question of how to live richly and self-reflectively, the literary work was a supreme example of moral practice. (Ibid.)

Eagleton goes on to say that the form of a literary work is key to the work's moral value as much as its content is. He does not prescribe one form over another (as Hale does when preferencing features of the novel) but suggests that form brings varying points of access. I assert that the hybrid form articulates the connective tissue (becoming that tissue), between its fragments, parts, or layers of 'content' as well as the resulting effect of the whole, whose conceptual purpose offers 'new' scope for exploring and challenging moral value.

Eagleton proposes that for certain writers morality is a matter of 'imagination' as it enables a kind of affinity, and in this manner, "…we can feel our way empathetically into the inner lives of others" (p. 60). But Eagleton also points out, that the process of imagination leading to empathy does *not* equate to knowledge; to know someone by reading about them is not as likely as it is to know oneself as reader and responder to the text. Eagleton writes: "'Becoming' Lear will only yield you the truth of Lear if he grasps the truth about himself, which would seem to be far from the case" (p. 62). However, becoming Lear will offer you knowledge about Lear's anguish and the depths of his unknowing, and *that* would be (some) knowledge. So, it seems that there is a case for the self-reflexive reader to find morality or truth as a process of acquisition across a 'lifetime' of reading. The space in which other readers find similar or other truths or morals is the space of connection between readers, the founding of a shared and morally charged ethics.

Jameson writes that the eighteenth century purged 'us' of the theological meaning of good and evil (Jameson 1991, pp. 289–290). He suggests that the binary didn't go away but got "sexualized" and politicized and passed "down to us" (p. 290). Jameson suggests that 'the Other' exemplifies this binary, the existence of which results in the "…revitalization of ethics as a set of mental categories" used to sort, sift, and weigh that which we feel compelled to judge (p. 289). He suggests that we are using a hard scaffolding of ethics when we set up seemingly un-bridgeable binaries of right/wrong, true/false, self/other (p. 290).

In the New Ethical Theory, in Hale, and also for Redemptive Hybridism (as additive, or as a foil), 'Othering' and 'Otherness', are the becoming-Other. This amounts to possibility *with*, and the maintenance of empathy *with*, the Other. It is reparation performed inside the very word that might once have signalled empathy's opposite. It is a redemptive reversal; a hybridizing act that moves beyond postmodernity while building on it. Hybridizing manoeuvres perform the poetics of unfinished-ness, difference, multiplicity, heteroglossia and/or polyglossia, which alterity requires.

Leaps in the dark

If mutuality, reciprocity, and difference are as far as the ethical can reach, then practitioners and consumers of the literary text must have a lot more (moral) rope as yet unused. Mutuality can be known by a standoff; reciprocity can be evident in reprimand or revenge; difference can be known by ghettoism. The drumming-up of appreciation for ethicality, and the seeing, caring, learning about factors that naturalize and instate 'difference', is where the ethical begins to make a difference and move, morally, in practice. The residue is the expansive part; the unknown which lingers, even ghostlike, as an increasing mass of possibility.

The practice of redemptive hybridizing (whatever that looks like) performs the Self-Other (becoming-Other) but with no loss of the self. Whether the fictive/creative/hybrid work (there are nuances) is made of narratives or not, it will be 'about' the Other and the self—potentially redemptively, and always hybridly so.

The matter of ethics and social alterity recalls Emmanuel Levinas' *Totality and Infinity* ([1961] 1969) in which is developed the idea of the *physical* presence of the other as the source of 'infinity' apropos connection and possibility between self and Other. Counter to this, written communication between a *self* and an *other* is past as soon as it is produced and so belongs to 'totality'. In Levinas, the face-to-face encounter of dialogue and physical gesture (the face), is socially ethical in comparison with the (less ethical) textual encounter in which the author takes authority over what is said and how.

The ethical-physical – which is the visible author in Wallace, whose *The Pale King* is a "vocational memoir" (*TPK*, p. 70), and the saturated atom in Woolf— may become pertinent to the 'testimonial turn' observed in post-postmodernity. For example, post-postmodernly, Nelson presents a lot of her-self; not *only* a textual persona, to her reader. She uses the terms 'love' and 'family' because these signify territory she claims not only theoretically but also physically and experientially as she inserts her autotheory into hearts as well as minds.

Hale writes that Hillis Miller calls ethical decisions, "leaps in the dark" (from *Conduct*, in Hale 2007, p. 195). According to Hale, the 'leap' is "…predicated on the will to believe in alterity, in the possibility of a law outside and different than the self, the possibility of translation and the limits to translation" (p. 201). Hale writes that according to New Ethical Theory, the reader's 'leap' is not drawn from the outside: "…the necessity of making decisions for oneself that places 'I alone' at the centre of ethical judgements that cannot be verified by any outside source" (p. 195). While liberating in the existential sense, the exclusive "I alone", makes for difficulty where an ethics must negotiate with an Other. It becomes difficult to reconcile "I alone" as part of a collective; the relationship of 'I' to the Other/s surely involves reciprocity, each subject informing and affecting the other and revealing "…the possibility of a law outside and different than the self" (p. 201).

High, low, high, low, it's off to blend we go . . .

In her book *American Hybrid Poetics: Gender, Mass Culture, and Form* (2014), Amy Moorman Robbins views hybridity "…as an innovative and specifically feminist poetics of critical difference" (p. 13). She specifies the marginality of the woman poet-hybridist within a totalizing culture:

> …we can read the term 'hybrid' as both an aesthetics of the mix as well as a politics of the socially constructed in-between, a space from which marginally positioned individuals, through development of innovative and nonconforming art, can wage critique of the totalizing culture within which they find themselves. (Ibid.)

Hybridity in Robbins is a "…political strategy, one that forces encounters between hitherto incompatible literary traditions and that thereby brings to the surface competing ideologies and their implications for lived experience" (p. 2). In my own project, hybridizing (the becoming-hybrid) makes 'incompatibility' somewhat more redundant, at least in its negative sense, while *difference* is the quality that conveys complexity, texture, and possibility. *Difference in unity* necessitates incompatibilities (as differences) and synchronizes them; meanwhile competing-with but not cancelling-out becomes *unity in difference*, that is, unity held by the dynamic of dialogism (differences in dialogue). Robbins seems to not disagree, while holding to her central idea that the female poet is a marginalized figure who writes herself into a-not-the frame via a strategy of hybridity as defence and offence. Robbins adds that "…mixings of high with the feminized low are rarely treated as serious forays into oppositional art" (ibid.) and she goes on to outline a women's practice for which hybridity is reaction and strategy.

"Mixing" implicitly allows distinct parts to remain distinct while participating Otherly (unity in difference). If, instead, the term *blending* is used, elements might be merged or made invisible as they thicken the whole (difference in unity). There is a case for both/and (more) in hybrid practice. In my reading of it, Robbins's is an image of juxtapositions rather than assimilations. There is a sense of a hybridity which safe-guards undiluted components in avoidance of a crushing totality while honouring the differences that make the unifying whole. This would reflect Robbins's hypothesis that political hybridities perform a compartmentalizing function (in relation to women writers). Robbins (p.10) asserts that women's hybrid poetics argue against established notions such as Huyssen's where high culture is "…implicitly masculine" and Theodor Adorno's where "…there is no outside to the mass culture that has replaced official culture as the dominant mode of social control in our time". Robbins identifies a compelling contingent of women hybridists as outsiders or reactionaries, however, these might also be viewed as forward-thinking practitioners at the centre of things.

In *Prisms* ([1955] 1997), we see Adorno in the 'act' not only of an implicit femicide (women are engaged in the reproduction of life that he denounces) but also of calling for an embodied delusion and grandiosity that diverts from the lived reality of a majority of humans and the art they would produce. He writes:

> Only the mind which, in the delusion of being absolute, removes itself entirely from the merely existent, truly defines the existent in its negativity. As long as even the least part of the mind remains engaged in the reproduction of life, it is its sworn bondsman. (pp. 25–26)

Adorno is a product of the "existent" business of reproduction that he denounces in his call to become 'mind'. What he says is problematic (as identified by Robbins) for women other than as grit to use as friction in the making of a pearl. I agree with Robbins that it is important to set women (and other insufficiently represented groups) apart for protection and elevation for a time, but the way she frames it, women writers from the hybridity zone have been sectioned there – forced to re-camp on the margins, speak in code, and make a reactionary art of hybridity because of adversity.

As a way of reading or viewing, redemptive hybridity proposes the subsumption of the patriarchy or élite, favouring its over-writing or re-purpose. Hybridizing manoeuvres are strengthened by their taking in and surpassing of the 'enemy' until it is no longer 'enemy' but necessary texture. Robbins refers to an art of complicity, an idea which fits with the pervasive sense in her book of the feminist hybridist as a guerrilla tactician meeting opposition:

> ...an art of complicity can also be an art of revolution. As I will show, what connects these two modes of thinking is a feminist drive to imagine new worlds out of familiar ones (and mass culture is nothing if not familiar) together with a sincere doubt about ever finding a secure place therein. (2014, p. 11)

Robbins's use of "complicity" makes a useful construction apropos hybridity, articulating something near the 'taking-in-of-enemies' (after Hassan) in its imagining of new worlds after-and-because-of mass culture. However, her "sincere doubt about ever finding a secure place therein" while also 'imagining new worlds' tends toward a metaxically unstable place from which to build. One might instead commute "sincere doubt" to a more agnostic 'jury's out'-type view on possibility, requiring only a suspended belief.

In relation to the postmodern context of the 'long now',[11] Andreas Huyssens writes in 'Mapping the Postmodern' ([1984] 1990) that the tension between coexistent modalities and ideologies is productive:

> The point is not to eliminate the productive tension between the political and the aesthetic, between history and the text, between engagement and the mission of art. The point is to heighten that tension, even to rediscover it and to bring it back into focus in the arts as well as in criticism. (p. 271)

Tension-resolving might be preferable to 'tension-heightening' in relation to the women's movement, various feminisms, and the relationship of these with mainstream modernisms and matters patriarchal. An agenda to productively heighten the tension between the modernisms with, in particular, its busyness of flags at the (late postmodern) summit, may be an engagement with tension while being illustrative of a state of circular conflict which is counterproductive, even squashing the difference that makes the tension. Engaging with tension and difference, is what redemptive hybridism does.

In *Prisms*, Adorno refuses the blending of 'high and low' forms in favour of an élitist purity: "...culture originates in the radical separation of mental and physical work" (1997, p. 25). For Adorno, radical artistic experimentation, especially involving status/class collapse, becomes a form of self-mutilation, bringing a debilitating loss of control to its creator. On page 26 he writes: "Modern bourgeois cultural criticism" [enjoys the separation of] "'high' and 'popular' culture" [...] "Its anti-philistinism exceeds that of the Athenian upper

---

[11] This 'long now' extends from 1984 when Huyssen's essay was first published. Later published in the 1990 collection edited by L.J. Nicholson.

classes to the extent that the proletariat is more dangerous than the slaves" (all, p. 26). Adorno skews legitimate individual expression into a regulatory linear purism that disregards the creative forms of the "proletariat" such as: jazz, automatism, spontaneity, and certainly hybridity.

An analysis of Gertrude Stein's *Blood on the Dining Room Floor* (*BotDRF* [1948] 2004), inspired by Robbins (2014), is pertinent here. Robbins observes that the critical take on Stein's book at the time of its posthumous publication was that it proves that popular genre and the avant-garde don't mix. Stein's short novella investigates and challenges numerous conventions as it combines the genre of the (Victorian) detective novel, autobiographical content, word-sound-rhyme-meter play, and interruptions (Robbins 2014, p. 14). There are political insinuations and Stein does not always name the characters who 'live' via their attributes; being subjectively 'real' based on the shifting sands of point of view.

Robbins writes that Stein mixes, "…matters of high importance [e.g. the atomic bomb] with the mundane details of daily living" (p. 20). But it isn't a mixing of adjacent terms and co-habiting phrases in Stein; it is more like a blending in which the performance of hybridity arrives via the author's embodying of the Other. In the following example, the embodiment is a stepping into Helen as a child, (in the manner that Woolf and Wallace step into characters), demonstrating the fallibility but also the veracity of memory:

> Helen was an orphan, that is to say her mother was put away and her father the major was killed in the war. You all remember the war. Some can forget a war. It is not necessary to remember or to forget a war.
>
> Who remembers a door. Anyone who remembers a door can remember a war. He went to the war to be killed in the war because his wife was crazy. She behaved strangely when she went to church. She even behaved strangely when she did not. She played the piano and at the same time put cement between the keys so that they would not sound. You see how easy it is to have cement around. (*BotDRF*, pp. 37–38)

BotDRF is a "…textual hybrid merging mass culture form with experimentalist aesthetics and interspersing historical events with fictional ones" (Robbins 2014, p. 22). It is Stein's "…serious attempt to bridge in her writing the two realms she straddled in life—the realms of the middle class and of modern art" (p. 43). Robbins points out that critics of Stein's novella at the time of its publication said it was neither one thing nor another ipso facto it was a failure. Robbins writes that this "…is deeply informed by an overarching desire to see modernist high art as entirely distinct from mass culture, as Adorno would have it, rather than as reliant upon mass culture in a dialectical relation" (p. 23). Hybridity is not the preserve of the avant-garde. Élitism becomes subsumed by the *redemptive* hybrid as exemplified by Stein, Levé, and Wallace among other practitioners of 'high-low' collapse.

According to Robbins, women's (hybrid) practice has been relegated to the margins because a patriarchal mainstream has considered women's practice intrinsic to femininity and 'thereby' to *failure* (p. 28). The problem has been multiple, as woman's relegation increases her risk when exerting herself as a writer/artist alongside the male counterpart. Robbins problematizes the situation apropos of *BotDRF*; a personal story seeking a reader who's willing and 'self-binding' (Hale) to receive such a hybrid offering, one that contains the new (form) inside the old (form) or vice versa.

Stein's work, as Robbins shows, features 'high' literary trickery within the 'low' form of detective fiction, underpinned by the series of auto-biographical events that inspired it. All things considered, *BotDRF* was relegated to the margins. Its 'failures' Robbins argues, were because it is 'woman's fiction'; a woman-authored detective novel; and ultimately, a non-persuasive instrument of persuasion (not winning over the mainstream to its hybrid cause). Robbins suggests (in different words) that *BotDRF*'s 'redemption' might come from a reading which does not ignore:

> ...the novel's innovative hybrid structure and blended aesthetics in which recursive form and the carefully orchestrated assemblage of other texts work in tension with the strict rules of conventional plotting. (2014, p. 24)

Adorno-esque patriarchal élitism meets marginalia in antithesis (each characterized by apartness). But, is a poetics of antithesis (like an ideology based on an observation of metaxy) able to move art forward productively?

Hartsock calls for women to make an account of the world from the margins: "...we need to dissolve the false 'we' I have been using into its real multiplicity and variety and out of this concrete multiplicity build an account of the world as seen from the margins" (1990, p. 171). However, I would also make a case for infiltration; a poetics of pushing out from within rather than lobbing parts of oneself at the mainstream, from the margins. This is a life-and-art in which the "concrete multiplicity" (ibid.) might presume and uphold difference from within.

A writer like Nelson reclaims the centre with her hybridizing work, the value of which would be less efficacious if she set her position to 'apart', 'marginal', or 'fringe'. Her project of reclamations—of visibility, love, the centre, the self as an authoritative free agent—is not a 'being-marginal'.

While there are a range of points of view that identify as feminist, some would feel an empathy attachment to the image of marginality Robbins gives, and the underground hybridity—a kind of self-encryption—of that, while others, perhaps Nelson, might assert the visible centre where one places oneself in full view, as an overriding of old relegations.

A history of degradation may have forced female practitioners to leave bits of themselves in places; perhaps attempting to infiltrate the mainstream via fragments and moments (even codes and pseudonyms) as Robbins shows, rather than via grand entrances and impressive slabs of text that draw attention to *her* 'self and sex' and the relation of that to women's work. In this manner, 'perfecting' the language of habitual fragmentation, brevity, and distilled gestures might have enabled some to claim ground and to refuse perpetual nomadism, fringe dwelling, and presumptive expectations of a women's literary form.

Robbins points out a cultural disdain for, but inextricable connection with the hybrid form, as if it were the preserve of a separatist feminism: "the work of women poets is ever under threat of erasure [and effacement] as new movements come to the fore [...] the concept of 'hybrid' is both on the rise and under fire" (2014, p. 19). However, practicing "under fire" is what the radical, the cutting-edge, and the resilient do. As suggested previously, once the trail-blazing has done its work, the margins may be less of a place of incarceration and more of a reclamation of the centre.

But there are other minorities and minority practices that forge ahead with new or personalized methods that show their author caring less about commercial viability or mainstream visibility and more about art for art's sake. High-low collapse is evident, for example, in Levé's *Autoportrait*, which embodies interdisciplinarity via paratactical autobiographical fragments which might once have been called 'high' or 'low', but in the context of his work's hybridity, distinctions are blurred, subverted, inverted, or have become irrelevant. A flattening or levelling of values may result when high and low are given equilibrium in a text after filtration through the 'mesh' of the author-character. Here is an example from inside the frame of Levé's abutted and paratactical sentencing: "I have written several love letters but no breakup letters, I saved that job for my voice. I would rather paint chewing gum up close than Versailles from far away. I touch white for luck" (Levé [2005] 2012, p. 19). "I would rather paint chewing gum up close than Versailles from far away" is an exemplary stitching of the micro/macro and low/high. That sentence works alone as well as it works surrounded by the distilled banalities that frame it—all of which is important for Levé's emphasis on the jewel-like quality of moments like husks stripped of emotion. A rhythm emerges, as the form metonymically encapsulates something akin to the writer reflected in a broken window—or—the texture of words and ideas re-contextualized in the arena of page or screen.

Redemptive Hybridism does not necessitate the relegation of oppositions, it mobilizes collaborations and apprehensions productively. It is a turn or tendency that works with differences in unity towards unity in differences. It is a 'making flesh' from words, beyond matters of genre but also because of them.

Part Two

Figures of Redemptive Hybridism

4

Woolf's Atom; the Image of Hybridity

Begin with the atom, Virginia Woolf

As alluded to throughout this Work, Woolf's diary entry of Wednesday, 28 November 1928, expresses a desire (essential to this project) to saturate the atom and get to the core of the matter. Woolf's atom is at the nucleus of hybridity. Here is an expanded quote for context:

> The idea has come to me that what I want now to do is to saturate every atom. I mean to eliminate all waste, deadness, superfluity: to give the moment whole; whatever it includes. Say that the moment is a combination of thought; sensation; the voice of the sea. Waste, deadness, come from the inclusion of things that don't belong to the moment; this appalling narrative business of the realist: getting on from lunch to dinner: it is false, unreal, merely conventional. Why admit anything to literature that is not poetry—by which I mean saturated? (*Diary*, np)

Woolf's saturated atom is essential to the picture I am drawing of hybridizing as being and *becoming* on a continuum. From *Jacob's Room*: "Sandra, floating from the particular to the universal, lay back in a trance" (Woolf [1922] 1989, p. 149). This epigraphical sentence encapsulates Woolf's modus operandi and themes, which become her 'saturated atom'; a hybridizing of the innermost with the outermost.

In *A Thousand Plateaus*, Deleuze and Guattari write that according to Henry James "…it is necessary to 'begin far away, as far away as possible,' and to proceed by 'blocks of wrought matter'" (p. 329). "Far away" suggests a long view of unfolding experience, of stages or phases, like the scientist magnifying the atom. Meanwhile, Woolf moves in reverse: her commencement and unfolding begin close up at the "particular", knowing the fibres and distilling the essence. She is moving away by degrees to the "universal". She is 'eliminating waste' and giving "the moment whole". "Such is the link between imperceptibly, indiscernibility, and impersonality—the three virtues" write Deleuze and Guattari about Woolf's strategy for 'saturating the atom' ([1980] 2014, p. 280). In reference to Woolf's previously cited diary excerpt, they write:

> She says that it is necessary to 'saturate every atom,' and to do that it is necessary to eliminate, to eliminate all that is resemblance and analogy, but also 'to put everything into it': eliminate everything that exceeds the moment, but put in everything that it includes—and the moment is not the instantaneous, it is the haecceity into which one slips and that slips into other haecceities by transparency. To be present at the dawn of the world. (Ibid.)

However, only something with form can be saturated, which might suggest (if not explicitly determine), that future forms or the becoming of forms, are nascent at an atomic level. The image of a 'saturated atom' is useful for creative practice, despite atoms having borders and a particular way of moving or being moved; ergo, objectivity interrupting subjectivity.

To eliminate yet put everything in (like Woolf) is to make the impossible possible. However, in Woolf, saturation and attenuating intensities make art that is particularizing *and* universalizing (the 'Sandra' quote a few quotes back) and analogy holds the particular.[1]

The haecceity in Woolf gathers with other truths and builds a multiplicity within her becoming-fluid. Clarissa Dalloway for example, is continually expanding her awareness via her haecceitical thought in its saturating and flooding. Clarissa's perfectionism is intrinsic to her ill-ease, an exquisite aberration in *Mrs Dalloway* and a different and fascinating trajectory for *saturation*.

But what *is* the saturating substance? Is it the writer becoming-atom? And what about the effect of saturation on negatively charged electrons, positively charged protons, and the neutral core nucleus? Can analogies be so far removed from their source material? Possibly not, and certainly not if the analogy is to have a full and hybridizing range of possibilities – but we can extend Woolf's analogy. For example: if one saturates the atom with oneself, one is, in a way

---

[1] To 'eliminate resemblance and analogy' as Deleuze and Guattari suggest, might eliminate *A Thousand Plateaus*, a catalogue of analogies becoming a text.

becoming-atom (a kind of implosion or sub-acute consciousness). To saturate, is imagistically productive in terms of creative intensity while it is also a colonizing or consuming manoeuvre. The contradictions make an interesting texture, but where they undermine atoms, something will break or flood the boundaries. That then is the perpetual risk, the vulnerability or instability of which works into Redemptive Hybridism's narrative modus operandi.

Woolf's *The Waves* ([1931] 1998) is awash with allusion to saturation, but it also emulsifies its arborescent and rhizomatic movements in a way that makes a complex garment from the fabric of the text where no one moment stands as obviously more saturated than any other, but where the whole is texerically 'even' and musical; a poetic arrangement where one 'part' cannot be pulled out of the music without destroying it. This is very different to a work like *The Pale King* or one of Levé's texts, which rattle with loose parts that are given to be unified by the reader. *The Waves* articulates a carefully determined pattern of archetypes and their heteroglossic interrelationships, plus the macro-micro complexity of all interrelationships – whether human to human, or human to non-human spaces and objects:

> What vast forces of good and evil have brought me here? he
> asks, and sees with sorrow that his chair has worn a little hole in
> the pile of the purple carpet. (*TW*, Dr Crane, p. 39)

From the "vast forces" to 'the hole in the carpet', here is *everything* in a brief distillation. The musicality of *The Waves* shows a reliance on parts, but the parts work univocally – like *Mrs Dalloway's* 'world in a day': a single day in June where new life (flowers/Clarissa's enthusiasm), old life (Doctors and the regimental world), and tragic life (Septimus and also Clarissa on the brink) are collectively intrinsic to *the* concept of the Russian-dolls effect of a world unpackable down to atoms and back up, like: "Sandra floating from the particular to the universal" in *Jacob's Room* (Woolf 1989, p. 149).

Woolf's saturation can be imagined in various ways, suffice here to say it is a becoming-other in the flood into and beyond the character-self. The saturation is constrained by its (stretched or maximized) parameters, its textual form, and its writer's biases; especially when compared to a work like *TPK* in its unfinishedness—a comparison which makes Woolf's work appear radically contained while Wallace's is pock-marked with caveats where 'stuff' escapes but might also come in with the reader.

Saturation in Woolf and Wallace

Woolf and Wallace, from different locations on a spectrum, both *saturate* where authors, characters, places, moments, and truths overlap. Both perform something like an authorial 'stare'. Woolf's is meditative though not without anxiety, and Wallace's is closer to mental absence caused in part by boredom.[2] In Wallace the negation whereby, "Something goes out of you—you can feel your face merely hanging loose" (*TPK*, p. 116), is a reversal of the productive becoming played out in Woolf who makes an expansive gesture towards, not only becoming-other but also 'becoming magnificent' apropos of the "fertile" natural order, which is fertility of the mind in its becoming-other. Here for example, in *To The Lighthouse*:

> Mrs Ramsay sat silent. She was glad, Lily thought, to rest in silence, uncommunicative; to rest in the extreme obscurity of human relationships. Who knows what we are, what we feel? Who knows even at the moment of intimacy, This [*sic*] is knowledge? Aren't things spoilt then, Mrs Ramsay may have asked (it seemed to have happened so often, this silence by her side) by saying them? Aren't we more expressive thus? The moment at least seemed extraordinarily fertile. (*TtL*, p. 161)

'Obscurity' and 'fertility' are related via complexity, suggesting the centrifugal and centripetal movements of life and practice in which contradictions make the necessary tension. Bakhtin's centrifugal and centripetal movements are useful here, as explained by Booth in his Introduction to Bakhtin's *Problems of Dostoyevsky's Poetics*:

> Human existence, created as it is *in* many languages, presents two opposing tendencies. There is a 'centrifugal' force dispersing us outward into an ever greater variety of 'voices,' outward into a seeming chaos that presumably only a God could encompass. And there are various 'centripetal' forces preserving us from overwhelming fluidity and variety. The drive to create artworks that have some kind of coherence – that is, formal unity – is obviously a 'centripetal' force; it provides us with the best experience we have of what Coleridge called 'multeity in unity,' unity that does justice to variety. But we are always tempted to follow that drive too far in the direction of imposing a monologic unity. (2014, pp. xxi–xxii)

---

[2] Reference to *TPK*, p. 116: "being in a stare". There is more on 'boredom in *TPK*', in Chapter Six.

In Bakhtin, the centripetal reflects (or mimics) the centrifugal as an inverse movement. And the liminality at the intersection of opposing forces is hybridly vitalizing to the potentialities of practice. The *centrifugal* "chaos" in Bakhtin belongs in the outward-leaning authorial (God-like) terrain, which contains or innervates the *centripetal* exemplars of practice such as 'our' close characters, our intensity and intentions. Woolf's saturated atom belongs here: an image of a both/and movement which is, in this setting, less about 'flood' and more about fulfilment.[3]

Wallace's apparent empathy for Toni Ware in her ordinariness, stuck-ness, and despair, may—considering his tendency to authorial hovering—be an empathy-disgust for himself: his treatment of and interaction with Ware is a push-me-pull-you which defies the binary monologism-dialogism and instates balance or tension concerning dynamic movement.

Wallace writes that Ware was: "Begat in one car and born in another. Creeping up in dreams to see her own conceiving" (*TPK*, p. 59). If Toni Ware creeps up to see her own conceiving, she is either suffocatingly solipsistic, she is the author, or she is both. But fertility is of natural rhythms, and these are suppressed beneath technological ones in *TPK*.

Woolf's fertile moment and Wallace's 'creeping up to see one's own conceiving' involve saturating the self-other space, but in recognition that one can only saturate the object of one's *own* thought. So, the question arises of the excess of that which remains beyond the saturating manoeuvre which makes the fully saturated object; where does it go? I will discuss this shortly in relation to *Mrs Dalloway*. Meanwhile, in *To The Lighthouse*, the death and subsequent absence of Mrs Ramsay (mainly) and also Prue (and others), shows that death as a fertile space, is 'on the cards' all along. Rather than becoming a negation, the space left by Mrs Ramsay is filled by Lily Briscoe who previously embodied Mrs Ramsay's wings or flailed in her undertow while that woman roamed the story like Athena. When Lily steps into the Mrs Ramsay space, she becomes swollen as a character as if she has taken in or replaced *each* of the dead. In keeping with Woolf's exhortation to make literature a poetic saturation, Lily is hybridizing in her redemptive uptake of not only Mrs Ramsay but of death itself.

---

[3] I am no scientist. This is a mash-up of Bakhtin, intuited images, and careful attention to the mechanics of the literary work of others.

Mrs Dalloway as fertile ground

"...she had always had the feeling that it was very, very dangerous to live even one day" (*MD*, p. 11). Clarissa Dalloway believes that things live on in each other, and that she has immortality in "the trees at home" (ibid.). Woolf's 'saturation' enacts a high value on becoming multiple.

Deleuze and Guattari mention Mrs Dalloway's walk through the streets as an exemplification of haecceity (2014, p. 263), which is the '*it*-ness' of her experience. Haecceitical moments, as shown in D&G, configure becomings-multiple, in an instant or moment un-time-bound (not representing a given amount of time). Saturation is also exemplary here: "Taking a walk is a haecceity; never again will Mrs. Dalloway say to herself, 'I am this, I am that, he is this, he is that'" write D&G (ibid.). Here, taking a walk is a process of saturation and an example of how the haecceity works or appears in long moments: "Haecceity, fog, glare. A haecceity has neither beginning nor end, origin nor destination; it is always in the middle. It is not made of points, only of lines. It is a rhizome" (ibid.).[4] They speak of intensity as an overflow, beyond saturation; a flood into the territory; even the blending of overflows from differently saturated atoms (or objects or ideas) via the haecceity and/or line of flight. The saturation fills – and then in terms of the haecceity – it moves beyond its 'maps', its 'words', or simply its 'outlines' (perimeters), which lose concentration and specificity in the process, and new territory emerges through the excess.

> 'But when we sit together, close,' said Bernard, 'we melt into each other with phrases. We are edged with mist. We make an unsubstantial territory.' (*TW*, p. 11)

The "unsubstantial" is the hybridizing of the "territory". In *The Waves* explicitly, but also in her other works, Woolf encapsulates the borderless-ness and timelessness of the textual human. These are matters of saturation but also of excess, which concerns the substance that cannot be absorbed once saturation is maximized, and which might flood the territory seeking another site of saturation. The post-saturation movement is rendered in the post-postmodern moment of authorial connection with the reader whereby a saturation like Woolf's becomes a shared effort, requiring 'extra' vessels or space for the overflow beyond the atom or text.

---

[4] Partially quoted earlier apropos the idea of middle-ness but reiterated here in a different context.

A day in June

Within the frame of one day (various sources say, possibly 13 June 1923), Woolf enacts the micro-macro in reciprocal reflection, to the point where the micro is saturated with desire. The thick air-space between characters and their shared intensities, is rife with performances of archetypal behaviour constrained by type, circumstance, and plot. The macro is a post-WW1 London with all the strictures of class structure beyond which is Woolf herself, filtering it all through Clarissa Dalloway, Septimus, and a day-full of others.

As Clarissa re-lives Septimus's suicide, she is fully 'gone over' into possession of him in his absence: "Always her body went through it" (*MD*, p. 203). In this way, Woolf shows Clarissa expanding into the fertile ground of the Other; but she is 'flooding' even beyond Septimus in a redemptively hybridizing manoeuvre of aggregation and empathy. This brings to mind Wallace's possession of Toni Ware who is fertile ground for her author's inhabitation in *The Pale King*.

To be freest, in Woolf, is to be at liberty to immanently (Deleuze) share the consciousness of others – to flood into them – particularly of other types, in order to become more complete or to transcend subjectivity and attain (some) objectivity while not forsaking the type/base (root) of one's own becoming. 'Consciousness sharing' is exemplified in *The Waves* where characters are constructed as if parts of a pattern or musical score. But Clarissa Dalloway is an epicentre around which everything she observes and experiences works centripetally as she embodies her desire for Other-possession. She remains unsuccessful in that quest due to her dependency on the opinions of others. She is stuck or perpetually saturating; held in place, with no agency other than what is released by her becoming-other.

Septimus, on the other hand, is a philosopher-poet defeated incrementally by his body and mind, ostensibly because of the war (his PTSD monster, convoluted by the guilt he feels about Evans's death). Septimus is highly developed even though relatively briefly. He is endemic madness, not becoming any-one-or-thing else, nor is he becoming enlightened – unless death is a passage there, and I do not think Woolf is suggesting that. Thus, with Woolf, Septimus and Clarissa form an assemblage that depicts the interactivity between sanity and insanity, and the relationship of that to creativity and a profound humanity…

> Sounds made harmonies with premeditation; the spaces between them were as significant as the sounds. A child cried. Rightly far away a horn sounded. All taken together meant the birth of a new religion. (*MD*, Septimus, p. 26)

Septimus believes that because of his un-feeling, he has become, "...so pocked and marked with vice that women shuddered when they saw him in the street. The verdict of human nature on such a wretch was death" (p. 101). The unbearable Doctor Holmes is that "human nature". And: "Human nature, in short, was on him – the repulsive brute, with the blood-red nostrils. Holmes was on him" (p. 102). Holmes as "human nature" is effectively handing down a verdict of death. He registers in Septimus like a poison that kills insidiously. "You brute! You brute! cried Septimus, seeing human nature, that is Dr Holmes, enter the room" (p. 104). And: "Once you fall, Septimus repeated to himself, human nature is on you. Holmes and Bradshaw are on you" (p. 108). Perhaps through Septimus, Woolf can do and say potent things about the war, depression, madness, and society that she can't say in any other voice or genre; ergo, Septimus is forged out of necessity, and redeemed by the role he plays as his *self* stands for other lost selves.[5] Clarissa too is unstable, but held in place by the rhythms of her environment and her becoming-other at every turn, which is both her redemption and her undoing.

Woolf provokes the question, 'what is madness?' which she answers by rhetorically showing that it is sometimes a symptom of genius: the anguish of bearing extreme capability inside a limited frame (a body, a suite of emotions, an era, or class) and/or simply one's ill fit with normativity. Woolf is brutal about Sir William's, and England's, values and the constituent repression of the already weakened:

> Sir William not only prospered himself but made England prosper, secluded her lunatics, forbade childbirth, penalized despair, made it impossible for the unfit to propagate their views until they, too, shared his sense of proportion – his, if they were men, Lady Bradshaw's if they were women. (*MD*, p. 110)

Septimus's poetic mind searches for sense and order. In frequent reference to scientific methods but always in conjunction with his poetic sight, he determines that tangibles work in tangent with the mysteries of life, making *beauty* or something like the haecceitical 'it-ness' of things the truth:

> Up in the sky swallows swooping, swerving, flinging themselves in and out, round and round, yet always with perfect control as if elastics held them; and the

---

[5] Differently here, is the lost/absent 'self' of Jacob Flanders from Woolf's *Jacob's Room*. He is another victim of the circumstances of War. And in so far as an author's works cross-pollinate; the two young men are embodied in Woolf.

flies rising and falling; and the sun spotting now this leaf, now that, in mockery, dazzling it with soft gold in pure good temper; and now and again some chime (it might be a motor horn) tinkling divinely on the grass stalks – all of this, calm and reasonable as it was, made out of ordinary things as it was, was the truth now; beauty, that was the truth now. Beauty was everywhere. (pp. 77–78)

"…if elastics held them", and "it might be a motorhorn", are grounded moments that provide a contrast with the pathos showing Septimus's wavering mental capacity and complexity. Meanwhile time and its conformities, the Doctors and Lucrezia (Septimus's wife), remain cruel. Here, Rezia is the prison guard announcing imminent death…

'It is time,' said Rezia.
The word 'time' split its husk; poured its riches over him; and from his lips fell like shells, like shavings from a plane, without his making them, hard, white, imperishable, words, and flew to attach themselves to their places in an ode to Time; an immortal ode to Time. (p. 78)

Time is shown for what it is (in a text): a loaded pod that splits and gives flight to words that "attach themselves to their places" (or are impeded in the process). In Septimus, Woolf commits author to character and vice versa—whether or not affects and effects of tied-ness or visibility are in play. In her diary, Woolf writes that she is depressed and that it has to do, at least in part, with the death of Septimus: "A feeling of depression is on me, as if we were old and near the end of all things […] Then, being at a low ebb with my book—the death of Septimus—and I begin to count myself a failure" (*Diary*, Saturday, 2 August 1924, np).

Society values "Proportion, divine proportion, Sir William's goddess" (*MD*, p. 110). In the manner that Woolf uses it, proportion is a word of immense pomposity signifying the upright and the inflexible, "But Proportion has a sister…" (ibid.). And 'she' is much worse: "Conversion is her name and she feasts on the wills of the weakly" (p. 111). Here, Woolf performatively exemplifies the travesty of the class (and sex) barricade that seeks to repress outsiders and non-conformists.

In the moments where Clarissa observes or thinks about Septimus, she becomes an assemblage with him; when musing on his death she 'goes through it' herself; this moment of intimacy seems to reflect Woolf's own embodiment of characters as per the diary entry about depression and Septimus, as well as her exquisite desire to 'saturate the atom':

> He had killed himself – but how? Always her body went through it […] her dress flamed, her body burnt. He had thrown himself from a window. Up had flashed the ground; through him, blundering, bruising, went the rusty spikes. There he lay with a thud, thud, thud in his brain, and then a suffocation of blackness. So she saw it. But why had he done it? And the Bradshaws talked of it at her party! (*MD*, p. 203)

Clarissa's illness is alluded to but not dwelt on in specificity. The "spasm" (shown below) is preceded by musings on her age and situation, and a parallel may be drawn wherein the pain originates in her mind (like Septimus's pain):

> Laying her brooch on the table, she had a sudden spasm, as if, while she mused, the icy claws had had the chance to fix in her. She was not old yet. She had just broken into her fifty-second year. Months and months of it were still untouched. June, July, August! Each still remained almost whole, and, as if to catch the falling drop, Clarissa (crossing to the dressing table) plunged into the very heart of the moment, transfixed it, there. (pp. 41–42)

Clarissa wants the trappings (fortifications) of her life (husband Richard, friend Peter, daughter Elizabeth, benevolent associates, servants et al.) "…to come about her and beat off the enemy" (p. 50). The enemy is her own mind: "…while she mused, the icy claws" (p. 41) as her mind reacts to the body, sex, social circumstances, and time/era. But she is capable of haecceitical bliss as she "…plunged into the very heart of the moment" (p. 42). However: "It was all over for her. The sheet was stretched and the bed narrow. She had gone up into the tower alone and left them blackberrying in the sun" (pp. 52–53).

Mrs Dalloway's narrative shows not one point of view but the visible part in a galaxy. No-one is swayed or changed beyond the possibilites for their type (and no author asserts her own voice inside or outside the narrative); each character is a piece, which remains interconnected with each other – just as bodies in solar systems (or atoms in molecules) are. The author invisibly inhabits her manipulations of each one as they tip and flow into and out of each other in their hybridizing.

> The only way to get outside of the dualisms is to be-between, to pass between, the intermezzo—that is what Virginia Woolf lived with all her energies, in all of her work, never ceasing to become. (D&G 2014, p. 277)

It certainly seems so.

Inter-genre Woolf

Woolf's final novel, *Between the Acts* of 1941, is an unfinished and experimental hybrid work.[6] It appears variously comical, musical, and greatly fragmented by shifts of mind, style, and reference to real-world events mixed in fiction. This gives it a staccato and un-novelistic texture. The work's hybridity goes beyond its formal qualities as it is embedded with metaphor and genre movements that exemplify Woolf's hindsight across a life of multiplicity. As a play within a play (and more), *BtA* is an immanently hybrid exploration of strategies not previously used with such veracity by Woolf. It seems that in *BtA* Woolf explores a final list.

In an introductory note to *BtA*, Jackie Kay writes that Woolf shows us what it is like to be both/and:

> She creates tension, by forcing us to imagine what it is like to be both visible and invisible, inside and outside, real and unreal, actor and audience, beast, and woman, silence and noise, drowning and floating, public and private, high culture and jolly human heart. (Kay 2000, in *BtA*, p. xii)

BtA presents an array of problems, stalemates, and impossibilities for the 'play' of life and indeed for creative expression which, Woolf shows,[7] may not always match the creator's intensity of feeling (or their efforts at atomic saturation). The play is amusing and stifling. As the title indicates and the text bears-out, the substance is in the space between the acts where the audience-reader is acutely significant, ultimately carrying the story forward, cued by actors who never really turn back into 'regular' people once the spurious pseudo-fiction of the play has ended. "Each still acted the unacted part conferred on them by their clothes" (*BtA*, p. 121).

To confer identity according to clothes or by other societal markers, is problematized in Woolf for whom the physical is both momentary and monolithic, while true selves move between, beyond, and through 'it all'. In relation to *BtA* I ask, almost rhetorically: are the play, its story, Woolf's history and our own ever singular, subtractable, separable, or are they multiple, blur-edged hybrids incorporating creative argument and strife or necessary tension? How might a fictive textual life ever be richly conveyed without attention to its

---

[6] Unfinished, as per Leonard Woolf's note in the 2005 edition of *BtA*. Also, in her introductory note Lisa Jardine explains that in the margins of a letter, Woolf asked Leonard to "destroy all my papers" (Jardine, in *BtA*, p. xviii), but he did not and so we have *Between the Acts*.

[7] In her diaries and when reading between and on the lines of her creative work.

hybridity and the hybridity of the writing process? Might argument and strife (internal and external) become (redemptively) necessary for the intensity that saturates atoms? "Before they slept, they must fight; after they had fought, they would embrace. From that embrace another life might be born. But first they must fight" (p. 136).

Lisa Jardine picks up an interesting point about the nemetic (though brief) friendship between Woolf and Katherine Mansfield. Glancing across a broad field, Jardine suggests it's possible Woolf held onto an early critique by Mansfield of her *Night and Day* (1919), which Mansfield criticized for its leaving out the overwhelming reality of the First World War and being 'cold and indifferent' (Jardine 2000, in *BtA*, pp. xx–xxi). Jardine suggests that Mansfield's feedback might have informed Woolf's subsequent efforts to develop a style which is relevant and truthful, not leaving out anything important.[8]

If any specific origin for Woolf's hybridity is needed, this can be encapsulated by her exhortation in 1928 to saturate the atom. That desire for distillation, intensity, truth, and satisfaction is evident within the particular and experimental features of her work. In the essay 'Modern Fiction' ([1925] 2003) Woolf shows this in a paragraph that moves from the atom to the 'big', illustrating the sense throughout Woolf that inner and outer worlds are distinguished only by moments of apprehension and framed via language:

> Let us record the atoms as they fall upon the mind in the order in which they fall, let us trace the pattern, however disconnected and incoherent in appearance, which each sight or incident scores upon the consciousness. Let us not take it for granted that life exists more fully in what is commonly thought big than in what is commonly thought small. (Woolf 2003, np)

Woolf's craft essays describe her atomic desire, in exhortations and critiques that show us her community of influence, and also her capacity for fusing stylistic approaches. Here is an example from 'Craftsmanship' ([1942] 2012):

> Written up opposite us in the railway carriage are the words: 'Do not lean out of the window.' At the first reading the useful meaning, the surface meaning, is

---

[8] Woolf, suggests Jardine, brings Mansfield back as the character Mrs Manresa (Jardine, in *BtA*, p. xxiv). Manresa is a coarse antipodean without inhibitions who 'gulps her cup of tea' (p. 66), and 'squats on the floor' (p. 67). But, any insult Mansfield might have levelled at Woolf, is matched by Woolf's own cutting criticism (in her diary) of Mansfield several months before Mansfield critiqued *Night and Day* in the review of November 1919 (Jardine, in *BtA*, p. xx). In her diary entry of 7 August 1918, Woolf writes: "I threw down *Bliss* with the exclamation, 'She's done for!' Indeed I don't see how much faith in her as woman or writer can survive that sort of story." (np)

conveyed; but soon, as we sit looking at the words, they shuffle, they change; and we begin saying, 'Windows, yes windows—casements opening on the foam of perilous seas in faery lands forlorn.' And before we know what we are doing, we have leant out of the window; we are looking for Ruth in tears amid the alien corn. The penalty for that is twenty pounds or a broken neck. (Woolf 2012, np)

Recalling the relative intensities of the 'small trumping the large' (Woolf, 'Modern Fiction'), Kafka's train image and Nabokov's bored clock (both mentioned in Chapter Two), Woolf's essay 'Craftsmanship' features similar poetic 'flights' ("perilous seas in faery lands") in conjunction with blunt concretizations (the "broken neck") to convey authoriality with poetic inserts. The images are like brain flashes, flickers, atomic saturations, and evidence of the life of the author engaging with the material it critiques. The visibility of the author in the essay form is vivid and unsettling for Woolf compared to the hidden author of the novel, which is of *visions*: "Where the novelistic voice is authoritative and always, necessarily, in control of its fictive world, the essayistic voice is unmoored: explorative, open to self-doubt and prone to risky exchanges with its audience" writes Randi Saloman ([2012] 2014, p. 3). Woolf's interest in both the essay and the novel leads to a hybrid form:

> I find myself infinitely delighting in facts for a change, and in possession of quantities beyond counting: though I feel now and then the tug to vision, but resist it. This is the true line, I am sure, after *The Waves—The Partigers*—this is what leads naturally onto the next stage—the essay-novel. (*Diary*, Sunday, 2 October 1932, np)

The 'risky exchange' (Saloman) may serve genre hybridity well. The "risky" idea goes out to the "audience" who meets it, not with indifference. Of course, novelistic voices may also involve risky exchanges, but the effects are buffered by the fiction author's distancing strategies. *The Voyage Out* (1915) and *Night and Day* (1919) are examples of Woolf's early essayism, placing her in the text. She then proceeds to hide in the novelism of her mid-career before finally achieving her "own style" (*Diary*, np)[9] in *The Waves* (1931), and the eventual genre-mixing of the textural *Between the Acts* (1941).

The following excerpt from 'Craftsmanship' is a critique in Woolf's essayistic voice of the effect of words, and in particular of writing and eventually of the potential for truth as constructed by the reader. Here, Woolf implies (and I extrapolate), that what characters and indeed their authors do is live and write

---

[9] Quoted in Chapter One.

essayistically in attendance to moments of tedium, fear, and even glory, held together by the gaze of the other and distilled and created over and over via subsumptions and mergings towards new languages:

> If we insist on forcing them [words] against their nature to be useful, we see to our cost how they mislead us, how they fool us, how they land us a crack on the head. We have been so often fooled in this way by words, they have so often proved that they hate being useful, that it is their nature not to express one simple statement but a thousand possibilities—they have done this so often that at last, happily, we are beginning to face the fact. We are beginning to invent another language—a language perfectly and beautifully adapted to express useful statements, a language of signs. There is one great living master of this language to whom we are all indebted, that anonymous writer—whether man, woman or disembodied spirit nobody knows—who describes hotels in the Michelin Guide. (Woolf [1942] 2012, np)

It might seem that Woolf was tending towards the essence of that "language of signs" by distilling consciousness into essential words. The plain language and concision of the reviewer's rating scale in their task to be unequivocal is fraught with unacknowledged possibilities and lacking in nuance, which Woolf acknowledges in her cynical depiction of the Michelin reviewer, while envisioning a not-dissimilar language as an ideal of sorts, the ultimate *saturation*, which does not lose the density of language.

So, hybridizing distillations that particularize *and* universalize, are for Woolf, the thing to do. In 'Between Sensation and Sign: The Secret Language of *The Waves*' (2012) Maureen Chun argues that in *The Waves*, Woolf achieves a return to words as things. She writes: "[*The Waves*'] original vision establishes the continuity of words, narrative, and world through a physicalized consciousness" (p. 55). Woolf certainly gives everything to words in *The Waves*, but it could also be said that Work performs a becoming *un*-physicalized in its engagement with flights and fluidity, and in tension with the necessity of words to achieve a musicality, like a score of consciousness, which is also becoming a score of *collective* consciousness in collaboration with the reader.

In reference to Woolf's *The Cinema* (1926), Chun asserts that Woolf seeks a "secret language" (p. 56),[10] one that is visual and textural, which:

---

[10] Woolf articulates the search for a "secret language" in 'Craftsmanship' with her cynical proposition of the reviewer's system of star-rating.

...operates beneath narrative language as a system of representation, and occasionally surges to view in moments that reassert that there remain elements of language, life, and the real world that resist the human work of signification. (Ibid.)

The emergence of a "secret language" necessitates work against the psychic weight of established narrative significations in order to supply writer and reader with a more expansive method of immersion in the 'art' of words as triggers of feeling and lines of flight, or as the un-signified.

It ends where it begins, with the atom

The atomic level is where human ontologies commence (at least *figuratively*. I am only a gleaner). This connects conceptually at least to Tillich's notion of becoming from the ground of being (1954), and dialectically to Deleuze's univocity (floating, shifting, 'un-inscribed' particles, collectively). While Deleuzoguattarian univocity eschews the stability of any micro-order or rather, in their terms, the rigidity of molecular segmentarity (D&G 2014, p. 213) they simultaneously hail Woolf's desire to saturate the atom. Both atom and molecule as building blocks derive from or contribute to the arborescent systems Deleuze and Guattari decry, but isn't *any* system of interdependent parts an arborescent one even if also rhizomatic and in this case 'saturated'? Rhizomatic systems also *begin*, and move through a process, which like a (arborescent) tree, depends on specific irrevocable factors for growth.[11]

From an atomic beginning comes Wittgenstein's 'family resemblance' which as previously discussed in Chapter Three, argues that family traits are what binds the members of the group involving: "...a complicated network of similarities overlapping and criss-crossing" (Wittgenstein, in Eagleton 2012, p. 20). The differences among the group render its individuals distinct while connected. This is inevitably a model of difference in unity, the post-structural/ postmodern approach to a difference which is always contingent to the extent of the eventual loss of the subject; whereas unity in difference values and rallies around difference.

---

[11] Why not invent new words and language to host ideas inside words which make concepts that are not in conflict with their own meaning?

Bringing it back to texts, the comparison is in terms of the meaning of 'literature' and decisions about what is contained or excluded genre-wise. The argument is open, and Literature is hybrid, even while its parts might not be easily described that way. Eagleton quotes Derrida with whom he agrees on the 'duplicity of literature' in so far as meaning is derived by the reader via her secondary "uptake" (2012, p. 82) or the unique meaning-making of the words she reads: "In a minimum autobiographical trait can be gathered up the greatest potentiality of historical, theoretical, linguistic, philosophical culture…" (Derrida, in Eagleton 2012, p. 83). And, Eagleton writes: "…any particular literary statement packs a wealth of general connotations into itself. It is thus that the singular comes to behave as a microcosm, condensing whole possible worlds in its slim compass" (ibid.). The collaborative unity of the micro/macro (in life and art) is not monologic or self-gazing, it is dialogic and even interdependent in moments.

Woolf's self-seeing-others (e.g. Bernard, *The Waves*; and Isa, *Between the Acts*, etc.,) become other-self hybrids of the kind involving rhizomatic movement one to the other. Woolf's saturation-style accommodation of her characters is her multiple embodying. Hers is a hybridizing movement towards *flood*, always and only when served by constraint. So, saturation is not the key; it is the (verbing of it) *saturating*, which continues via saturation's excess beyond the saturated thing (the noun).

In casting broadly across Woolf's *oeuvre*, it becomes apparent that redemptive hybridity is present in the manner, methods, and intensities by which her characters are shown to view theirs and others' humanity. Redemptions are available or lost within a moment, while having been written since the beginning of time. They are affirmatively or negatively robust—that is: foretold or prescribed by character type and circumstance.

Claire Colebrook (2012) writes that according to Deleuze, moments like those described in Woolf, have a force that transcends individuals while being experienced by them. The force is 'individuating' not individualistic. "Becoming-woman", for example, is what happens when "the force of what is experienced takes the self beyond its organic and selfsame limits" (p. 70). Thus, moments have "eternal power" (ibid.).

It is the way the atomic (sub-momentary or sub-molecular) or what is seeded or coded impacts on redemption (whether cause and effect are ever extricable), that is important to Woolf's hybridity. Because it is not possible to continue to saturate an atom without destroying it, as a non-scientist filtering this through a non-linear creative mind, I wonder; would the concept rely on each atom in the molecule being similarly as saturated (intense/complete/pure)? Regardless of what works or does not work in the thick space where nonfigurative and figurative truths coincide with speculation, what *is* valuable to know is that the atom is the smallest beginning, the original building block, the holder of a *part* of truth, which is also truth because parts make the whole.

The distillation of intensity (apropos of the atom) which interests Woolf must be sustained beyond the saturated atom, and out-or-up into the molecule (a frame shared by a variance of atoms), all of which risks a great deal, adding magnitude to the image.

In *The Waves* for example, there are enactments of the atomic principle via portraits of *becoming*, like windows onto atomic (seeded, coded, inscribed) redemptions where perfection is not the goal:

> I remarked with what magnificent vitality the atoms of my attention dispersed, swarmed round the interruption, assimilated the message, adapted themselves to a new state of affairs and had created, by the time I put back the receiver, a richer, stronger, a more complicated world in which I was called upon to act my part and had no doubt whatever that I could do it. (*TW*, Bernard, p. 218)

In a broad conceptual sweep, assisted by what is gleaned in Woolf, articulated by Deleuze and Guattari, and extrapolated here, the redemptive atom makes up molecules of redemption (or, at least those tinged by redemption) which go through stages to become (or to move nearer) redemptive hybridity in literary practice. This atom can be thought of as *the* mutable receptive-and-reactive particle, the measure of being; a micro-reflection of (whole) being and crammed full of sub-atomic creative potential—which may or may not infect the whole (person) with transformative power!

A redemptive atom becoming redemptive hybridizing makes a heuristic conceptual image, but one with an internal logic—'it *exists*', at least for literary purposes, and it articulates an impetus for writing below/into/beyond and between the sub-or-micro layers that compromise the lisible surface. The intensity of possibility arrives via manoeuvres of saturation, overflow, and flood. It is this intensity, populated by multiplicities, that innervates the redemptively hybridizing manoeuvres of the post-postmodern paradigm past, present, and future.

5

Finding a Name for Possibility

Postmodernism, feminism, and agency

Post-structuralist and postmodern perspectives concern "...insurmountable barriers to ever knowing the world beyond texts authoritatively" writes Nick J. Fox (2014, np). Within these ideologies contingency might seem invigorating where it is read as 'truthlessness for all', however, such negative egality is problematic for various minority groups, some women, feminists, the unwell and vulnerable, etc., if brushed-over by the flattening paint of contingency with its corruptive effect on lived experience. This is where 'unity in difference' might be asserted to enable the seeing of difference and the support of it, not constraining or demanding that it throw open to postmodernity's game. This makes way for the contestation of what is vital, to the extent that impossibility becomes thoroughly wrapped around necks.

Postmodernism builds "...identity assemblages rather than social structures" (Fox 2014, np), which matters to the aforementioned necessities of life, and here also to feminism as a culturally pertinent arena for hybridizing, polarizing, and for continual renovations of ideology.

In her 'Introduction' to *Feminism/Postmodernism* (1990), Linda J. Nicholson, writes that postmodernism might offer feminism an expansion of its terms of reference:

> ...for some feminists, postmodernism is not only a natural ally but also provides a basis for avoiding the tendency to construct theory that generalizes from the experiences of Western, white, middle-class women. This position, qualified, is taken by Nancy Fraser and myself. As we note in 'Social Criticism without Philosophy', postmodernism offers feminism some useful ideas about method, particularly a wariness toward generalizations which transcend the boundaries of culture and region [...] feminist theorists have most frequently claimed to base their theories in observation and to acknowledge their construction as rooted in the concerns of the present. (p. 5).

Nicholson's postmodernism is one of inclusivity and diversity apropos of feminist voices. However, other essay writers in the collection argue that postmodernism only serves feminism if feminism is prepared to become a game of indefinite parts with little to do with the more guttural concerns of lived-realities.

There are feminists who would shift the emphasis from Nicholson's 'rootedness in the present' to a formulation whereby making a workable present means attending to a dysfunctional past, which can only happen by acknowledging and respecting distinct voices, bodies, and the groups with which they identify. To progress the latter, Christine Di Stefano makes a case for keeping feminism separate from masculinist postmodernism because women have not benefited from the privileges afforded their male counterparts. In her essay 'Dilemmas of Difference: Feminism, Modernity, and Postmodernism' she writes: "…postmodernism expresses the claims and needs of a constituency (white, privileged men of the industrialized West) that has already had an Enlightenment for itself" (Di Stefano 1990, p. 75). Does Di Stefano's view perpetuate the separateness that becomes the problem, or does she bring to light an important matter for feminists (even now) who are on the lineage going back to suffragism? A lineage which according to Koa Beck in *White Feminism* (2021), is white and privileged, causing problems for a feminism of inclusion.

For Judith Butler, feminism is problematic where it attends only to the totalizing idea of *woman* as a binary opposition or cause or identity concerning fixity. So, instead of using 'women', Butler opts for the "category of women" (1990, p. 326).[1] Butler's postmodernity of surface treatments (similar in Foucault) makes 'generalizations'—I am thinking of Nicholson's use of that word (1990, p. 5) quoted previously—via its perpetual moments of specificity, which disconnect the subject from the substance of its three-dimensionality in favour of a façade.

Wary of postmodernism's erasure of substance, Susan Bordo claims, in her essay 'Feminism, Postmodernism, and Gender-Scepticism' (1990), that perpetual movement and fragmentation deny the substance of bodies and their obvious/actual lived limitations and specificity. "If the body is a metaphor for our locatedness in space and time and thus for the finitude of human

---

[1] I discuss this in my introductory chapter.

perception and knowledge, then the postmodern body is no body at all" (Bordo 1990, p. 145). She sums this up concisely: "...one is always *somewhere*, and limited" (ibid.).

While feminism re-groups in individual (textual) forms and diverging theories, the pluralism 'of it all' is broadly legitimizing of difference/s: we are able to engage in a broad use of play and rigor with simultaneous theories from across a broad span of knowledge where we incorporate our reactivity, our humility in the presence of alterity, our effort to understand, and our acknowledgement of naivety and any bewilderment—but necessarily, all towards testing and formulating concepts that give to a core of purpose albeit mutable.

With a suite of interrelated concepts, Deleuze and Guattari effectively reframe what's already there, which has nothing to do with being helpful to causes (like feminism), but as Massumi identifies in his Translator's Foreword to *A Thousand Plateaus*, Deleuzoguattarian concepts can be used in other settings, even being changed in 'translation' and making the becoming-fiction, the auto-theoreticality, the ficto-criticicality, and the art-fictionality of theory-and-practice. All practice involves intertext. All practice and theory takes in enemies, even if, as in D&G it defers the pause in which one (individual or group) might rehearse their autonomy while imprinting a memory of what that looks like before scattering into multiplicities (molecularities) again.

Despite the deconstruction of individual and group legitimacy (any concrete features) and because of the very imagistic Deleuzoguattarian multiplicities, I am emboldened (for a moment) to appropriate their world-making analogies and re-use these inside redemptively hybridizing manoeuvres (like this project) within a lineage of women's practice on one hand, while on the other hand within a space where gender is not front and centre, unified and convoluted as it is by multiplicities. My points of reference within and across any one or more of the suite of frames in which I act as woman, mother, writer, artist, person, etc., is my pluralism, while I hold for reasons of identity to those aspects which are *fixed* in subjective and/or objective meanings, and shall be defended despite and because they are necessary, while necessarily always changing.

Finding names and building frames

The perpetuity and multiplicity within Hassan's 'host-enemy' matrix is central to the/this modernisms continuum. 'Co-existent enemies' articulates a key feature of an emergent *post*-postmodernism; a harmonizing term that not only houses modernism and postmodernism, but also any other movement or ideology that feeds into the continuum.

According to Hutcheon ([1989] 2002), what is required is a new name for what is being produced. Names are identifiers or "heuristic" placeholders (below), as may be the case with post-postmodernism, as it articulates continuity—but that may not be enough. She writes:

> The postmodern moment has passed, even if its discursive strategies and its ideological critique continue to live on – as do those of modernism – in our contemporary twenty-first-century world. Literary historical categories like modernism and postmodernism are, after all, only heuristic labels that we create in our attempts to chart cultural changes and continuities. Post-postmodernism needs a new label of its own, and I conclude, therefore, with this challenge to readers to find it – and name it for the twenty-first century. (Hutcheon 2002, p. 181)

Hutcheon could not have known the extent to which she would (directly or indirectly) be taken up on that challenge. In no particular order, there have been digi/meta/alter/hyper/uber/(etc.,)-modernisms each a different perspective on the machinations of the cultural climate around the dawn of the twenty-first century. There is now quite a cluster of flags on top of the post-postmodern mountain.[2]

Given my metaphor of subsumed or housed 'enemies' after Hassan in particular, it seems inconsistent not to call the current paradigm simply 'post-postmodernism' (despite the awkwardness of adding 'posts' ad infinitum). However, the paradigmatic reach gets exponentially larger with all that taking in, to the extent that *post*-postmodernism does not connote any particular style or genre, while certainly holding tendencies. It is here that I insert Redemptive Hybridism to add (all this) suggestively, observationally, and collegially.

If any other name is to be deployed, it would need to encapsulate the multiplicity of co-existent cultural tendencies while not discrediting or interrupting the non-hierarchical structure of the continuum: modernism →

---

[2] Including the flag of Redemptive Hybridism, which prefers to decorate a birthday cake than a mountain top, and is content to sit alongside (some) others.

postmodernism → post-postmodernism. While I agree with Hutcheon about the benefit of finding a new name, 'post-postmodernism' is useful for an overt relationship to its forbears and for its hosting of multiple points of view. But this must surely be the last *post*. 'Post-post', we are already attempting to define what comes next, while the multiplicity, simultaneity, and splitting-off that has always occurred and which instated the problem and advantage of *difference*, now suggests the logical way forward in unity—and time will reveal the most explicative mountain-top flag/s. But in terms of a name for the hybrid work being produced, it is useful to consider how we situate ourselves in relation to names, identity markers, and other framings like these.

In an interview with Attridge, Derrida identifies the need to name the work that 'deforms the limits of literature' while not elevating new forms above 'old':

> I would not say that we can mix everything up and give up the distinctions between all these types of 'literary' or 'critical' production (for there is also a 'critical' instance at work '*in*' what is called the literary work). So it is necessary to determine or delimit another space where we justify relevant distinctions between certain forms of literature and certain forms of… I don't know what name to give it, that's the problem, we must invent one for those 'critical' inventions which belong to literature while deforming its limits […] These new distinctions ought to give up on the purity and linearity of frontiers. (Derrida, in Attridge [1989] 1992, p. 52)

To name a recurrent practice or tendency is key to the task of encapsulating its traits and effects. A name is a frame (or map) as Derrida implies, and ideas shift and move inside frames that plot the course. It may be seen then, that while the space-between comprises the territory, the space of possibility is elevated in hybrid forms comprised of both negative and positive space. This does not necessarily require a giving up of "purity", but only if purity might be thought of as being within the perfect process—the exactitude where intention and practice or subject and object align and make a 'perfectly' flawed imperfection.

Ficto-criticism

Stephen Muecke (2002) suggests that the name "…we would have given" Derrida to describe the kind of literature he speaks of is "ficto-criticism". Muecke says: "When criticism is well written, and fiction has more ideas than usual, the distinction between the two starts to break down" (all Muecke 2002, p. 108). But the breakdown doesn't move us into a hybridizing multiplicity; it is not genre and form at their 'best' that kick-start a redemptive hybridity, it is the state of collapse as it coincides with hope's energy and the creator's[3] conception of possibility, that constructs the path.

A collaboration of genre-collapse and possibility can be read in *The Space Between: Australian Women Writing Fictocriticsm* edited by Heather Kerr and Amanda Nettelbeck (1998). This work exemplifies authorial/testimonial and vernacular texts in tangent. The work of the writers is curated inside the frame 'ficto-criticism' where a shared space enables performance and projection of difference within a unity of women. Ania Walwicz's *Look at Me, Ma – I'm Going to be a Marginal Writer!* is an example of how hybrid forms pass through their author collecting DNA (multiplicity, possibility, and authorial tone):

> I have failed to place myself anywhere. But you said that you are avant-garde, before! I've named myself Polly. I am very fancy. Is one allowed to be contrary? I am never serious. I am ironic. How do I conclude now? [Gap] How do I end? A text becomes finite, conclusive, limited, strained here, uneasy, shush… I don't want to play the game. I don't want to play this game anymore [in a child voice, with a French, I think, accent]. (Walwicz, in Kerr & Nettelbeck 1998, pp. 276–277)

The 'unresolved' texture and tone in Walwicz, and her choice of words make a humorous 'jab' at a postmodern delimiting of agency and possibility. As well as being ficto-critical, this collection could be considered auto-theoretical and auto-fictional; however, *none* of these categorical names articulates the breadth and scope of the work in this collection as it 'deforms the limits' (Derrida) of literature while seizing (some) specificities of 'being a woman'.

Collective responses require a name to indicate direction and stance. This may be why paradigm-defining 'isms' proliferate exponentially in this *post*-postmodern era of coexistent and burgeoning multiplicities. A genre name is seized, announced, and immediately becomes both limiting and specifying while furnishing the reader with certain assumptions and expectations.

The Argonauts and autotheory

Like fictocritcism, autotheory has a ring of ingenuity about it—of composing terrain in a space where there is formerly none. But autotheory does not write fictions—unless it does; the 'auto' being the author-self, is the unreliable and intimate aspect of the duality, and so, there is every chance of deceit. In fictocriticism the game is announced up-front.

---

[3] Creator = writer, artist, anyone who creates.

Maggie Nelson's *The Argonauts* (2015b) combines the autobiographical with the theoretical, becoming 'autotheory', which she discusses with Michael Silverblatt (2015). Named after Barthes's ship builders and heroic crew and in relation to Nelson's appropriation of that analogy, *The Argonauts* is an authorial response to love's incarnations and specific complexities. Nelson also invokes and interacts with various theoretical points of view throughout.

'The Argonauts' references the Greek myth which Roland Barthes discusses in his multi-media autobiography *Roland Barthes* ([1975] 1994). Barthes employs the anecdote of the ship, the *Argo* and its 'Argonauts' from the Greek myth of Jason and the Argonauts: a crew of heroes who sailed on the ship named *Argo*[4] in pursuit of the 'Golden Fleece' (the taking of which would bring utmost authority and grandeur). Barthes uses the image as an illustration of the idea that a name (in this case, the *Argo*) has a mutable veracity—a name is like a head of seeds that grows myriad ideas and instates myriad trajectories. While the *Argo*'s properties change over time as it is re-built or added to, the name remains (an embodiment inscribed with memory) and comes to signify a quality or essence rather than a particular entity:

> …the ship *Argo* (luminous and white), each piece of which the Argonauts gradually replaced, so that they ended with an entirely new ship, without having to alter either its name or its form. [Then at the end of the same paragraph]: …by dint of the combinations made within one and the same name, nothing is left of the origin: *Argo* is an object with no other cause than its name, with no other identity than its form. (Barthes 1994, p. 46)

The object changes but the name remains as a *substitution* or frame that signifies or nominates the lineage of a concept (ibid.). The Barthesian Argonauts are the agents of change who alter the object, the *Argo*, giving it a new-or-fluid materiality that requires new-or-fluid definitions (while keeping the name) and its investiture with divine grandeur (apropos the first *Argo*). Nelson tells us that after her pronouncement of love, she sent the following to (Harry) "you":

> I sent you the passage from *Roland Barthes by Roland Barthes* in which Barthes describes how the subject who utters the phrase 'I love you' is like 'the Argonaut renewing his ship during its voyage without changing its name.' Just as the *Argo*'s parts may be replaced over time but the boat is still called the *Argo*,

---

[4] According to Greek mythology, the *Argo* is said to have been constructed with the help of Hera or Athena and consecrated to Poseidon. The *Argo* is said to have been the first ship. Jason was killed in his sleep by a rotten beam that fell from the *Argo*.

whenever the lover utters the phrase 'I love you', its meaning must be renewed by each use, as 'the very task of love and of language is to give to one and the same phrase inflections which will be forever new.' (Nelson 2015b, p. 5)

As Barthes says, the *Argo*, and also love, are not the name (an edifice), they are the form they take. Nelson performs a kind of truth-telling which is nothing like the smoke-and-mirrors truth of Wallace's *TPK*; Nelson's purpose is sincere like Wallace's but conveyed essayistically, non-fictively, and with a sharper focus on a particular and authorial subject. Nelson's project has layers while retaining a crystalline focus on a contemporary and personal situation apropos of gender, difference, and love (and various tones between and of those).

The Argonauts illustrates a redemptive hybridity via its auto-theoretical monologue on being Maggie Nelson; a woman, writer, academic, mother, and lover/partner in a relationship with her transgender partner Harry, while also being human; exemplifying desires and choices that are embodied by humans across spectrums. Nelson and her partner are the Argonauts re-defining love while being worked on by love's past, present, and future-common attributes. But Nelson's *Argo* is also in relation to the/her 'self', "…we develop, even in utero, in response to a flow of projections and reflections ricocheting off us. Eventually, we call that snowball a self (*Argo*)" (Nelson 2015b, p. 95).

In an interview with Silverblatt, Nelson says that no existing name for her writing will do, hence she applies the most suitable term, 'autotheory'. Hers is a hybrid approach to practice and semantics: one name needs changing while another vastly-used one—'love'—does not, even *should* not according to Nelson, who, with her partner, is on a continuum of re-building whatever is meant or felt when 'love' is invoked. And while love means different things to different people, it has gravitas. For Nelson, 'love' is perpetually re-cast or added to (in Silverblatt 2015, and *The Argonauts*). She suggests that one's capacity for love is limitless but that as time passes the attributes change inside the name.

The Argonauts neatly refers to other re-buildings, such as those performed via intertext and meta-nonfiction.[5] The following example is of a testimonial and intertextual moment in *The Argonauts*, which stretches across time and culture to Charlotte Brontë's "Reader, I married him" from the end of *Jane Eyre*:

Reader, we married there, with the assistance of Reverend Lorelei Starbuck. Reverend Starbuck suggested we discuss the vows with her beforehand; we

---

[5] Formulated here to suggest a non-fictionality that becomes 'unreliable' when it includes an autobiographical aspect.

said they didn't really matter. She insisted. We let them stay standard, albeit stripped of pronouns. (Nelson 2015b, pp. 24–25)[6]

This is parodic of the R/romantic genre while enacting a 'rebuilding' of it too. It is dialogic of long-politicized issues pertaining to marriage, and becoming in its multiplicity a moment of heightened contemporary hybridity. It invokes the intertextual (the reference to Brontë), the paratextual (main text takes in what might have been a footnote), the meta-nonfictional (exemplification of textual possibility), and of course also the lived-reality of a couple and their family.

Nelson's 'Argonauts' are the lovers re-defining love. It is the *Argo*-self forming over time. It is the 'off-site' re-builders, such as the cast (and crew) of the Greek myth, Barthes himself, *and* Nelson together in a frame and complicit in the production of this autotheory. The reader is also an *Argo* being shaped and re-formed by each experience (each moment).

Paracriticism

Hassan's use and definition of the term 'postmodernism' reached critical and pivotal mass with *Dismemberment of Orpheus: Toward a Postmodern Literature* (1971), in which he configured a mechanism of collaborative-combative exchange via his infamous chart comparing the features of modernism with those of postmodernism (p. 269). Then with *Paracriticisms: Seven Speculations of the Times* (1975), Hassan enacts a genre-collapsed metonymic textuality from the 'thick' of postmodernism. *Paracriticisms* reaches from premodern romanticism to post-postmodern authorial visibility at a time when postmodern strategies and ideology are becoming 'commonplace'.

Hassan embodies the liberality of the paradigm, to express "…a desire to break out of criticism" (1975, p. xi). He unfolds his point of view across seven essays and extends his speculations via curated inserts or fragments that show different aspects of thought; having the effect of emphasizing the fragmentary, accretive, autobiographical, and randomly-gleaned nature of personal knowledge. There are 'digressions', 'anecdotals', and 'propositions' that demonstrate caveats-becoming-integral to empirical ideas. Hassan says that the work includes "…fictions of the heart" (ibid.).

---

[6] If you are addressed as 'Reader' it is no longer possible to peep in at key holes; you've been brought into the frame.

As a neologism, *paracriticism* is the *beyond* of criticism, where the status quo is pushed into its former nemesis becoming a fortified hybrid. Paracriticism also performs the postmodern liberty to subjectively arrange and define the world-as-self.

> ...paracriticism: essays in language, traces of the times, fictions of the heart. Literature is part of their substance, but their critical edge is only one of many edges in the mind. I would not protest if they were denied the name of criticism. Perhaps I should simply say: in these essays I write neither as critic nor scholar—nor yet impersonate poet, novelist, or playwright—but try to find my voice in the singular forms that speculation sometimes requires. Yet what, finally, is singular? Every voice is cursed by its echo, blessed by an answer this side of mortality. (Ibid.)

As a trans-modern expression beyond, while according to, the modernisms continuum, Hassan's monologue pulls back just in time from solipsism while maintaining a personal voice to fuse with opinion, and elsewhere with tested truths or facts. In its capacity of broadening authorial visibility in 'non-fiction' while searching for a 'para'-something, his work becomes transgeneric (intermedial) within the modernisms.

The work moves between various characteristics of multiple genres 'tipped out', such as: empirical material, opinion, metafictional moments, and metonymic poetic expressions of concepts, and "fictions of the heart" (ibid.). For example, at the beginning of the chapter titled 'FICTION AND FUTURE: An Extravaganza for Voice and Tape', Hassan commences with the fragment: '1. BEGINNING NOW', in which he speculates that "man" is a generalist and the author or reader "we", might "begin anywhere." He writes:

> A generalist may find in graffiti a start [...] The handwriting on the wall reminds me of Marx. History repeats itself, according to Marx, the first time is tragedy and the next time as farce.
>
> I will come to my topic, contemporary fiction, by and by. I am at my topic, on various levels, now. (p. 97)

There are numerous allusions to socio-political revolution, as well as examples of romantic heroism, authorial intrusion, and insinuations about liberties in the practice and form of textual work, *as well as* great intimacy with the reader via Hassan's use of first person.

The creative splicing of material in *Paracriticisms* does not detract or minimize the knowledge-impartation of its parts, but life is breathed into the whole by the continued presence of its author who extends the possibilities and the potential audience via generous genre multiplicity (collapse and collaboration). Hassan's work performs an enabling of conjoint experience of conjoint process, within (theoretically,) an unlimited postmodern frame, which he begins to draw in the 1970s – an era in which, "...our motives speak in a babble of tongues" (p. xvi).

Call me[a]taxy: some recent pre-fixes

As a denotive framing of era, *post-postmodernism* captures only a suggestion of forward movement; meanwhile, there are any number of other prefixes attached to modernism that flag their own brand of restlessness and change (for example again: cos/meta/alter/hyper/digi/uber). Each incorporates particular lenses and preferences and shows the splitting-off effect caused by chagrin with postmodernism and late culture.

Working within a *post*-postmodern frame, which is sometimes an extension, sometimes a subsummation rather than a cancelling of postmodernism, the various nominative markers tend towards an operation of (Plato's) 'metaxy', or the 'in-between'. In Simone Weil, metaxy (*metaxu*) is approximately 'the absent as present' in relation to the human necessity to problematize a position at the in-between of death and life, or contradiction and edification:

> Given that reality is itself *metaxu* [...] the real (*le réel*) itself is an obstacle that represents contradiction, an obstacle felt, e.g., in a difficult idea, in the presence of another, or in physical labor; thus thought comes into contact with necessity and must transform contradiction into correlation or mysterious and crucifying relation, resulting in spiritual edification. (Rozelle-Stone & Davis [2018] 2020, np)

"Contradiction into correlation" would neatly describe the redemptively hybrid use of tension and subsumption in a process of strengthening and a reflection of heterogeneity (in literary in art). Contradiction need not always be resolved as we see in Wallace's *The Pale King* where it emphasizes transformative in-stability. However, and arguably, the available anecdata[7] shows that 'we' have a preference for movement towards resolution.

Metamodernism frames the instability of the *post*-postmodern moment (the 'what have we become'?) and its chagrin with postmodernity. It appropriates

---

[7] Anecdata = a buzzword mashing up 'anecdote' and 'data'.

Romanticism's sincerity and mixes it with an inherited irony in the contemporary moment. Its 'meta' derives from a combination of metaxy, meta-physical, and meta-narrative. In her *Interconnections in a Blakean & Metamodern Space* (2007) Alexandra Dumitrescu describes metamodern ideas as maps being continually revisioned (after J.L. Borges [1967] 1997).[8] Her thesis *Towards a Metamodern Literature* (2014) develops these ideas further. In Dumitrescu, there is an overt leveraging of Metamodernism as a salve *against* Postmodernism. There is an organic inevitability about, or subjection to, the biological and other networks, with William Blake as an example of metamodern values incorporating the majesty of nature and its spiritual and unifying connection with humans. Dumitrescu's *metaxy* is insufficiency becoming sufficient. She sees: "A boat being built or repaired as it sails" (2007).[9] This suggests a becoming or a completing *in-situ*, having therefore a distinct timbre of forward momentum.

Meanwhile, in their *Notes on Metamodernism* (2010), Timotheus Vermeulen and Robin van den Akker's Metamodernism features perpetual oscillation between poles:

> ...it is a pendulum swinging between 2, 3, 5, 10, innumerable poles. Each time the metamodern enthusiasm swings toward fanaticism, gravity pulls it back toward irony; the moment its irony sways toward apathy, gravity pulls it back toward enthusiasm. (2010, np)

Attraction to the other/opposite might be the "gravity" that pulls the "metamodern enthusiasm" back. Vermeulen and van den Akker emphasize the part that postmodern irony still plays as it operates in conjunction with sincerity to forge the oscillatory (metaxical) response worked out in metamodern culture.

Vermeulen and van den Akker emphasize the contemporary Internet-driven fragmentation, which works with their analogy of perpetual oscillation. Of course, instability is inevitable in a twenty-first century of co-existing multiplicities, and this becomes the paradigmatic condition; one must be content to live either in a *tabula rasa*[10] state of imminent decision or face impossibility in acceptance of a complex state of indecision: "Metamodernism moves for the sake of moving, attempts in spite of its inevitable failure; it seeks forever for a

---

[8] This resembles the (Greek) Jason and the Argonauts myth, particularly as it is taken up by Barthes (1994), as discussed in this chapter.
[9] 'Repair under sail' is close to what Barthes (1994) articulated on Jason and the Argonauts.
[10] *Tabula rasa*, in John Locke, is in relation to the idea that individuals are born with their mind in a condition of 'blank slate' for knowledge building.

truth that it never expects to find" (Vermeulen & van den Akker 2010, np). They assert that a metaxical position is always the *figment* of a position that never occurs, because of oscillation. Theirs is a high value on postmodern irony stitched to sincerity.

Where Metamodernism emphasizes the oscillatory it emphasizes im/possibility, and each variation is a multiplicity.[11] Meanwhile, a *redemptive* trajectory might take in the past/the enemy (postmodernism) and see this as distinct while altered at the taking-in, thus restoring power to subject (selves/minorities/outliers) and process.

Briefly, in addition and for contrast, Christian Moraru's theories of Cosmodernism and Planetarism bear some resemblance to Metamodernism in terms of the sincerity and simultaneity articulated. However, a key feature of Moraru's figuration diverges where he figures a kind of a centripetality as he stakes out a planetary boundary and works as though towards a 'centre' from nearer the "greater elsewhere" (cited more fully shortly). While the planetary as a context is an anthropogenically urgent one, the beyond of the planet, in this heuristic, is also begging to be named.[12] Moraru's *Reading for the Planet: Toward a Geomethodology* ([2015] 2018):

> …restages the cosmodern 'algorithm' of interpretation […and] the role of relationality […] teasing out the inscriptions of planetarity, the world's reemergence *qua* planet, in early twenty-first-century literary, cultural, and theoretical practices. (p. 6)[13]

The "…cultural geography of relationality" (p. 5) expounded in Moraru's theory and in his book *Cosmodernism* (2011), becomes in *Reading for the Planet*

---

[11] Here are some significant contributions to metamodernism's online presence, which is of course synonymous with fast dissemination and change. This list is by *no* means exhaustive: 1. The website established by Vermeulen and van den Akker in 2009 and edited/shared with others, functions now as an archive. These two were at the forefront of metamodernism's popularity. See: https://www.metamodernism.com/about-2/. 2. Dumitrescu (a.k.a. 'Balm') and colleagues known as Metamoderncreatives, set up *becoming* "a metamodern magazine of arts and literature" launched synchronously with their Jan 2023 symposium on metamodernism. See: https://www.metamoderncreatives.com/. 3. Linda Ceriello and Greg Dember curate and author gatherings, conversations, and texts among other media, which discuss and "catalogue" examples of metamodernism. See: https://whatismetamodern.com/.
[12] Perhaps even a *galactic* framing of life, theory, and texts, etc., would be *the/a* truly anthropocentric take, allowing for centrifugal movement, with all the unity-difference of that.
[13] But is the world the planet? Is the world also not the planet? And where does perception come in?

a: "…characteristic *geocultural logic*: the heterotopic copresence deployed by the greater elsewhere's ever more aggressive bid for redefining the cultural 'here'" (p. 6). The 'here' is the planetary position, which is not a 'globalizing' one (p. 24). This helpful configuration of the situation figures a post-neoliberal *beyond* of the subjective gaze or reality endorsed by globalism. There is an emphasis on relationality towards an ethical planetary re-*worlding*, which "…imagines a world yet to come" (pp. 58–59). The methodology is a *geomethodology*, toward 'worlding' via, among other things, an ethical 'reading-with' (the other).[14]

Each of these 'modernisms' has discourse with and defines the 'current structure of feeling' through specific lenses.[15] What they, and redemptive hybridism do as frames in post-postmodern territory is push up through the paradigmatic 'relatives' which formed us, to assert the re-emergence of possibility; even if articulated very differently in each frame.[16]

David St. John ends his Introduction in *American Hybrid: A Norton Anthology of New Poetry* (Swenson & St. John 2009) with a pleasing exhortation to a participatory reading and the generative path ahead: "The purpose of this anthology is to celebrate these exquisite hybridizations emerging in the work of all our poets. Let the gates of the Garden stand open; let the renaming of the world begin" (p. xxviii). The 'renaming of the world' invokes the limitations of language. However, as a possibility it *might* be done in the hybrdizing arenas of art-and-text.

---

[14] An ethical 'reading-with' brings to mind D.J. Hale on self-binding in alterity, as discussed in Chapter Three.

[15] Coined by Raymond Williams "…in Preface to Film (1954), to discuss the relationship between dramatic conventions and written texts." Structure of feeling refers to the simultaneous different ideologies and ways of thinking that coincide in time. "Williams uses the term feeling rather than thought to signal that what is at stake may not yet be articulated in a fully worked-out form, but has rather to be inferred by reading between the lines. If the term is vague it is because it is used to name something that can really only be regarded as a trajectory." From *Oxford Reference* (online): http://www.oxfordreference.com/view/10.1093/oi/authority.20110803100538488 (retrieved 13 March 2016).

[16] I am sure that anyone who is occupied with constructive assemblages of theory and practice for revisioning and adding to the modernisms continuum is hemmed-in by names as well as by the pressure of garnering the essence-and-possibility that defines their quest.

6

The Pale King's Constellation; Factoids, Ghosts, and Boredom

Tell the truth, David Foster Wallace

A postmodern gaze at particulars (Eagleton 2012, pp. 14–17) is evidently the root cause and also the effect of the problem that Wallace identifies inside and outside *The Pale King*. But universal truths come down via the particulars that encode them.[1]

In relation to this, Eagleton cites Iris Murdoch's character Annadine from *Under the Net*: "We must be ruled by the situation itself and this is unutterably particular" (Murdoch, in Eagleton 2012, p. 14). But, wonders Eagleton, *how* can we speak of the particular without ultimately giving it a context; that which lies or lives outside of the particular? (pp. 14–15). Hybrid forms and hybridizing processes specifically engage with particulars *in*, or *and*, the outside of the particular, via collapse and collaboration of spaces and hierarchies.

By gazing at particulars, Wallace constructs (with the posthumous input of his editor), a semantic heterotopia (Topinka 2010)[2] akin to a 'magic-eye' picture[3] offering the author-and-reader a precarious yet reflexive engagement with their own mind. But there is in *TPK*, slippage in and out of particulars – such as the specific doubts, dense observations, and perceptions of truth – and into a space *around* particulars which is blocked by the inevitable overlaps that come with

---

[1] Similar to 'gazing at particulars' is Sterne's *interruption*, a closed particular that would eschew the Kierkegaardian universal. Kierkegaard's 'feeling the lack' = an 'open universal'. In this sense, Sterne could be said to be a precursor of Postmodernism from the eighteenth century.
[2] Topinka discusses Foucault's use of Borges's *'Funes the Memorius'*; Funes cannot forget, thus his memory becomes non-linear, a heterotopic or alternate space for contemplating history and time; a new order or way of organizing, in this case, memories.
[3] Into which one gazes and finds other images—even worlds—during the gaze.

unfinishedness and fragmentation. This is fascinating for what it reveals about Wallace's hybridity, as I will show.

TPK's reader is offered an authorial lens that focuses, blurs, and re-focuses. This troubled gaze evokes the impossibility Wallace identifies at the pointy end of postmodernity and late capitalism, and as evident in the material gathered into his final book.

Passages showing the neuroses of the first protagonist Claude Sylvanshine are interspersed with the ins and outs of taxation; the effect metonymically engages the difficulty, boredom, dubiousness, but also a redemptive-ness discussed in this chapter. Reading Sylvanshine is like running to the length of a short chain, choking, and falling back.

> What if he was simply born and destined to live in the shadow of Total Fear and Despair, and all his so-called activities were pathetic attempts to distract him from the inevitable? Discuss important differences between reserve accounting and charge-off accounting in the tax treatment of bad debts. Surely fear is a type of stress. Tedium is like stress but its own Category of Woe. Sylvanshine's father, whenever something professionally bad happened—which was a lot—had a habit of saying 'Woe to Sylvanshine.' There is an anti-stress technique called Thought Stopping.[4] (*TPK*, pp. 14–15)

Throughout *TPK* Wallace uses disjunctive strategies that hail 'truth' without committing to it (in case it is a lie in disguise?). This becomes his 'truthiness'[5]—his approach to hybridity. The fragmented and anxious Sylvanshine reflects the particularity of the reader'/s' disjointed mind as well as his own in a para-*tax*-ic[6] stream of consciousness that adds up to the truth/s that is/are beyond the particular, e.g. the 'fact' of the body/time imprint in the creation of a manuscript, and the simultaneous desires of its writer, which are of course sub-truths to broader truths, and on it goes.

In a postmodern sense, anything written or uttered can be 'true' within its art-fictional frame and for the duration of the narrative or conceptual space made by the language. As Eagleton says about the writer:

> A writer may 'fictionalise' a factually true account, casting it in dramatic form, fashioning memorable characters, shaping it into an absorbing narrative and

---

[4] Capitalization per *TPK*.
[5] Not a Wallace-specific 1980s–90s buzz word, mentioned in another footnote soon.
[6] Tax joke.

organising its features so as to highlight certain moral themes and general motifs [...] You might then read the book not for the sake of the empirical truth or falsehood of its account but precisely for these 'literary' qualities. (2012, p. 114)

And literary qualities *become* truths in terms of their ability to resonate with an emotional or conceptual force. Hartsock writes that according to Foucault, "...truth [is] simply an error hardened into unalterable form in the long process of history" (1990, p. 165). This summation of Foucault on truth, shows truth as error's chronic sickness. Whereas, while early post-postmodernity (Wallace) wrestles with truth and with what to do about the lies handed down, the truth thereof is an unspecified goal which encounters and takes in error, a reversal of the Foucauldian observation.

The reader is a collaborator apropos of truth-building. They ascribe and define subjective truths that operate in tension with any beliefs that underpin or give traction to the poetics of the writing. The reader's work also concerns the hybridization of fact and fiction into an amalgamation with constituent exaggeration or alteration. But Eagleton goes on to say: "...it is how they [the factually true statements] function strategically or rhetorically that counts, not their epistemological status" (2012, p. 115). Presumably this assertion would work for factually *untrue* statements as well—that the manner and placement of statements is what 'matters' in making fiction, as well as what the true or false or in-between statement builds.

> A reader might still put aside the truth-value of the non-fictional utterances, or might still 'fictionalise' the whole work, fictional and non-fictional statements together, in the sense of assigning it some exemplary import, or using it as an occasion for make-believe. (p. 117)

The text's believability may be an effect of its accessibility to the reader and their degree of identification with it (after Eagleton 2012, pp. 117–118). Eagleton writes: "A good deal of human behaviour is marked by this duality: doing something yet performing it at the same time" (p. 120). Via embodiments, we inhabit truth while breaking it down. The performance is then taken in by the viewer and filtered there, and truth is caught in the space between.

A note about context

Wallace studies as a cultural frame has been largely upheld by white males—I could add 'young' (as in, younger-than-me and younger than Wallace).[7] While there are obvious reasons as to why this might be, and also some obvious exceptions, Wallace *also* transcends those cultural frames via the hybridity of his final work and also via the convolution of himself with that work.

In relation to the commodity value of Wallace, Lee Konstantinou writes, "Wallace has been transformed into an empty literary brand name" (2018, p. 49). Konstantinou suggests that whether the reader places their Wallace book in a prominent position on their bookshelf or actually reads him, Wallace might be seducing and manipulating them either way via his fashionable infamy or sparkling writerly tricks (p. 50). But despite the various uses for Wallace's books, from objects of pretension, to life-changing or paradigm-defining texts, Clare Hayes-Brady indicates *TPK*'s transmodern hybridity: "*The Pale King* combines the figure of the romantic hero with that of the ironic hero" (2018, p. 143). *TPK* is, she writes, commonly considered to be "…one of Wallace's more uplifting works," despite any down-beat themes. I agree. "*The Pale King* offers reversal and renewal, struggle and continuation" (both ibid). The in-roads it makes are because of its hybridizing, including its unfinishedness and the room it makes for the reader.

I would like to think that while I have let Wallace take up a lot of space in this project, I become immune to seduction (Konstantinou) because of a poetically forensic interest in Wallace's tricks, dovetailed with a wariness about his attitude to women (more in my concluding chapter) and a great deal of empathy for his view towards a post-postmodernity, which is ultimately a redemptively hybrid one.

Here we go, boredom is encouraged…

---

[7] I am aware that this is anecdata.

Discordant parts in harmony

Kurt Vonnegut's novel *Cat's Cradle* ([1963] 1970) opens with: "Nothing in this book is true."[8] This is the mirror-image of, but also fairly similar to, Wallace's, "All of this is true. This book is really true" (*TPK*, p. 67). It is, to draw a line around this generational disparity in parity, as though Vonnegut as 'founder' of (his fictional) Bokononism, a religion based on lies, has a heretic in Wallace, but one who uses similar language. Vonnegut's 'foma' can be compared with Wallace's 'factoid';[9] both engage with the notion that untruths are harmless ironic gestures that reverse-engineer, and/or in the case of the factoid in particular, *approximate* the truth, 'rounding it up' in the absence of facts.

In an 'Author's Foreword' in '§9', commencing page 66 of *TPK* and finishing on page 85, Wallace writes: "Author here. Meaning the real author, the living human holding the pencil."[10] He proceeds to write that the aforementioned is

---

[8] Vonnegut 'invented' the religion Bokononism, which is explored in the *Cat's Cradle*. Bokononism is based on the concept of 'foma', which are 'harmless untruths' (elsewhere, 'useful lies'). The religion, including its texts and songs, is made up of 'lies' and lying, which it celebrates as a legitimate way to live pain-free. Adherents to the religion do or can live a life of peace (the 'bliss' of denial). In the un-numbered few pages before the contents page, sits the exhortation: "Nothing in the book is true. 'Live by the foma that make you brave and kind and healthy and happy.'" Bokononism presumes that religion is all lies, hence the *bettering* of religion in Bokononism by 'honestly' admitting the lie but, ironically, living according to the lie, religiously. On pages 13–14 the *Cat's Cradle* narrator says: "The first sentence in *The Books of Bokonon* is this: 'All of the true things I am about to tell you are shameless lies.'" And the parodic and ironic context is well and truly set.

[9] "Norman Mailer [...] coined the term ['factoid'] in his 1973 book *Marilyn*, about Marilyn Monroe. In the book, Mailer explains that factoids are 'facts which have no existence before appearing in a magazine or newspaper, creations which are not so much lies as a product to manipulate emotion in the Silent Majority.'" Merriam Webster online dictionary, retrieved 19 September 2019, https://www.merriam-webster.com/dictionary/factoid#note-1. *TPK*, Footnote #33, p. 281, uses but doesn't explain 'factoid' and its other appearances seem similar to Mailer's. The factoid is similar to 'truthiness', a 1990s–2000s buzz word.

[10] *TPK*, Chapter 9 Author's Foreword: "Author here. Meaning the real author, the living human holding the pencil [...] this right here is me as a real person, David Wallace, aged forty, SS no. 975-04-2012, addressing you from my Form 8829-deductible home office at 725 Indian Hill Blvd., Claremont 91711.CA, on this fifth day of spring, 2005, to inform you of the following: All of this is true. This book is really true" (pp. 66–67). Wallace goes on to explain that the 'disclaimer' on the copyright page at the front of book 'disclaims' [keeping the tautology]; "...this very Author's Foreword. In other words, this Foreword is defined by the disclaimer as itself fictional, meaning that it lies within the area of special legal protection established by that disclaimer. I need this legal protection in order to inform you that what follows [here he inserts a footnote explaining that 'everything that surrounds this Foreword is essentially true' footnote #2 p. 67] is, in reality, not fiction at all, but substantially true and accurate. That *The Pale King* is, in point of fact, more like a memoir than any kind of made up story" (p. 67). Wallace also writes that if you believe the legal page, you can't believe him now... Then on page 68, after repeatedly going on about the disclaimer, there is the enormous footnote #3 explaining the 'publisher's' involvement or lack thereof in these issues. The footnote takes up more than three quarters of page 68 and is continued on page 69. During this footnote Wallace writes: "...and don't think the whole book will be like this" (p. 69). It both *is* and is not.

important and worth repeating, "All of this is true. This book is really true" (*TPK*, p. 67). Or at least, it is a 'factoid'... Given the context for *TPK*: posthumously assembled by a third party and published unfinished, the many mentions of truth make a slippery slope as well as a deep irony in a text which paints a portrait of a figuratively 'many-headed' hybrid author-editor-reader.

Prior to one of *TPK*'s many extreme footnotes, Wallace asserts the truth of the rest of the book again: "...it's a mainly true and accurate partial record of what I saw and heard and did [...] at IRS Post 047, the Midwest Regional Examination Center, Peoria, IL, in 1985-86" (p. 69). And here:

> The point I'm trying to drive home here is that it's still all substantially true— i.e., the book this Foreword is part of—regardless of the various ways some of the forthcoming §s have had to be distorted, depersonalized, polyphonized, or otherwise jazzed up in order to conform to the specs of the legal disclaimer. (*TPK*, p. 72)

The interplay between main text and footnotes challenges and performs *TPK*'s repeated assertions of 'true'. This also serves up a useful supply of issues in relation to deceit, yearning, self-delusion, and writing 'fiction' inside which truth begins to clang meaninglessly, ironizing the very idea of truth, and challenging genre.

Wallace claims that even while he distorts and 'jazzes' up the truth, it remains 'true' (ibid.). This does of course open up the field to a 'truer than true'; the *actual* truth, or at least the truly possible. And this is where it (all) becomes specifically hybridizing and redemptively so. In contestable spaces of truth and possibility, where the reader is inoculated by the many wearying assertions of 'truth', they 'know' only factoids. But 'factoid land' is an insupportable though necessary port enroute through or to hybridity. It is here that we experience our preferences and beliefs as we filter information. What I believe Wallace would have us do, is wade around in factoids to see what effects that dizzying space might raise up. Then, in the future, near or far, and after much filtering and sieving, we might find that truth, like gold, has finally been adequately tested.[11]

One of *TPK*'s (few) 'key' female characters, Toni Ware, epitomizes the fine-line between truth and lies; she is all creatures, all things highly strung and reaching breaking point. Ware is her own harsh judge. Her built-in truth-teller is faulty and she encapsulates the stuck-ness and paradigmatic self-annihilism that

---

[11] I will not surmise on *adequacy*; the openness of this exhortation precludes any measurement of that.

arrives post-truth at the burnt-out shell of an undead postmodernity, a space of despair and searching, made worse by endless repetitions.

Hayes-Brady suggests that the character Toni Ware is "...one of the most disturbing in Wallace's whole body of work" (2018, p. 148). She writes that Ware's "...self-denial is in fact the strongest affirmation of her self-sufficiency" (ibid.). Ware's space of despair is of white noise, inadequacy, and paranoia; it is constructed from a difficult pastiche of irony and empathy:

> There were five other US citizens in the store and then a sixth when the woman sans child came in to pay, and while Toni selected enough items to fill a bag she observed them interact or not and felt again the acquaintance she always assumed all strangers in rooms she entered enjoyed, the conviction that everyone in the room all knew each other well and felt the connection and sameness they shared by virtue of what they had in common, the quality of not being her. (*TPK*, p. 513)

Wallace's empathetic treatment of Toni Ware inside a cynically-drawn sketch of a conservative right-wing America, e.g. the "five other US citizens", which suggests 'entitlement', seems also an empathy-anger at *himself* in being Toni Ware and *stuck* (in ways) since they were a child. Toni Ware was, "Begat in one car and born in another. Creeping up in dreams to see her own conceiving" (p. 59). This is similar to the disembodiment enacted in Wallace's short story 'Good Old Neon' in *Oblivion* ([2004] 2005). And the moment Toni Ware, standing in the 'ramp tumour' (a motorway's on-off-ramp shop, *TPK*, pp. 512–513) wipes (and is later is seen to have wiped) the large wad of her own carefully harvested snot on her lapel—brooch-or-brand-like—is a highly effective tragic crescendo:

> Which she carefully wiped onto the left lapel of her cream-colored coat, with enough pressure to give it some length but not enough to compromise its adhesion or distort the nougat at its heart. (p. 514)

Toni Ware is then confronted by the 'truth' of her own repugnancy. It is a profound moment of tension where what is ultimately surmised by the reader (and not by Ware herself) is the complex simplicity of Toni Ware and the truth about her:

> ...her strongest impulse had just been to drive half-blind with tears home to throw the coat that cost months of going without to buy so she could take her two babies to church in something they didn't have to feel ashamed to be with into the low-income housing development's dumpster and spend the rest of

the day praying God to help her make some sense out of the senseless violation she just had happen and to avoid forever thereafter this QWIK 'N' EZ out of degradation and horror. (pp. 515–516)

The presence of *TPK*'s hovering, actual, real, author and his confessional authorial telling and obsession with truth-until-it-rattles is succinct in the appearances of David—sometimes F.—Wallace the 'fictional-non-fiction' narrator as per the Author's Foreword (pp. 66–85). On page 72, the narrator gives seemingly paranoid instructions to the reader about how to read and what to believe:

> The point I'm trying to drive home here is that it's still all substantially true [...]. This is not to say that this jazzing up is all just gratuitous titty-pinching; given the aforementioned legal-slash-commercial constraints, it's ended up being integral to the book's whole project. The idea, as both sides' counsel worked it out, is that you will regard features like shifting p.o.v.s, structural fragmentation, willed incongruities, & c. as simply the modern literary analogs of 'Once upon a time...' (p. 72)

Importantly, the truth-or-not of the narrator-author's (memoiresque) obsessions and intensities is the overarching 'truth' that *TPK* asserts in its claustrophobic spaces between. But whether or not we are reading a 'true story' is the lingering and animating question, while the 'fact' that truth is so rigorously challenged via *TPK*'s many even contradictory assertions makes *truth* (and truthless-ness) the subject in those moments.

Truth in a flash

"*The Pale King* is [...] a kind of vocational memoir. It is also supposed to function as a portrait of a bureaucracy" (*TPK*, p. 70). *TPK* is also an unfolding testimony of working at the IRS while doing research for the book, and an exemplification of deep weariness *and* wariness. Caught as it is as 'work in progress', *TPK* gazes at its own navel and beyond in its quasi-private but overwhelmingly public exploration of place, value, and meaning. On the whole, *TPK* is a summary of the cultural state of play, nationally, globally, and of Wallace's own mind.

The use of non-fictional strategies helps impart a hybridizing veracity, bringing Wallace's text closer to the reader in terms of their 'self-binding' (Hale 2007) to reading and waiting and reading and waiting (in 'factoid-land') to see what effect the experience of being locked into the dull-and-dry IRS will have on their psyche: will they too find enlightenment via boredom's spiritual potentiality? They will certainly find a lot of footnotes that affirm the text's hybridity in conjunction with the slippery matter of genre:

> [Footnote #] 3: N.B. I'm not going to be one of those memoirists who pretends to remember every last fact and thing in photorealist detail. The human mind doesn't work that way, and everyone knows it. (*TPK*, p. 257)

This declaration of intent recalls Levé's stochastic marbles (Chapter Three), and the "everyone knows it" makes a dialogic requirement of the reader, continuing Wallace's predilection for a (utilitarian) visibility in his writing style and form. It has a function similar to Genette's "and some others which have escaped me" (also Chapter Three) in so far as the reader is immediately drawn into an awareness of the author as directorial, the text as metafiction, and their own partaking of and willingly believing in a bunch of words.

At bottom of page 283 in *TPK*, the narrator says that all the detail mentioned on the page is "…being perceived and processed in nothing more than a distracted flash." It is interesting to retrospectively spurt forth so much detail in a "flash". And: "…the myriad details and impressions (of which there were thousands or even millions, all obviously incoming at the same moment) of arrival" (*TPK*, pp. 284–285).

This "flash" is not an epiphany, which is (in James Joyce for example) a moment of knowing that touches everything subsequent to it and implicates everything past. No, in *TPK*, the flash is an impressionistic fragment of an elusive object-goal. It is like a neurological brain zap, as if chemically induced, rather than a momentous or prolonged epiphany.

The inference for truth then is pertinent when information is taken up in a 'flash' then expressed in a myriad written words. The modalities of flash and text, do not articulate an equitable understanding; the text is the *translation* of the flash and 'everyone knows' material gets lost there—ergo, truth is the victim *or* the contingent salient point that the writer/philosopher chases and attempts to find ever more concise translations of, within for example, redemptively hybrid forms.

Even unfinished, *TPK* employs the 'enemy', reconstituting it and its game to present the problem of trickery and ploy by *using* trickery and ploy. The result is, a perpetually hybridizing work (in the manner that only unfinished works can be) and one that redeems the writer-and-reader from previous limitations while articulating the lack of individual autonomy under the predicament of capitalism that Wallace identifies.

Everyday ghosts, souls, and phantoms

Divine voice/s

Bakhtin makes an analogy of the formerly "single-languaged, geographically and socially united people" (Ruth Coates [1998] 2005, p. 108) of the (Old Testament's) Tower of Babel, whose post-fall polyglossia (Genesis 11:7) delimits their power by causing confusion and division. The prose writer, "…takes into account 'the Tower of Babel mixing of languages that goes on around any object'" (Bakhtin, in Coates 2005, p. 108). So, after the creator has reigned-in the created who has misused their power, the created becomes linguistically unintelligible: "…linguistic unity […] is equated with arrogance and the will to power" (Coates 2005, p. 108). However, according to Bakhtin, the *ideal* novel works out its dialogic relations via attention to the particularities of a new, post-babel polyphonic form after Dostoyevsky (in Bakhtin [1929] 2014), which transcends any unitary/monologic control becoming redemptive for the created. Coates shows Bakhtin's commitment to a kind of linguistic nomadism and all that is refined by that:

> The novel begins by presuming a verbal and semantic decentring of the ideological world, a certain linguistic homelessness of literary consciousness, which no longer possesses a sacrosanct and unitary linguistic medium for containing ideological thought. (Bakhtin, in Coates 2005, p. 110)

Then there is (the New Testament) Pentecost, in the book of Acts,[12] where the human and the divine work in a relational frame while still beset by linguistic difference and selective intelligibility. This time there is an in-filling of a *supernatural* linguistic power towards a luminously *relevant* literature, like Dostoevsky's polyphonic model, according to Bakhtin (2014).

---

[12] "¹When the day of Pentecost came, they were all together in one place. ²Suddenly a sound like the blowing of a violent wind came from heaven and filled the whole house where they were sitting. ³They saw what seem to be tongues of fire that separated and came to rest on each of them. ⁴All of them were filled with the holy spirit and began to speak in other tongues as the spirit enabled them" (Acts 2:1–4).

Post-postmodernly, the divine may (re)enter the fray; conceptually at least, it may hybridize all voices in itself. *We* feel the need of that indwelling voice to make us conscious of a spiritual-self—the last and least mined part, and (very) arguably we feel this even more than the need to colonize other planets or elevate ourselves to other unsustainable heights. The missing or buried voice is not one we need to interpret but one that communicates in 'yearning too deep for words' (Romans 8: 26) while *needing* words, and that is where the hybridizing of forms, languages, words, character, and more is tested and engaged.

God with a squeaky voice

There's no getting away from "me"/"the real author" (*TPK*, p 66). This is the container for and flavouring of each voice in the work. The fictional-non-fictional 'David Wallace' narrator-author-character (referred to in Hering 2017) is a compound becoming fortified in its hybridizing. Regarding the authorial character-figure of 'David Wallace', Hering writes that all of the "…voices are all implicitly his voice: an unbalancing, and potential effacement, of the 'coexistence and interaction' model advanced by Bakhtin" (p. 146). However, any monologic tendency in Wallace becomes liminalizing and hybridizing where character and author difference is brushed over by a single unifying glaze. In Wallace and elsewhere, this 'brushing over' renders subjects as indistinct while *more than* they are in their singularity.

Wallace's taking-in (of the Other) might not always empower the Other in the manner, for example, that some feminists require, but the creativity in Wallace is not concerned with the social matters of fairness. Meanwhile, sincerity and author visibility may impact constructively on those matters and for the emergence of art-and-text forms that enter fully into the relational interplay pronounced by the restless post-postmodern moment.

The David Wallace (character) as David Foster Wallace (author) and vice versa, becomes a vector for all of the characters, and as a multiple it hosts the narration. But inserted amidst the authoriality in *TPK* are some notable stand-alone character portraits, thought-games, and 'set pieces' which enable us to lose the sense of Wallace micro-managing his characters. These are, for example, the Rand-Drinion dialogue, Lane Dean's boredom, the Chris Fogle 'novella', the self-kissing boy, and Toni Ware – the "standard-sized woman", a 'multiple' with "twenty different voices" used in different situations in her job at the IRS (*TPK*, p. 510).

Bakhtin suggests that the consciousness of the creator of a polyphonic novel is "…constantly and everywhere present in the novel, and is active in it to the highest degree" but does not transform the consciousness of the characters into objects and does not give them second-hand and finalizing definitions (2014, pp. 67–68). Wallace emulsifies characters in *TPK* a little too much for a solid claim on any stylistic bracketing or a distinct ideological bent, and likewise the work is (permanently) liminal in its unfinishedness. The layering, overlap, and uncertainty in the work reach *not quite* the categorically monologic due to Wallace's intermittent backings-off to give way to character life in vignette; and reach not quite the dialogic because of the way he grinds the gears between sections[13] in which characters are cogs in the machine, and because everything seems filtered through himself via enough unmasked authorial interruptions.

A pale king is a haunting

The author-character David Wallace with ambiguous middle F—ambiguous because the F. could refer to Foster or Francis; that is, "David Francis Wallace, incoming high-value transfer" should not be confused (but of course is confused) with "David Foster Wallace, incoming low-value contract hire" (*TPK*, footnote #4, p. 413). The 'David F. Wallace' version might appear in duplicate and confuse things (the ambiguous 'F.' could stand for Francis or Foster). Wallace shows this by engaging with the idea of names and identity, and names and functionality, and how these intersect with bureaucracy: "David F. Wallace, GS-9, age twenty, of Philo IL, did not exist; his file had been deleted, or absorbed into, that of David F. Wallace, GS-13, age thirty-nine, of Rome NY's Northeast REC" (p. 411). Wallace shows the mess caused by 'red tape' and "systematic bugs and problems" (p. 410) courtesy of machines/computers and systems that disallow simplicity. Also exemplified is the convergence of character, hover-y author, and the 'real' 'actual' Wallace, within a hybrid one with many parts (as well as no parts at all where he is ghosted).

Footnote # 4 on page 413 refers to, "…my initial misassignment." The voice here belongs to one "David F. Wallace" describing how he was placed in the

---

[13] Or they are ground on his behalf via his editor's best-guess.

wrong setting by the system that confused his name with another. The very long footnote (followed by others) explains that the IRS computer couldn't distinguish between David *Francis* Wallace and David *Foster* Wallace, and in the 'main text' (between footnotes) on page 414, the story is similar: "In short, the name David F. Wallace fell in that statistical middle area where the original debugging's consequent 'ghost conflation' bug could still cause significant problems and woe."

The "ghost conflation" is a hybridizing conflation as it blends names, makes difficult entities, and encapsulates the bulked-up genre of Wallace's novel where truth and lies (like the accuracy and inaccuracy of a name) become 'factoids' as the possibilities mount impossibly, and "David F. Wallace" becomes both Wallaces/Wallace's and none.

The author *is* identified in the text while also not identified, due to the complex illusions and difficult assertions of truth. But the hybridization of truth and lies is the point, with its view to the past and the future in portrayal of a logjammed present.

The Pale King is riddled with ghosts and ambiguity about ghosts but it also features souls, phantoms, and an author with shapeshifting powers. Generally speaking (when speaking about unprovable material) a *ghost* might eventuate after something sentient has died; they are imagistic of photons or plasma, while, the *soul* is the essence of a person, living or dead. *Soul* is the transcendent part—and innervating of—the "fucking human being" (Wallace, in McCaffery [1993] 2012. See my Introduction), which Wallace hopes to preserve and articulate.

Wallace tells McCaffery: "Once I'm done with the thing, I'm basically dead, and probably the text's dead; it becomes simply language, and language lives not just in but *through* the reader" (in McCaffery 2012, p. 40). In this analogy, language is the ghost that haunts or moves, unrestrained by corporeal matters. Wallace/the author is simultaneously written into his text in so far as it lives in the reader who hosts him as they host his words. The ghost-image prevails in *TPK* for its haunting insinuations of intertext and metafiction. But, there are two "actual" ghosts at the IRS, a 'fact' which momentarily debunks any allegorical allusions while simultaneously setting the phantasmagorical in print: "The truth is that there are two actual, non-hallucinatory ghosts haunting post 047's wiggle room […] The ghosts' names are Garrity and Blumquist" (*TPK*, p. 315). Here is consciousness seeking its connections. The language about death for example shows it as a shift in consciousness and more meaningful than a lifeless body. Wallace writes about one of the ghosts: "Blumquist is a very bland, dull, efficient rote examiner who died at his desk unnoticed in 1980" (p. 315). This is a present-tense ghost, narrated not by a ghost-author but by a living one who manipulates the text to evoke the truisms: 'life over death' and 'death in life'.

Then there are the phantoms at the IRS; these are not paranormal: "*Phantom* refers to a particular kind of hallucination that can afflict rote examiners at a certain threshold of concentrated boredom" (p. 314). And, "…the phantoms are always deeply, diametrically different from the examiners they visit. This is why they're so frightening." They hail from the "examiners' repressed side" (both, ibid.). At the behest of its hover-y author and its ghosts, *TPK* becomes a machine hybridizing life, death, and the in-between (where there are ghosts).

Wallace works in what Jameson (not referring to Wallace) calls "…the imaginary museum of a now global culture" (1991, p. 18), rather than reviving "dead styles" (ibid.). The ghosts in *TPK* are not revived flesh but are shadows of the past haunting the present, enlarging it, and reminding the reader that nothing is disconnected (art and ideas do not die). The textual ghosts are thickening absences becoming presences, and are known by the reader in spaces of insinuation and non-completion where the author hovers.

From his work on Wallace at the Harry Ransom Center's David Foster Wallace archive, Hering locates the origins of the 'ghost story' in *TPK* within Wallace's notes there. He shows Wallace exploring an 'undead' narrator: "Your mind and capacity for thought are the enemy of your ghost. Your ghost is essentially you. […] I am soul. The mind is the enemy. It will not let go" (Wallace, in Hering 2017, p. 140). Here, as Hering enables us to see, Wallace rehearses the idea before and beyond the published *TPK*, of a true self as soul. However, in my reading of *TPK*, it appears that Wallace is not resolved in this conception, because the two concepts, ghost/soul, are not interchangeable.

Presumably, given the narrative sprawl of *TPK* in its many textual parts (peri-, para-, even *post-* text) the soul-ghost-self enables artistic licence and unlimited scope. If the previous Wallace note is taken 'literally', that is: the soul is the essence of the living *or* dead self, while the ghost is a trapped post-death anachronism, then Wallace's "I am soul" (ibid.) suggests that the soul is addressing "your ghosts" (ibid.) as if it were the *true* narrator, and 'you' the manipulatable character are an assemblage belonging to the soul-narrator (author-creator-god) which enables the author to move in and out of your persona/e... The soul-narrator performs versions of consciousness.

Ambiguity and contradiction in *The Pale King*

Poetic tension

The Pale King comprises a complex spatiality; to me it is reminiscent of Andrei Tarkovsky's 1972 film *Solaris* (after the book by Stanislaw Lem). Both Wallace and Tarkovsky feature a hybridizing claustrophobia due to the confluence of various insinuations of mental ill-ease converging with contested truths. Both invigorate unnerving, artificially lit, mechanistically controlled interior spaces where various kinds of monotone and monochrome and an emphatically overbearing sense of uncertainty play out via set-pieces which collectively hold poetic hostilities in equilibrium.

William Empson might call the narrative tension an *ambiguity* by negation or by contradiction (Empson [1930] 1966). *TPK*'s context and poetics move in and out of ambiguity in terms of its writer-reader relationship and the effects of slippage there, making an ambiguous carrier for its concrete images and resulting in an affectual both/and—a duality which is one aspect of the Work's value. For example, Wallace acknowledges the reader (again) in the 'main text': "Now it's becoming clear that I could spend an enormous amount of both our time just on describing this initial arrival" (*TPK*, p. 288). The irony is overt, while Wallace's intention becomes ambiguous: if the reader's time is on his mind, why not avoid so many repetitive authorial insertions? The answer of course is that these are intrinsic to the hybrid text where 'interruptions' have an essential, caveating, disambiguous, and definitive place.

In a post-postmodern frame like *TPK*, contradictions, oppositions, or negations may sit alongside or in overlap even with antonyms, becoming dynamic without the need for ideological scales to weigh elements and make hierarchical schemes. According to Empson (1966), contradiction, vagueness, rhythm, repetition, enactments of synaesthesia (where senses cross-over), and something akin to stream-of-consciousness[14] as well as negation or denial, may

---

[14] Empson's fifth type of ambiguity is in relation to ambiguity's expression of the writer's fluctuating mind, and vice versa (Empson 1966, p. 155).

all be employed to create dynamic ambiguities for the purpose (in Shakespeare among others) of enlivening the poetic substance of the text and making it live in the reader who straddles possibilities, takes sides, or formulates a response at the behest of ambiguity. Referring to *Macbeth*, Empson shows how Shakespeare uses strategic ambiguity to make richer the possible readings and multiplicity which comes with a range of readings from the same words and punctuation marks:

> '…Receive what cheer you may,
>
> The Night is long, that never finds the Day.'
>
> (Act iv, end. *Macbeth*, in Empson, p. 202).

Here, writes Empson, it is thanks to the word choice and importantly the commas, that there is ambiguity. I paraphrase: 'The night is long *if* it never finds the day', as well as 'the night is long *because it will not* find the day'; the former is contingent while the latter is certain death.

In *TPK*, the poetics of the collaboratively assembled work drag the reader away from *TPK* as fiction and into its being-memoir. This includes the 'heavy glitter' of Wallace's obsessive-style footnotes, which bring the (necessary) 'ambiguity' in paratextual movements that make caveats and contradictions.

The aura of *TPK*'s textual circumstances (its 'tragic' unfinished-ness) adds to its ambiguity. Max wrote that Wallace wanted to write a novel about the tax code "…out of which mystical clarity might emerge" (2013, p. 292).[15] And while "mystical clarity" is ambiguous, it also has direction and meaning, leaving everything—the author—in limbo.

Empson suggests that readers (given as male) may 'ignore meanings', becoming subject to the "weapon" of contradiction: "Since it is the business of the reader to extract the meanings useful to him and ignore the meanings he thinks foolish, it is evident that contradiction is a powerful literary weapon" (1966, p. 197). If there is a range of possible (true) meanings, it is the fact that there is contradiction or an activation of a semantic spectrum, deliberate or not, that matters. The multiplicities become significant to the reading of the work and do not need to be (even *should not* be) ignored.

---

[15] No specific source is given in Max for the assertion about Wallace.

Sometimes, as in *TPK*, where convoluted purpose is at its most ambiguous (because the author did not complete the work), one must reside in the inbetweening of it, the uncertainties, with no need to look for solid ground. Beyond any scholar's exhaustive study, the text remains an unfinished and torturous memoiresque work-in-progress full of ambiguities that look like compound images or multiplicities.

Empson expounds the unifying properties of "antithesis" (1966, p. 215), which seems to be key: that negation in its contradiction or denial might perform an affirmative or balancing role, for example: within shade there is light, within death there is life.

An ambiguity described in Empson which I find significantly relevant to my figuration of redemptive hybridity, is the condition of *synaesthesia*. As a method of delivering ambiguity, possibility, and a richness of description by the senses, synaesthesia enables the synaesthete to experience a multiplicity of senses, or a complication in one sense in response to particular sights, sounds, aromas, textures, and tastes. They move and are moved beyond a single-sense experience of something, to a state where for example, colours might have flavour or sounds trigger aromas… Empson writes that a synaesthetic view:

> …throws back the reader upon the undifferentiated affective states which are all that such sensations have in common; perhaps recalls him to an infantile state before they had been distinguished from one another. (1966, p. 13)

Though ambiguous to the non-synesthete, synaesthesia may bring a creative advantage and is not *only* the primitive 'state' depicted in Empson. Meanwhile, ambiguity is one of the effects of a mind working on an idea via its available and particular tools and in conjunction with the forces that underpin nuance and shade in literature. To pull out phrases, sentences, and key words and speak of these as mechanisms of ambiguity, is only the tip of the iceberg. However, a significant mode of ambiguity in *TPK* is the author-self and author-character at the place where boundaries between these shimmer. Significant too, is the pervasive question: what is fact and what is fiction and at what point does it matter? But even that, in a work so paratactically busy and unfinished can only be decided in moments that change according to the reader's zooming out to 'optically blend' matters of truth, which are in turn, matters of proximity and of the particular lens in use.

Boredom: between crisis and epiphany

Are we there yet?

Wallace takes on boredom by *becoming* bored and boring – almost sacrificially as if *for* us (at a stretch, the way Christ took on sin). We know this because boredom is thematized, demonstrated, exemplified, and embodied throughout the text.

The real skill required to succeed in bureaucracy is, "…the ability to deal with boredom" (*TPK*, p. 438). "It is the key to modern life. If you are immune to boredom, there is literally nothing you cannot accomplish" (ibid.). This is the kernel of the spiritual aspect of boredom in *TPK* where it is a conduit of transcendence.

The character Lane Dean sees beyond the IRS paradigm (to something grander). He invokes Kierkegaard: "…see for example Kierkegaard's '*Strange that boredom, in itself so staid and solid, should have such power to set in motion*'" (p. 385). Occupying the space between un-boring activities, boredom may lead to associative thinking such as Lane Dean's, and hover between crisis and epiphany, hybridizing extremes, and holding the thinker in limbo.

"The French of course had *malaise, ennui*. See Pascal's fourth *Pensée*, which Lane Dean heard as *pantsy*" (p. 383). Lane Dean is working at the IRS to make ends meet for his young family. He is overcome by the boredom he encounters as a newbie, and observes the "*soul murdering*" (p. 385) qualities of working there; "He let himself look up and saw that no time had passed at all, again" (ibid.). But: "How do you write about dullness without being dull?" Wallace wondered (Max 2013, p. 281). "The obvious solution, […] was to overwhelm this seemingly inert subject with the full movement of your thought" (ibid.). That is, "overwhelm" by the manner and complexity with which dullness is conveyed—the contrast and the irony between the content and its delivery, constructing contradiction, contrast, and quandary even—spikes that are less boring than they are challenging (while boring) and therefore redeemed somewhat.

Wallace wanted to depict the IRS as a "secular church" (Max, p. 256). And because it was the "…dullest possible venue he could think of" (ibid.). Wallace seems to suggest that lack of purpose or direction (also, lack of God?) is part of the problem of boredom, but also that via boredom and its meditative opportunity, one *might* find God. Therefore, between boredom as death and boredom as life there is scope for the full movement of thought, and scope (in *TPK* and in Wallace's agenda) to exercise the full movement of poetic choices in so far as author and text are liberated from any prerequisite to follow a particular format—liberated even to *exemplify* boredom as a sort of Petri dish site for the 'new' to coalesce. 'New' that is, with a precedent in the twentieth century with 'modernists on boredom' like Nabokov and Beckett.

TPK tests the idea that boredom can be a conduit of enlightenment. For example, into one of the book's various mashups of Christianity and boredom, arrives a Jesuit priest and substitute teacher who tells his audience about the heroism of labour and drudgery:

> …the less conventionally heroic or exciting or adverting or even interesting or engaging a labor appears to be, the greater its potential as an arena for actual heroism, and therefore as a denomination of joy unequaled by any you men can yet imagine. (*TPK*, p. 230)

It becomes a religious cult of accounting, reminiscent in timbre and allusive in sentiment of James Joyce's *A Portrait of the Artist as a Young Man* ([1916] 2000). Here, a Jesuit is calling the boys to their upcoming retreat:

> He who remembers the last things will act and think with them always before his eyes. He will live a good life and die a good death, believing and knowing that, if he has sacrificed much in this earthly life, it will be given to him a hundredfold and a thousandfold more in the life to come, in the kingdom without end—a blessing, my dear boys, which I wish you from my heart, one and all, in the name of the Father and of the Son and of the Holy Ghost. Amen. (Joyce 2000, p. 119)

Lane Dean, Christian family man, new to the IRS and its mind-numbing attributes, begins hallucinating with boredom. He starts to see his "…baby's photo's face melting" (*TPK*, p. 382). Boredom is shown to elaborate what is already in the mind of the bored; the grotesque is 'unleashed' in cahoots with (Lane Dean's) fear. Throughout *TPK*, boredom is an antidote to powerfully innervating emotion and an entrance into the zone of nothingness (considering Wallace's chagrin with postmodernism of which 'nothingness' is characteristic). Boredom is nullifying, sedating, and sometimes euphoria-inducing in its opportunity for psychic transportation beyond the physical – but it is also hellish.

There is, in *TPK*, a Joycean magnificence about dread and impending doom. In both *TPK* and Joyce's *Portrait* there is a condition, a time, a *something* paradigmatic that pesters and represses. There is a similar sense of lingering possibility for redemption or annihilation, but unlike *Portrait*, the conclusion is lacking at the 'end' of *TPK*.

Boredom kills

In 1996 Wallace took university classes in accounting as preparation for the novel. He then took a class in federal income taxation in summer 1997, and in advanced tax later that year (Max 2013, p. 256). He conducted interviews with IRS workers, and went to Peoria (near where he grew up in Champaign-Urbana, Illinois) where there was a large IRS facility, which becomes a symbol of contemporary dullness (and the Midwest), and ironically, also a 'secular church' (as mentioned) and so, a place of redemption.

Tax forms sent Wallace into a Zen-like trance (p. 291). His boredom connects to meditation and possibility, but ultimately it is annihilative in its machinistic performance of mindlessness and mental and spiritual death. This 'trance', is a type of (negative) freedom from the spikes of feeling that are integral to living.

One of the questions activated in *TPK* is, what happens to a person's internal life when they work in a dull job for a very long time? "The agents' jobs were tedious, but dullness, in Wallace's conceit, was what ultimately set them free" (Max 2013, p. 257). But after the passionate sermonesque responses Wallace makes in the 1993 interview with McCaffery (2012), and in his *This is Water* speech and essay ([2005] 2009), and particularly in the extremes of feeling endemic in *TPK*, it is apparent that Wallace's 'boredom' incorporates a testing of its scope and capacity for destruction and creativity. Also tested is the character's capacity to embody various boredoms.

An IRS worker is found dead at his desk after four days and no one had noticed. This suggests two things; firstly, that boredom 'kills' and secondly, that boredom (before it 'kills' you) stops you from feeling and seeing. Ironically, the deceased man, Blumquist, was examining the tax affairs of medical partnerships when he died (*TPK*, p. 27). And there is also this: "Training officer Pam Jensen had a .22 revolver in her purse—she had promised herself a bullet in the roof of her mouth after her 1,500th training presentation" (p. 332).

"…being in a stare" (p. 116), is gazing into space as if looking, but not actually looking or seeing. You are not doing anything in this state, "…but you are doing it fixedly" (ibid.). There is danger *and* providence in zoning out; the emptying of one's mind can be a constructive meditative endeavour, but it can also, as Wallace points out, make you 'die' a little, like the dog who "…never noticed the chain. He didn't hate it. The chain. He just up and made it not relevant" (p. 117).

Like 'boiling the frog slowly', unseeing and neglect are symptoms of the problem. Wallace puts his man or woman (himself, the hover-y author) on that 'chain' (or in that pot); the metaphor could also be the mouse-wheel of perpetuity. For Lane Dean, "This was boredom beyond any boredom he'd ever felt" (p. 377). And the associative/creative aspect of boredom emerges. "…unbidden came the thought that *boring* also meant something that drilled in and made a hole" (p. 378). Wallace tells the reader that he is sure that he is the only living American who's read all the transcripts, records, studies, white papers, code amendments, revenue rulings, and procedural memos of the IRS (footnote #25, p. 84). All of which are available to the public, he says, with irony (p. 85).

The most boring and the most interesting conversation

The Meredith Rand and Shane Drinion conversation animates its extra-diegetic material: the absent-but-present writer, the reader's aching back, the feel of the book's paper, the slightly too-small-for-comfort size of the font—the hermeneutics of (textual) unfinishedness. Rand-Drinion is a *necessarily* tedious but amusing dialogue *about* dialogue, truth, sexual attraction, mental ill-health, aloneness, the subjective versus the objective rights and wrongs – shown via a game of conversational table tennis. It is ultimately suggestive of boredom again. The dialogue takes up most of '§46', that is pages 444–509 of *TPK* and painstakingly explores what happens when one (person or character) is seen in veneer and used as a foil by-or-for another. This orchestrates an authorial dialogical set-piece.

Meredith Rand is troublingly beautiful according to the heterosexual men at the IRS: they *want* her but don't like her. Women are jealous of her and don't like her. She does most of the talking while the robotic Shane Drinion speaks like a zombie with an editorializing role for much of the conversation. The irony here is majestic, that these two should have been allowed to blunder on (and on) is wrong and yet so *right* in terms of the flow and fractures between the two and in each one, and the humour this slippage-but-traction sets up (humour redeems boredom). Here, Rand questions Drinion about what she has been saying:

> 'Is this boring?'
> Drinion responds: 'The major part of it isn't, no.'
> 'What part of it is boring?'

'Boring isn't a very good term. Certain parts you tend to repeat, or say over again only in a slightly different way. These parts add no new information, so these parts require more work to pay attention to, alth—' (*TPK*, p. 501)

And Rand interrupts halfway through the word that would probably have been 'although'. Drinion is often represented inside Rand's monologue, by ellipses that indicate his presence and *potential* dialogue; his *opportunity* to speak and his choice not to. Meredith Rand refers to herself as a "fox" numerous times (pp. 486–487), and the discomfort we might feel at her 'self-foxing' is a distaste for shallow vanity—but, we begin to wonder, perhaps she's correct and knows it. But while Rand's self-absorption is no major transgression, the fact that it makes her painfully boring comes close: "Rand's rep at the REC is that she's sexy but crazy and a serious bore, just won't shut up if you get her started" (p. 489). Wallace implies that Rand is tolerated because although she is boring she is also beautiful. And the reader shudders at the thought of how things would be for her if she were boring and ugly.[16]

Rand-Drinion is an exploration of (almost) affect-free dialogue: each character is boring partly because their connection to the other is stripped of subterfuge and mystery—other than in Rand's apparently self-obsessed effort to see herself mirrored back amply in Drinion. If they do not utter it, it/life/ the outside the bar, doesn't exist. Rand would tell her co-worker later, that "[Drinion] paid such close, intense attention to what she was saying" (*TPK*, p. 473). Meanwhile, Drinion levitates while Rand is talking (several mentions, e.g. p. 485) This quasi-sexual mystical reaction shows the problematic provenance of attraction plus boredom. And while normative conversational reciprocity does not feature, that is also not relevant here.

Hering suggests that Rand-Drinion comprises "scenarios of failed communication" (2017, p. 160), and that by the 'end' of their conversation, "no dialogic change has been effected" (ibid.). While this might be true, especially if these were 'real' humans in dialogue or characters inside a more plot-and-character-driven text, the Rand-Drinion conversation is also an exercise in dissecting, problematizing, pathologizing, and illustrating self-other dynamics and dialogic 'rabbit holes'. It shows failure, but in my reading, any such normative assessment criteria need not apply. The conversation is a successful hybrid of

---

[16] In my Conclusion I touch on Wallace and sexism.

authorial game-playing and relatable sensations (boredom, attraction, irritation, humour). It is a masterclass in how to write flat characters whose substance exists courtesy of the suggestions and ideas that gather in their wake as pages are turned.

While Rand re-lives conversations she's previously had about her mental health and talks endlessly about herself, Drinion levitates with an abstract mix of sexual arousal, spiritual transcendence, and abject boredom, giving him the intense focus Rand reports later—ergo, the success of failure. The recursion in this set-piece amplifies Wallace's use of authorial/metafictionalizing moments throughout *TPK*.

"There is something kind of tiring about you," Rand tells Drinion. "It's like you're both interesting and really boring at the same time" (*TPK*, p. 461). Here's the crucial simultaneity that holds us enthralled, hopeful, and levitating as we read *TPK*.

Risking the final yawn

IRS recruits were wanted who could: "…maintain concentration under conditions of extreme tedium, complication, confusion, and absence of comprehensive info" (*TPK*, p. 247). The service was looking for "cogs, not spark plugs" (ibid.). The position of 'cog' is a 'divine' appointment; both pathetic *and* loaded with possibility – dualities again. Here, an IRS job ad is beheld like an answer to prayer:

> …a beam of light from the food court's overhead lighting far above fell through one of the star-shaped perforations in the tabletop and illuminated—as if by a symbolically star-shaped spotlight or ray of light—one particular advertisement among all the page's other ads and notices of business and career opportunities, this being a notice about the IRS's new recruitment-incentive program. (p. 239)

And redemption *from* boredom at the IRS may come in the Buddhist sense of transcendence or via the immanence of acceptance and submission. However, an acceptance of boredom turns boredom into a vestibule for possibility. The binary, 'despair versus joy' has been swallowed by boredom's nullifying tendency, like an anti-depressant might take the edges off, leaving no highs or lows. This could be redemptive or anti-redemptive in its nullification; so too might boredom be a black-hole-falling (after Deleuze & Guattari). Wallace defines boredom in metaphysical language, connecting it to transcendency and also ironically to imagination; hallucinations called phantoms, "...afflict rote examiners at a certain threshold of concentrated boredom" (*TPK*, p. 314). And, "...not every examiner gets visited" (ibid.). Not every. It makes boredom mystical and unpredictable and somehow, self-refuting.

The fragment quoted in my Introduction, "The new rebels might be artists willing to risk the [writing of the] yawn" from Wallace's *E Unibus Pluram* ([1990] 2014a, p. 707), suggests that Wallace considers 'yawn-inducing' work to be a marker of sincerity, even if ironically so. 'Risking the yawn', is suggestive of a levelling and overlapping of a proletariat-style worker-cog *and* worker-footnote (perhaps *any* worker-paratext). The "yawn" is symbiotic of person and poetics and reflective of the convergence of fragments and moments of human and literary doubt, faith, and urgency in the contemporary moment. Meanwhile, Wallace shows that weight of responsibility and sense of running out of time creeps up on person, poetics, and practice as an urge the opposite of boring—turning boredom into an anaesthetizing luxury we can no longer afford.

A Conclusion, of Sorts: This Is Not the End

> Redemptive hybridism makes fluids of solids, compiles flesh and soul, and stitches genres to generate the new or the re-worked gesture. Among other things...

This project makes a speculative analysis and enactment of a redemptively hybridizing *room*, in a post-postmodern *house*, in the *neighbourhood* of the living trajectory of the modernisms continuum. The paradigmatic *becoming* that I have figured occurs on a continuum in which there are no deaths while there are productive takings-in. Suggestion and heurism are mobilized for their capacity to open up, out, and towards, and the lenses or frames through which I view any singular aspect, become collectively formative.

I have discussed and shown that the modernisms continuum features redemptively hybridizing manoeuvres that encapsulate and enable a productive-progressive self-other collaboration in texts; an alterity that attends to the repair, restitution, and necessary (or at least a relevant) wholisim despite and because of an anthropogenic neoliberally-afflicted world where conceptions of endangerment necessitate shared *and* singular voices.

I have exemplified a span of practice from (before and around) Virginia Woolf to (around and beyond) David Foster Wallace, incorporating a curated suite of others who collectively and/or individually exemplify my project's formulation of Redemptive Hybridity and enable me to show how and why this is *post*-postmodern.

Whether a deistic etymology for *redemption* is palatable or not, that reading is suggestive and full of scope, expanding the pragmatic and the unequivocal, those sites fed by incremental proofs which make a flimsy basis for possibility while simultaneously being necessary for daily self-making. I use the term *redemptive* because it suggests an antidote to the contemporary condition as identified by Wallace, and also because it is, I believe, constructively provocative when placed in the arena with postmodernism—and simply because it makes way for imagination and aspects of being human which reflect and exemplify the as yet unknown, and the hoped for.

No other (English) word can do what *redemptive* does, which when coupled with hybridism, takes concepts like the human and their texts towards the Other and into a transformative communion or collaboration—even collapse, of genre and other categories into hybrid re-makings.

Enactments of multiplicity in texts may be felt or performed by way of inference, allusion, and slippage within the interactions of fictive or (auto) biographically believable characters in non-character-centric literary art as well as in other textual forms. The magnitude of divine/creative possibility in and beyond the human subject makes relevant reflexively, a certain ethical humility which applies a harmonizing of difference while also upholding difference/the individual;[1] safeguarding for example, voice, body, and soul – those aspects that give flesh to texts and heart to narratives of difference.

Hassan's word-flesh is also word-to-mind and mind-to-flesh; each construction adding complexity to the hybridization of writer-word, text-reader, and more. Elsewhere, in a postmodern frame, there is only *something* (a word) in relation, and so there is *nothing* (no word) until *someone* performs it and someone else hears. But where does the *something* (the word) come from if it has no precedent? There are no paradigm deaths. Everything is a building block.

In this project I have shown after close reading, speculation, and heuristics (a hybrid process of knowledge formation) that all precedents are contained and continued in subsequent or simultaneous movements and ideas. The life of a creator is an intertextual one, and postmodernism contains its enemy modernism (Hassan). Everything leaves a trace, and is ultimately (that word is totalizing) hybridizing (not totalizing), a contradiction, a hybrid itself, a reparation – as is thought and its process.

Deleuze and Guattari's "tool box" of interrelated concepts helps with the figuration of hybridizing images (images are moments fixed in time, whether or not they proceed to dissolve and reform).

This Work's process takes on concepts like redemption, hybridity, postmodernism, the modernisms continuum, the convoluted 'post-post' and

---

[1] A broad image of the divine in texts is formulated among Kant, Kierkegaard, Bakhtin, Hassan, Eagleton, with Woolf's atom and Wallace's soul/ghost/yearning. The divine is (often) infantilized and/or 'cancelled' in a postmodern view, where 'God as autocrat' is invoked. A Redemptively Hybrid position suggests an opening of windows to possibilities, in pursuit of the divine *and/or*, the beyond-the-self-towards-the other (all others) or the Other (particular other).

the risk of a future 'post-post-post', God, truth, death, life—boredom, and puts everything into it (Woolf saturating her atom again). Doubts are worked over and raised, work is made, communities engaged, and any outcomes-as-objects make distinct multiple tips of an iceberg that joins below the surface…

The gathering

The perpetuity of a fictive suite of beating hearts in Woolf, makes the standing-still of the "transfixed" (the following quote from *The Waves*), both impossible and thrilling:

> Down below, through the depths of the leaves, the gardeners swept the lawns with great brooms. The lady sat writing. Transfixed, stopped dead, I thought, 'I cannot interfere with a single stroke of those brooms. They sweep and they sweep. Nor with the fixity of that woman writing.' It is strange that one cannot stop gardeners sweeping nor dislodge a woman. There they have remained all my life. It is as if one had woken in Stonehenge surrounded by a circle of great stones, these enemies, these presences. (*TW*, p. 201)

Woolf's embodiments of the Other and of an environment or context for the self-other, reveal her exemplary atomic saturations. Her desire to express "the moment whole" identifies the possibility of textual intensity (wholeness) via 'saturating the atom', which is becoming-other and hybrid. She develops the intensity of a character's longing and awe, which moves with the type or kind of their nature, which, in turn, is embodied at the clash or junction of natures—that connective space between characters. Woolf's "enemies" (ibid.) perform as shadows, providing dimension to her hybridizing in scenes like the above in which she is as *other* and as monolithic as Stonehenge or an ancient Kauri tree,[2] and as ephemeral as the fleet of thoughts that made the paragraph in which textual images are locked.

Wallace's 'moment whole' in *TPK*, is an unfinished and fraying thing held together by particularities and continuities of authorial presence and matters of style. In *TPK*, possibility is affected by the unfinishedness which reveals a great deal about the post-author life of art and textual becomings. Whether he intended for the 'finished' work to be close to what we now have or not,

---

[2] The Kauri (Agathis Australis) is native to and revered in Aotearoa/New Zealand for its magnificence and *mana* (spiritually significant attributes of character). Kauri trees can live and grow for over a thousand years, giving them a majestic presence.

it *is* while it dances with failure and success, hybridly and humanly (which is of course contingent upon one's terms of engagement and point of view). But failure is a human enterprise, and human-authored texts are still preferable – if for no other reason, for the connection between the author and reader via the text which is *not* made by artificial intelligence (a can of worms). The failure (of *TPK* or any human-authored text) might also be the reader's failed reading, a shared and hybridizing enterprise.

In a post-postmodern frame, authorial presence is a feature of Redemptive Hybridity. This is exemplified in Wallace's final and posthumously published work, *The Pale King*. Wallace's strategies are of mixed modalities with juxtaposed enactments of infinite possibility in his striving to be fully human (in McCaffery [1993] 2012) of character and person. Authorial visibility necessitates an authorial stand-point on moral, ethical, aesthetic, poetic matters, adding counterbalance to the 'postmodern party' and supplying compulsion to the need (identified by Wallace) to become the returning 'parents' (ibid.).

The Pale King places Wallace and his surrogates at the IRS, and then speaks through them about a late culture which foments abject boredom. It also speaks about hope for boredom's transformativity. Wallace suggests the possibility of a sincere and spiritual experience, but one loaded with irony, born as it is out of the boredom endemic in a late capitalism tinged with postmodern and neoliberal agendas. In *TPK*, Wallace writes a redemptively hybrid account of a long moment—made longer by unfinishedness.

In *Autoportrait*, Levé writes: "Maybe I'm writing this book so I won't have to talk anymore" ([2005] 2012, p. 32). Like Wallace, Levé makes an act and admission of visibility. However, he uses himself as the visual and aural substance of a text stripped of (para)textual shenanigans—a contrast to Wallace. In Levé, autobiographical encounters are subsumed into each phase or moment of white space, change of font, or piece of used envelope providing a quick shopping list. In Levé, it all constructs the hybrid situation of the text. His reader realizes that there is value in each mark or space, while paratactical concrete images also become portable beyond the text.

Sarraute engages ellipses (like steppingstones) that trail forward implicating the page space, which works meditatively in and as the space of the text, all of it marking out the *tropisms* she maps. The mapping itself is a tropism (moving and responding to *everything* – the enormity of who, where, and when she is, while her textual art becomes metafictional. Her characters are her marks on the page as much as they are human metaphors. Sarraute plays with textuality, employing and articulating the in-between of a practice configured postmodernly while constructing heterotopic spaces of possibility.

Nelson's metonymically-given theory of familial, gender, and textual hybridity sharpens the reader's focus on the author as subject. She does not pull tricks in the manner of Wallace, whose assertions of truth can be like broken bits rattling around in a box; nor does she compromise the expansiveness of her material by forming it according to a tired academic method—nor does she push it towards niche or élitist conceptuality. Nelson tells her story succinctly, it is a making visible, which contributes to gains in genre hybridity. As well as being testimonial, *The Argonauts* reveals a theorist-self in relation to theorist-others, namely, Barthes of the titular "Argo", and goes on to theorize about the essential nature of love, that most fundamental of hybridizing practices.

The hybridizing process necessitates the reader's commitment to the text in all its parts, whether finished or not at the time of reading, and including, I assert, the reader's necessary placement of a high value on the voice of difference and being-Other and the integration of high with low forms (Robbins). Matters of agreement or judgment should be suspended in the process of gaining the whole text (and the author, by proxy).

Self-binding (Hale), taking in, containment, or subsumption (Hassan, Jameson, et al.), are mobilized in a conception of hybridizing, in so far as each conveys a sense of the shared task of going beyond the singular into conjunctions. Hassan's containment of 'enemies', Jameson's 'Flaubert becomes Joyce becomes Sarraute', and the Deleuzoguattarian 'becoming', each inform the hybridizing of the collective or housed, making the redemptive hybrid 'room', in the post-postmodern 'house', in the 'neighbourhood' of the modernisms continuum.

Even unfinishedness (closely allied to error and failure) such as Wallace's, or Woolf's in her last work, and each of the truncated lives, become spaces of possibility on this continuum as forms of truth-telling in their reveal of the jangling parts of process. If opposite to, but on a continuum with correctness, error is affiliated with truth as it demonstrates the human-and-hybridizing underbelly of process. Deleuze writes: "Error, therefore, pays homage to the 'truth' to the extent that, lacking a form of its own, it gives the form of the true to the false" (Deleuze [1968] 1994, p. 148). And then: the "…terrible trinity of madness, stupidity, and malevolence" is far worse because unlike error, these 'subvert' the "honest character of thought" (p. 149). While I cannot rank madness and error against each other, I agree that stupidity and especially malevolence seem worse. Error, giving "…the form of the true to the false" (p. 148), thickens the process, contests 'the truth' and perhaps makes it hybridly truer.

The writers and texts I have gathered were selected not only because of what they set up individually, but also because of what they contribute to a gathering. There are those who identify or perform as: modern, postmodern, or post-postmodern, etc., and there are those who defy easy categorization in the production of hybrid forms that reflect and articulate their difference.

The world has changed dramatically since I started work on what is now this book. My material has more company and peers than it did back then, such is the nature of a multi-year process. A manuscript takes in everything that happens along the way: that tedious book, that wonderful movie, that long moment of doubt, that captivating phrase, that illness, that beach, that tremendous discovery. This is the hybrid sum of its process.

As I review the many insights gained from analysing hybridity and its redemptive qualities in the texts I have looked at, I believe that the value of these arrives despite their authors, while also because of them. In relation to this, I want to end by briefly addressing David Foster Wallace's imperfection, which sits inside his contribution to literary art. This by no means launders bad behaviour, but it does resist moralizing attacks on literature and art.

In her essay 'The Last Essay I Need to Write about David Foster Wallace' (2021),[3] Mary K Holland suggests there is a kind of genius-washing of Wallace by his admirers and some academics. Holland suggests that Wallace Studies should not minimize the author's misogyny and alleged violence towards women.[4] However, I suggest, if the artistic value of a painting was decided in consideration of the artist's treatment of women, we might be asking 'Picasso, who?' There are *many* examples.

Why not take the 'bad' into company with the 'good' (if you can tell them apart)? Draw and write all over *it*; repair, learn from, disrupt constructively, until new categories or non-categories or reinvigorated categories emerge. The foxhole of misogynistic person-and-practice is long, broad, and dark.

---

[3] Source is Lit Hub online, which excerpts *#MeToo and Literary Studies: Reading, Writing, and Teaching about Sexual Violence and Rape Culture,* eds. Mary K. Holland and Heather Hewett. Bloomsbury Academic 2021.

[4] In her book *Lit* (2009, p. 321), Mary Karr mentions being abused by "David". Karr also indicates this issue on Twitter 11.59pm, 5 May 2018. In his Wallace biography ([2012] 2013), D.T. Max also writes about this matter, but in a manner that does not throw overt emphasis on any monster in Wallace's character.

A Conclusion, of Sorts: This Is Not the End 153

I have pushed the practices I have observed, through a redemptively hybridizing filter, which as well as the discreet points of view discussed, is also playfully suggestive of possibilities. In hybrid creative practices, harm or disagreement are not forgotten but may be 'processed' or taken in and thereby changed (like the enemy subsumed). This strengthening or thickening is *redemptively* hybridizing, and its ethic of re-use and re-purpose is an ideal that drives things forward. This is *not* to sanitize bad behaviour or belief (or bad writing or art), it is to see what sparks in combinations or in new contexts that might re-configure balance in acknowledgment of the fact (arguably) that one of art's movements is to capture lived realities—which are always hybridly multi-dimensional and flawed.

Holland asks rhetorically about Wallace, "What does it mean that *this* artist could not produce in his life the mutually respecting empathy he all but preached in his work [...]?" (2021, np). While an answer is impossible, there might be mitigating factors such as Wallace's self-consciousness and mental ill-health, which are everywhere apparent in his textual embodiment of deeply flawed people. By way of an example, *TPK*'s Toni Ware epitomizes the 'situation': Wallace has made one of his most eerily dysfunctional yet heart-wrenching characters a woman. This is unsettling when viewing Wallace as a misogynist. Like so many of Wallace's characters, Ware seems to have been created partly to explore an idea and partly so the author can either try on bodies or *other* them. But Wallace is unable to keep his own mind still, and Ware who has *that* coat to hide her frame is too much 'mind', hence her capacity for self-defacement. Ware's is Wallace's own solipsism,[5] and whether this is a flaw or something else, it contributes to being human, as does the character-author play in Woolf's last work:

> 'Did you feel,' she asked 'what he said: we act different parts but are the same?'
> 'Yes,' Isa answered. 'No,' she added. It was Yes, No. Yes, yes, yes, the tide rushed out embracing. No, no, no, it contracted. (*BtA*, p. 133)

To the fully human end, we saturate Woolf's atom[6] and play around like Frankenstein in a Deleuzoguattarian "tool box" where assemblages featuring differences emerge after taking in the paradigmatic enemy. This Work has 131

---

[5] Also see solipsism and Wallace as discussed by Holland (2018, p. 128).
[6] An image also held in Deleuze and Guattari's suite of concepts by virtue of their making Woolf an exemplar of *becoming*.

authors, 89 atoms, 87 saturations, 72 humans, 67 fragments, 46 ghosts, 39 fleshes, 34 Gods, 33 deaths, 25 loves, and 24 enemies. It weaves and threads authorial loose ends which the reader unpicks at will, and both/and/all collaboratively compose the substance of possibility and associated pathways within a post-postmodern frame where Redemptive Hybridism moves.[7]

---

[7] There is no end that we know of.

References

Adorno, Theodor [1955] 1997, *Prisms*, trans. S. Weber Nicholson and S. Weber, MIT Press, Cambridge, MA.

Attridge, Derek [1989] 1992, 'This Strange Institution Called Literature: An Interview with Jacques Derrida', in Derrida, J., D. Attridge (ed.), *Acts of Literature*, 33–75, Routledge, London and New York.

Bahun, Sanja 2014, *Modernism and Melancholia: Writing as Countermourning*, Oxford University Press, New York.

Bakhtin, Mikhail [1929] 2014, *Problems of Dostoyevsky's Poetics* (Theory and History of Literature, vol. 8), trans. C. Emerson (ed.), University of Minnesota Press, Minneapolis, MN.

Barthes, Roland [1975] 1994, *Roland Barthes*, trans. R. Howard, University of California Press, Los Angeles, https://monoskop.org/images/b/b3/Roland_Barthes_by_Roland_Barthes.pdf (retrieved 5 June 2019).

Beck, Koa 2021, *White Feminism*, Simon & Schuster UK Ltd., London.

Beckett, Samuel [1952] 1966, 'The Unnameable' in *Molloy / Malone Dies / The Unnameable*, 293–418, Calder and Boyars, London.

Bible New International Version: Exodus 3:2–3, Genesis 22:2, John 1:14, Matthew 4:4, John 6:63, Ecclesiastes 3:1, Romans 8:26, Acts 2:1–4, Genesis 11:7, Thessalonians 5:23, http://www.biblegateway.com (retrieved 5 August 2021).

Bloom, Harold (ed.) 2010, *Sin and Redemption*, Infobase Publishing, New York.

Booth, Wayne C. 2014, 'Introduction', in M. Bakhtin, *Problems of Dostoyevsky's Poetics*, xiii–xxvii, University of Minnesota Press, Minneapolis, MN.

Bordo, Susan 1990, 'Feminism, Postmodernism, and Gender-Scepticism', in L.J. Nicholson (ed.), *Feminism/Postmodernism*, 133–156, Routledge, New York and London.

Borges. J.L. [1967] 1997, *Historia Universal de la Infamia*, Madrid, Alianza.

Brodribb, Somer 1992, *Nothing Mat(t)ers: a Feminist Critique of Postmodernism*, Spinifex Press, Melbourne.

Burn, Stephen J. 2012, 'Introduction', in S.J. Burn (ed.), *Conversations with David Foster Wallace*, ix–xvii, The University Press of Mississippi, Jackson MI.

Butler, Judith 1990, 'Gender Trouble, Feminist Theory, and Psychoanalytic Discourse', in L.J. Nicholson, (ed.) *Feminism/Postmodernism*, 324–340, Routledge, New York and London.

Carson, Anne 2016, *Float: a collection of twenty-two chapbooks whose order is unfixed and whose topics are various*, Jonathan Cape, London.

Chun, Maureen 2012, 'Between Sensation and Sign: The Secret Language of *The Waves*', *Journal of Modern Literature*, vol. 36, no. 1, 53–70, Indiana University Press, Bloomington, IN

Cioffi, Frank L. 1999, 'Postmodernism, Etc: An Interview with Ihab Hassan', *Style*, vol. 33, no. 3, 357–371, http://www.jstor.org/stable/10.5325/style.33.3.357 (retrieved 2 November 2020).

Clark, Alex 2016, 'Between The Acts: Virginia Woolf's Last Book', *BBC Culture*, http://www.bbc.com/culture/story/20160321-between-the-acts-virginia-woolfs-last-book (retrieved 6 July 2019).

Coates, Ruth [1998] 2005, *Christianity in Bakhtin: God and the Exiled Author*, Cambridge University Press, Cambridge, UK.

Colebrook, Claire 2012, 'Woolf and Theory', in B. Randall and J. Goldman (eds), *Virginia Woolf in Context*, 65–78, Cambridge University Press, Cambridge, UK.

Deleuze, Gilles [1968] 1994, *Difference and Repetition*, trans. P. Patton, Columbia University Press, New York.

Deleuze, Gilles and Félix Guattari [1980] 2014, *A Thousand Plateaus: Capitalism and Schizophrenia*, trans. B. Massumi, University of Minnesota Press, Minneapolis, MN.

Di Stefano, Christine 1990, 'Dilemmas of Difference: Feminism, Modernity, and Postmodernism', in L.J. Nicholson (ed.), *Feminism/Postmodernism*, 63–82, Routledge, New York and London.

Dumitrescu, Alexandra 2007, 'Interconnections in Blakean and Metamodern Space', *Double Dialogues, On Space*, Issue 7, http://www.doubledialogues.com/archive/issue_seven/dumitrescu.html (retrieved 1 April 2015).

Dumitrescu, Alexandra 2014, *Towards a Metamodern Literature*, PhD thesis, Otago University, NZ.

Eagleton, Terry 2012, *The Event of Literature*, Yale University Press, Newhaven, CT and London.

Empson, William [1930] 1966, *Seven Types of Ambiguity*, New Directions, New York.

Fox, Nick J. 2014, 'Post-structuralism and Postmodernism', in W.C. Cockerham, R. Dingwall, and S.R. Quah (eds), *The Wiley-Blackwell Encyclopedia of Health, Illness, Behavior and Society*. Wiley, Chichester, https://www.researchgate.net/publication/320016117 (retrieved 28 April 2022).

Genette, Gérard [1987] 1991, 'Introduction to the Paratext', trans. M. Maclean, in *New Literary History*, vol. 22, no. 2, Spring, 261–272, https://doi.org/10.2307/469037 (retrieved 16 October 2020).

Gilbert, Matthew [1997] 2012, 'The "Infinite Story" Cult Hero behind 1,079-Page Novel Rides the Hype He Skewered', in S.J. Burn (ed.), *Conversations with David Foster Wallace*, 76–81, The University Press of Mississippi, Jackson, MI.

Grassian, Daniel 2003, *Hybrid Fictions: American Literature and Generation X*, McFarland and Co. Inc, Jefferson, NC.

Hale, Dorothy J. 2007, 'Fiction as Restriction: Self-Binding in New Ethical Theories of the Novel', *Narrative*, vol. 15, no. 2, May 2007, 187–206.

Hallward, Peter 1997, 'Gilles Deleuze and the Redemption From Interest', *Radical Philosophy*, January/February, vol. 81, 6–21.

Hart, Trevor 1997, 'Redemption and Fall' in C.E. Gunton (ed.), *The Cambridge Companion to Christian Doctrine*, 189–206, Cambridge University Press, Cambridge, UK.

Hartsock, Nancy 1990, 'Foucault on Power: A Theory for Women?', in L.J. Nicholson (ed.), *Feminism/Postmodernism*, 157–175, Routledge, New York and London.

Harvey, David [1990] 1994, *The Condition of Postmodernity*, Blackwell, Cambridge, MA and Oxford, UK.

Hassan, Ihab 1971, *The Dismemberment of Orpheus: Toward a Postmodern Literature*, Oxford University Press, New York.

Hassan, Ihab 1975, *Paracriticisms: Seven Speculations of the Times*, University of Illinois Press, Urbana, IL and Chicago and London.

Hassan, Ihab 1987, 'Towards a Concept of Postmodernism', in *The Postmodern Turn: Essays in Postmodern Theory and Culture*, 1–10, Ohio State University Press, Columbus, OH.

Hayes-Brady, Clare 2018 '"Palely Loitering": On Not Finishing (in) The Pale King', in R. Clare (ed.), *The Cambridge Companion to David Foster Wallace*, 142–155, Cambridge University Press, Cambridge, UK.

Heaton, John and Judy Groves (Illustrator) [1994] 2005, *Introducing Wittgenstein: A Graphic Guide*, Icon Books UK and Totem Books USA.

Hering, David [2016] 2017, *David Foster Wallace: Fiction and Form*, Bloomsbury Academic, New York and London.

Holland, Mary K. 2018, 'Infinite Jest' in R. Clare (ed), *The Cambridge Companion to David Foster Wallace*, 127–141, Cambridge University Press, Cambridge, UK.

Holland, Mary K. 2021, *The Last Essay I Need to Write about David Foster Wallace*, https://lithub.com/the-last-essay-i-need-to-write-about-david-foster-wallace/ (retrieved 6 March 2023).

Hopkins, Gerard Manley [1918] 1961, 'The Windhover', in M. Mack, L. Dean, W. Frost (eds), *Modern Poetry*, vol. VII, 2nd edn, 32, Prentice-Hall Inc., Englewood, NJ.

Huggett, Nick 2019, 'Zeno's Paradoxes', in E.N. Zalta (ed.), *The Stanford Encyclopedia of Philosophy*, https://plato.stanford.edu/entries/paradox-zeno/#Arr (retrieved 26 November 2019).

Hutcheon, Linda [1989] 2002, *The Politics of Postmodernism*, Routledge, London and New York.

Huyssens, Andreas [1984] 1990, 'Mapping the Postmodern', in L.J. Nicholson (ed.), *Feminism/Postmodernism*, 234–277, Routledge, New York and London.

Jameson, Fredric 1991, *Postmodernism, or, The Cultural Logic of Late Capitalism*, Duke University Press, Durham, NC.
Jardine, Lisa [2000] 2005, 'On Between the Acts' in V. Woolf, *Between the Acts*, pp. xvii–xxv, Vintage, London.
Josipovici, Gabriel 2010, *Whatever Happened to Modernism?* Yale University Press, Newhaven, CT and London.
Joyce, James [1916] 2000, *A Portrait of the Artist as a Young Man*, Penguin, London.
Kant, Immanuel [1790] 1952, 'The Critique of Judgement,' trans. J.C. Meredith, in *The Critique of Pure Reason, The Critique of Practical Reason and other ethical treatises; The Critique of Judgement*, 459–613, Encyclopaedia Britannica, (ed.) R.M. Hutchins, Chicago.
Kay, Jackie [2000] 2005, 'On Between the Acts' in V. Woolf, *Between the Acts*, pp. xi–xv, Vintage, London.
Kellaway Kate 2016, 'Anne Carson: I Do Not Believe in Art as Therapy', *The Guardian* Online, https://www.theguardian.com/books/2016/oct/30/anne-carson-do-not-believe-art-therapy-interview-float (retrieved 15 May 2022).
Kelly, Adam 2010, 'David Foster Wallace and the New Sincerity in American Fiction', in D. Hering (ed.), 2010, *Consider David Foster Wallace: Critical Essays,* 131–146, Sideshow Media Group Press, Austin, TX.
Kerr, Heather and Nettelback, Amanda (eds) 1998, *The Space Between: Australian Women Writing Fictocriticsm*, University of Western Australia Press, Crawley Western Australia.
Kierkegaard, Søren [1843] 2005, *Fear and Trembling*, trans. A. Hannay, Penguin, London.
Kierkegaard, Søren [1872] 1955, *On Authority and Revelation: The Book on Adler*, trans. W. Lowrie, Princeton University Press, NJ.
Konstantinou, Lee 2018 'Wallace's Bad Influence', in R. Clare (ed.), *The Cambridge companion to David Foster Wallace*, 49–63, Cambridge University Press, Cambridge, UK.
Ladin, Joy 2015, 'Autobiography of a Hybrid Narrative; Finding a Form for Trauma', in M. Sulak and J. Kolosov (eds), *Family Resemblance: An Anthology and Exploration of 8 Hybrid Literary Genres*, 101–110, Rose Metal Press, Brookline, MA.
Lerner, Ben [2011] 2013, *Leaving the Atocha Station*, Granta, London.
Levé, Edouard [2005] 2012, *Autoportrait*, trans. L. Stein, Dalkey Archive Press, Champaign, IL, Dublin and London.
Levé, Edouard [2008] 2017, *Suicide*, trans. J. Steyn, Dalkey Archive Press, Champaign, IL, Dublin and London.
Levinas, Emmanuel [1961] 1969, *Totality and Infinity: An Essay on Exteriority*, trans. A. Lingis, Duquesne University Press, Pittsburgh, PA.

Lilly, Joseph L. 1947, 'The Idea of Redemption in the Gospels', *The Catholic Biblical Quarterly*, vol. 9, no. 3, 255–261, http://www.jstor.org/stable/43719968 (retrieved 2 April 2022).

Lyotard, Jean-Francois [1979] 1984, *The Postmodern Condition: A Report on Knowledge* (Theory and History of Literature, vol. 10), trans. G. Bennington and B. Massumi, University of Minnesota Press, Minneapolis, MN.

Massumi, Brian [1987] 2014, 'Translator's Foreword: Pleasures of Philosophy', in G. Deleuze & F. Guattari, *A Thousand Plateaus: Capitalism and Schizophrenia*, ix–xv, University of Minnesota Press, Minneapolis, MN.

Max, D.T. [2012] 2013, *Every Love Story is a Ghost Story: A Life of David Foster Wallace*, Penguin, New York.

McCaffery, Larry [1993] 2012, 'Expanded Interview with David Foster Wallace', in S.J. Burn (ed.), *Conversations with David Foster Wallace*, 21–52, University Press of Mississippi, Jackson, MI.

Metcalf, Stephen 2017, 'Neoliberalism, the Idea that Swallowed the World', *The Guardian*, https://www.theguardian.com/news/2017/aug/18/neoliberalism-the-idea-that-changed-the-world (retrieved 22 June 2020).

Moraru, Christian [2015] 2018, *Reading for the Planet: Toward a Geomethodology*, University of Michigan Press, Ann Arbor, MI.

Morson, Gary Saul 1993, 'For the Time Being: Sideshadowing, Criticism, and the Russian Countertradition: Interdisciplinarity and Literary Theory', in N. Easterlin and B. Riebling (eds), *After Poststructuralism: Interdisciplinarity and Literary Theory*, 203–231, Northwestern University Press, Evanston, IL.

Muecke, Stephen 2002, 'The Fall: Fictocritical Writing', *Parallax*, vol. 8, no. 4, 108–112.

Nabokov, Vladimir [1928] 1968, *King Queen Knave*, trans. D. Nabokov, Heron Books, London.

Nelson, Maggie 2015a, 'Not Notes, Not Aphorisms, Not Fragments, Not Poetry; Composing Bluets' in M. Sulak and J. Kolosov (eds), *Family Resemblance: An Anthology and Exploration of 8 Hybrid Literary Genres*, 141–147, Rose Metal Press, Brookline, MA.

Nelson, Maggie 2015b, *The Argonauts*, Graywolf Press, Minneapolis, MN.

Nicholson, Linda J 1990, 'Introduction', in L.J. Nicholson (ed.), *Feminism/Postmodernism*, 1–16, Routledge, New York and London.

Paola Antonetta, Susanne 2015, 'Blurring the Magisteria; Science as Fact, Science as Metaphor', in M. Sulak and J. Kolosov (eds), *Family Resemblance: An Anthology and Exploration of 8 Hybrid Literary Genres*, 15–21, Rose Metal Press, Brookline, MA.

Phelan, James [2013] 2014, 'Narrative Ethics', in P. Hühn et al. (eds), *The Living Handbook of Narratology*, University of Hamburg, Hamburg, http://www.lhn.uni-hamburg.de/article/narrative-ethics (retrieved 12 November 2018).

Pietsch, Michael [2011] 2012, 'Editor's Note' in D.F. Wallace, *The Pale King*, v–x, Penguin, Victoria, Australia.

Project Gutenberg 2020, 'Sarraute, Nathalie', http://self.gutenberg.org/articles/eng/Nathalie_Sarraute (retrieved 25 May 2020).

The Poetry Foundation 2020, 'OuLiPo', https://www.poetryfoundation.org/learn/glossary-terms/oulipo (retrieved 4 April 2020).

Robbins, Amy Moorman 2014, *American Hybrid Poetics*, Rutgers University Press, New Brunswick, NJ and London.

Rozelle-Stone, A. Rebecca and Davis, Benjamin P. 2020, 'Simone Weil', in E.N. Zalta (ed.), *The Stanford Encyclopedia of Philosophy*, https://plato.stanford.edu/archives/fall2020/entries/simone-weil/ (retrieved 15 October 2020).

Saloman, Randi [2012] 2014, *Virginia Woolf's Essayism*, Edinburgh University Press, Edinburgh.

Sarraute, Nathalie [1939] 2015, *Tropisms*, trans. M. Jolas, New Directions, New York.

Sarraute, Nathalie [1958] 1959, *Portrait of a Man Unknown*, trans. M. Jolas, John Calder, London.

Sarraute, Nathalie [1963] 1965, *The Golden Fruits*, trans. M. Jolas, John Calder, London.

Sarraute, Nathalie [1968] 1969, *Between Life and Death*, trans. M. Jolas, Georges Braziller, New York.

Sarraute, Nathalie [1995] 1997, *Here*, trans. B. Wright, George Braziller, New York.

Shelley, Mary [1818] 1968, 'Frankenstein; or the Modern Prometheus' in P. Fairclough (ed.) *Three Gothic Novels*, 257–497, Penguin, London.

Silverblatt, Michael, 2 March 2006, 'David Foster Wallace: Consider the Lobster and Other Essays', *Bookworm*, radio KCRW, Los Angeles, https://www.kcrw.com/culture/shows/bookworm/david-foster-wallace-consider-the-lobster-and-other-essays (retrieved 28 May 2020).

Silverblatt, Michael, 11 June 2015, 'Maggie Nelson: The Argonauts', in *Bookworm*, radio KCRW, Los Angeles, https://www.kcrw.com/culture/shows/bookworm/maggie-nelson-the-argonauts (retrieved 16 November 2019).

Spivak, Gayatri Chakravorty [1985] 2010, 'Can the Subaltern Speak', in R. Morris (ed.), *Can the Subaltern Speak?: Reflections on the History of an Idea*, 21–78, Columbia University Press, New York, https://www.jstor.org/stable/10.7312/morr14384 (retrieved 14 October 2020).

Stein, Gertrude [1948] 2004, *Blood on the Dining Room Floor*, Virago Press, London.

Steyn, Jan [2010] 2017, 'Afterword' in E. Levé, *Suicide*, 119–128, Dalkey Archive Press, Champaign, IL, Dublin and London.

Sulak, Marcela 2015, 'Local, Organic, and Living: A Preface', in M. Sulak and J. Kolosov (eds), *Family Resemblance: An Anthology and Exploration of 8 Hybrid Literary Genres*, xi–xviii, Rose Metal Press, Brookline, MA.

Swenson, Cole and David St. John 2009, *A Norton Anthology of New poetry; American Hybrid*, Norton & Company, New York and London.

Tillich, Paul 1954, *Love, Power, and Justice: Ontological Analyses and Ethical Application*, Oxford University Press, London.

Topinka, Robert J. 2010, 'Foucault, Borges, Heterotopia: Producing Knowledge in Other Spaces', *Foucault Studies*, no. 9, September 2010, 54–70, https://doi.org/10.22439/fs.v0i9.3059 (retrieved 15 January 2017).

Vermeulen, Timotheus and Robin van den Akker 2010, 'Notes on Metamodernism', *Journal of Aesthetics and Culture*, vol. 2, no. 1, https://doi.org/10.3402/jac.v2i0.5677 (retrieved 7 April 2015 and 18 October 2020).

Vonnegut, Kurt [1963] 1970, *Cat's Cradle*, Dell Publishing, New York.

Wallace, David Foster [1990] 2014a, 'E Unibus Pluram: Television and U.S. Fiction' in *The David Foster Wallace Reader*, 656–707, Little, Brown and Company, New York.

Wallace, David Foster [2004] 2005, *Oblivion: Stories,* Abacus, Little Brown Group, London.

Wallace, David Foster [2004] 2014b, 'Consider the Lobster', in *The David Foster Wallace Reader*, 920–936. Little, Brown and Company, New York.

Wallace, David Foster [2005] 2009, *This Is Water: Some Thoughts, Delivered on a Significant Occasion, about Living a Compassionate Life*, Little, Brown and Company, New York.

Wallace, David Foster [2011] 2012, *The Pale King*, Penguin, Victoria, Australia.

Wallace, David Foster [2011] 2021, *Something To Do with Paying Attention*, McNally Editions, New York.

Woolf, Virginia [1915] 1992, *The Voyage Out*, Oxford University Press, Oxford.

Woolf, Virginia [1922] 1989 *Jacob's Room*, Triad Grafton, London.

Woolf, Virginia [1925] 1973, *Mrs Dalloway*, Penguin, Middlesex, England.

Woolf, Virginia [1925] 2003, 'Modern Fiction', in *The Common Reader; First Series*, Project Gutenberg 2003, https://gutenberg.net.au/ebooks03/0300031h.html#C12 (retrieved 12 June 2022).

Woolf, Virginia [1927] 1994, *To the Lighthouse*, Wordsworth Editions Ltd., Hertfordshire, UK.

Woolf, Virginia [1931] 1998, *The Waves*, Oxford University Press, Oxford.

Woolf, Virginia [1941] 2005, *Between the Acts*, Vintage, London.

Woolf, Virginia [1937 radio broadcast; 1942] 2012, 'Craftsmanship', in L. Woolf (ed.), *Death of the Moth and Other Essays*, Project Gutenberg, 2012, http://gutenberg.net.au/ebooks12/1203811h.html (retrieved 19 October 2015).

Woolf, Virginia [1953] 2014, *A Writer's Diary 1918–1941: Complete Edition*, e-artnow ebooks.

Index

Adorno, Theodor 83–6
Alterity 76, 80–1
　in Hale 77–9
Ambiguity
　in Empson 137, 137 n.14, 138–9
　synaesthesia 137, 139
　in Sarraute 52
　in Wallace (*TPK*) 135, 137–9
Anecdata 119 n.7, 126 n.7
Art-fiction 28, 111, 124
Assemblage 7, 28, 42, 44–5, 55, 86, 97, 99, 109, 122 n.16, 136, 153
Atom 47, 54, 105–7
　in *TPK* 28
　the saturated/*to* saturate 67
　in Woolf 8, 8 n.16, 17, 25, 25 n.3, 35, 67, 81, 91–2, 95–6, 99, 102, 105, 107, 148 n.1, 149
　in D&G 47, 92, 105, 107
　redemptive atom 107
Attridge, Derek 39
　with Derrida 113
Authenticity 18, 49, 50
Authorial 1, 11, 18, 30–2, 35, 37, 42, 56–7, 62 n.11, 63, 65, 68, 70, 72–3
　authoriality 7, 35, 50, 71, 75, 103, 133
Autofiction 31, 31 n.12
Autotheory 5 n.9, 72
　in Nelson 5, 81, 114–17

Bakhtin, Mikhail 6 n.10, 30, 30 n.8, 31, 37, 95, 95 n.3, 132–4, 148 n.1
　see also dialogic, dialogism, monologic, monologism
　glossia 30–1
　polyphony 30–1
　see also umbilical (cord)
Coates, Ruth 132
　Problems of Dostoyevsky's Poetics 29, 30, 31, 94
　Booth (*in Bakhtin*) 31, 94
　centrifugal and centripetal 94–5

Barthes, Roland 12, 120 n.8, n.9
　Argo 115–17, 151
Beck, Koa, *White Feminism* 110
Beckett, Samuel 24 n.1, 141
　The Unnameable 72
Becoming 4, 7, 9, 14 n.21, 16, 34–6, 45–6, 48, 57, 69, 71, 75, 91–2 n.1, 94–5, 97, 104–5, 107, 115, 117–18, 120, 133, 136–7, 140, 147, 151, 153 n.6
　becoming-atom 92–3
　becoming-complete 29
　becoming-fiction 111
　becoming-flesh 38
　becoming-fluid 92
　becoming human-and-divine 37
　becoming-hybrid 46, 82, 149
　becoming-Lear 80
　becoming-molecular 3 n.5
　becoming-multiple 13
　becoming-other 4, 13, 42, 49, 80–1, 93–4, 97–8, 149
　becoming-the-page-space 48
　becoming-redemptive 7, 107, 132
　becoming a redemptive machine 55
　becoming-saturated 47
　becoming truer (*TPK*) 76
　becoming-whale 47
　becoming-woman 3, 3 n.5, 46–7
Boring 146
　in *TPK* 140, 143–6
Boredom 45 n.1, 58, 140, 149
　in *TPK* 28–9, 94, 123, 126, 150
　and Claude Sylvanshine 124
　clock-related 58
　as death 141
　as hallucinatory 136
　at IRS 29, 143, 145
　and Lane Dean 141
　'being in a stare' 94 n.2, 142
　as negation 94, 146
　as pain 28, 94, 141

and Rand-Drinion 144–5
as redemptive 28, 140–1, 145,
as test 140
Burroughs, William 39, 42, 52 n.6
   the word as a virus 39, 40
   see also flesh

Carson, Anne, *Float* 44
Caveat 1, 30, 53, 70, 71–2, 75, 93, 117, 138
   caveating 16, 71–3, 75, 77, 137
Christ 24, 37, 140
Continental Theory 12, 12 n.17

Deleuze, Gilles, *Difference and Repetition* 7, 14
   univocity 14 n.21, 27, 151
Deleuze, Gilles & Guattari, Félix
   A Thousand Plateaus: Capitalism and Schizophrenia 3 n.3, 4, 4 n.7, 75, 91, 92 n.1
   arborescence 3 n.4, 26, 105
   arborescent 25, 41, 45, 54, 93, 105
   see also becoming, becoming-molecular, becoming-woman
   black hole 14 n.21, 25, 146
   body without organs 3 n.5, 13 n.18
   the book 41–2
   difference 4, 4 n.6, 7, 8, 10, 12, 14, 27, 46
   line of flight 8, 72
   see also middle
   molar 27 n.6, 46–7
   Massumi, Brian 3, 4, 4 n.7, 11, 25–6, 46 n.2, 111
   Mrs Dalloway 92, 96
   redemption 26, 107
   redemptive atom 107
   'tool box' 3, 4, 4 n.7, 26, 148, 153
   unconscious 67
   (on Woolf) 'saturate the atom' 92
Dialogic 6, 7, 53, 73, 106, 117, 131, 134
   in Bakhtin 30, 132
   in Hering 32–3, 144
   dialogism 31–2, 82, 95
Difference 7, 10, 13, 14, 42, 48, 50, 58, 62, 67, 77, 80–2, 84, 86, 110–11, 113–14, 116, 121 n.12, 132–3, 148, 151–2
   'difference in unity' 4, 7, 82–3, 105

'unity in difference' 14, 16, 47, 65, 82, 105, 109
Dostoyevsky, Fyodor
   with Wallace 29
   in Bakhtin 30–1, 94, 132

Eagleton, Terry
   The Event of Literature 27, 29, 58, 65, 79, 80, 105–6, 123–5, 148 n.1
Ectoplasm 8, 9
Élitism 10, 86
Enemy 4, 10, 83, 121, 153
   in Hassan 2, 10, 12, 112, 148
   in Woolf 100
   in *TPK* 131, 136
Enemies 16, 40. 84, 111
   in Hassan 1, 16, 112, 151
   in D&G 4
   in Woolf 149
Ethical 78, 81, 122, 122 n.14, 148, 150
   in Hale 76, 77, 77 n.10, 78–82
Ethics 78, 80–1
   'Narrative ethics' *in* Phelan 79

Factoid
   Mailer, Norman 75 n.8, 127, 127 n.9
   in *TPK* 75, 75 n.8, 127, 127 n.9, 128, 130
Family resemblance 65, 65 n.2
   in Wittgenstein 65, 105
   in Sulak & Kolosov
   Family Resemblance 66–8
Feminism 12, 40, 87, 111
Feminism/Postmodernism, ed. Nicholson, Linda J. 12, 14, 109–10
   Bordo, Susan 110–11
   Butler, Judith 13, 14, 110
   Di Stefano, Christine 110
   Hartsock, Nancy 12–14, 86, 125
   Huyssens, Andreas 84
   Nicholson, Linda 14, 84 n.11, 109
Ficto-criticism 113–14
Flesh 20, 37–8, 41–2, 48, 136, 147
   in Hassan 37
   Burroughs' word virus 39
   The Word (*and* flesh) 37, 42, 88, 148
Footnotes 7, 17, 32, 34, 71–6, 117, 124 n.5, 128, 131, 134–5, 138, 146
   see also paratext

Foucault, Michel 4 n.7, 5, 12, 12 n.17, 13, 110, 125
Frankenstein 153
  in Shelley, Mary 43–4
Fragment 3, 38, 44, 47, 62–3, 68–9, 80, 87, 146
  in Wallace 19, 32, 131, 146
  in Woolf 36, 68, 101
  in Hassan 38, 117–18
  in Carson 44
  in D&G 47
  in Sarraute 48–9, 51–4
  in Levé 56–7, 60, 70, 87
  in Nelson 66
Fragmentation 1, 3, 65–6, 87, 110, 120, 124
  in TPK 32–3, 75, 124, 130
  in Woolf 69

Gender 6, 13, 57, 82, 110–11, 116, 151
Genette, Gérard 73, 75, 131
Genre 6, 12, 23, 37, 65, 66, 66 n.3, 70, 70 n.7, 72, 78, 88–9, 106, 112–4, 148
  in Hassan 2, 117, 119
  in D&G 42
  in Woolf 98, 101, 103
  in Wallace 32, 34, 46, 63, 128, 131, 135
  in Sulak & Kolosov 66–7
  in Leve 69
  in Stein 85
  in Nelson 151
Ghost/s 33, 43, 68–9, 148 n.1
  in TPK 24, 34, 48 n.4, 58 n.8, 123, 135, 136
  in J. Joyce, Portrait 141
God 53, 78
  as author 24, 30–1, 133, 136
  in Bakhtin 94–5
  as hybrid 68
  as image 29, 69 n.4
  in the Bible 42
  in D&G 41
  as divine 148 n.1
  as redeemer
  in Wallace 130, 140
  in Tillich 50 n.5
  word of God 37

Haecceity 26–8, 54, 58, 92, 96
  haecceitical 7, 8, 27–8, 48, 92, 96

Hale, Dorothy J. 5, 67, 76, 77, 77 n.10, 78–9, 81
  see also alterity
  Butler 77 n.10
  New Ethical Theory 80–1
  self-binding 86, 122 n.14, 130, 151
Hallward, Peter 25–6
Harvey, David 15, 16
Hassan, Ihab 1, 2, 8, 10, 11, 84, 112, 148, 148 n.1, 151
  see also enemy
  Paracriticisms 12, 37–9, 117–18
  Sarraute 52, 52 n.6
Hayes-Brady, Clare 126, 129
Hering, David
  David Foster Wallace: Fiction and Form 32–3, 56 n.7, 74, 133, 136, 144
Hopkins, GM 27 n.5
  The Windhover 27
Hutcheon, Linda 1 n.1, 112–13
Hybrid form 4, 40–1, 43, 63, 65–9, 80, 87, 103, 113–14, 123, 131, 152
  Author, 128, 134
  Body 43, 68
  Novel 60, 86, 101
  Redemptive hybrid 23, 54, 151
  Space 30, 52, 68
  Text 78, 81–2, 85, 106, 113, 118, 137, 150

Irony 120, 121
  in Wallace 17, 18, 128–9, 137, 140, 143, 150

Jameson, Fredric 9–11, 57, 80, 136, 151

Kafka, Franz 8, 8 n.15, 24 n.1, 29, 58, 103
Kant, Immanuel 5, 10, 148 n.1
Kierkegaard, Soren 61, 78–9, 140, 148 n.1
Konstantinou, Lee 126

Lerner, Ben 57
Levé, Edouard 5, 30, 48, 61, 69, 86, 93, 131
  Autoportrait 56–7, 60, 87–8, 150
  Suicide 60, 60 n.10, 70, 70 n.7
  Oulipo 70
Lyotard, Jean-Francois 1, 9–11, 16

Max, DT 17, 29, 33–4, 56, 63, 63 n.12,
    138, 138 n.15, 140, 142, 152 n.4
McCaffery, Larry
    [1993] 2012 interview
    with DF Wallace 14–16, 19, 27 n.5,
        28–9, 33–4, 65, 67, 71, 76, 135,
        142, 150
McNally Editions 63
Metafiction 3, 32, 46, 48, 52, 55, 71, 76,
    118, 131, 135, 145, 150
Metamodernism 19, 119, 121, 121 n.11
    Dumitrescu, Alexandra 120
    Vermeulen, Timotheus & van den
        Akker, Robin 120
Metaxy 86, 119–20
    Weil's metaxu 119
Metonym 2, 6 n.10, 88, 117–18, 124, 151
Middle 30
    in A Thousand Plateaus 27, 45–7, 96,
        96 n.4
    in Sarraute 48
    in TPK 55, 59, 134–5
    in Wittgenstein's *Tractatus* 56
    in Levé 57
    in Stein 85
    in Woolf 46
    middle-class 109
'Modernisms continuum' 1, 5, 5 n.8, 6, 12,
    30, 42, 54, 112, 118, 122 n.16,
    147–8, 151
Molecular (*in D&G and not*) 3, 27, 46–7,
    105–6
    see also becoming-molecular
    molecular hijack 3 n.5, 46
    molecular woman 3 n.5, 46
Monologic 106
    in Bakhtin 30, 94, 132
    in Wallace 32, 133–4
    monologism 30, 30 n.8, n.10
    in Hering 32
Moral 17, 23, 24 n.2, 29, 43, 52, 78–80, 81,
    125, 150
    morality 15, 24, 79, 80
    morally 16, 80–1
Moraru, Christian 121

Nelson, Maggie 5 n.9, 30, 81, 87
    The Argonauts 115–17, 151
    Bluets 66

    see also Silverblatt (interview)
    in Sulak & Kolosov 66
Neoliberalism 15, 16, 18
Neurodiversity 67–8
Non-telic 52, 52 n.6

Other (*the*) 4 n.6, 6 n.10, 26, 29, 47, 53,
    76–7, 78, 80–2, 85, 94–5, 97–8,
    122, 129, 133, 144, 147–9, 151
    see also becoming-other

Parataxis 5, 54–5, 57
    Paratactical 48 n.4, 53, 60–1, 72, 87, 139
Paratext 73, 75, 146
    paratextual, 7, 49, 72–3, 75–6, 117, 138
    see also footnotes
Phantom 69, 136
Pietsch, Michael 32–4, 55, 62, 74
Plot (*the*) 5, 44, 73
    in Sarraute 48
    in Wallace 32–3, 144
    in Woolf 36–7, 97
Post-Postmodernism 2, 5 n.8, 12, 17, 18,
    45, 112–13, 119
Practice 2, 5, 5 n.9, 6, 19, 25, 31, 40–1, 54,
    72, 77 n.10, 78–9, 81–3, 86, 92,
    94–5, 107, 111, 113, 116, 118,
    122 n.16, 146–8, 151–3

Redemption 23–7, 29, 33, 43, 62 n.11, 76,
    86, 107, 147–8
    apolutrosis, hilasterion, lutron 23–4
    Bloom, Harold 24
    see also Deleuze, Gilles & Guattari,
        Félix
    in TPK 28, 141–2, 145
    in Wallace 28
    in Woolf 98, 106–7
Redemptive hybridism 2, 5, 6 n.11, 62, 65
    n.2, 80, 84, 88, 112, 112 n.2, 122,
    147, 154
Rhizomatic 2, 3, 3 n.4, 4, 14 n.21, 52–4,
    93, 105–6
    rhizome 27, 96
Robbins, Amy Moorman
    American Hybrid Poetics 82–3, 85–7,
        151
'Room, in house, in neighbourhood' 5, 23,
    42, 147, 151

Sarraute, Nathalie 11, 47, 48, 48 n.4,
    49–52, 54, 150–1
  Here 52–3, 57
  The Golden Fruits 48–9, 52
  Tropisms 50, 51
  tropism (*the*) 5, 47, 54, 150
'Shared Subjectivity' 13
Silverblatt, Michael
  interview DF Wallace 17
  interview M Nelson 115–16
Sincerity 18, 19, 34 n.14, 40, 57, 120–1
  in Wallace 17, 18, 33–4, 133, 146
  single-entendre 19
Solipsism 31, 118
  in Wallace 65–6, 95, 153 n.5
Soul 13, 42, 147–8
  in TPK 135–6, 140
Space-between 6–8, 20, 30, 39 n.18,
    45 n.1, 58, 69, 70 n.7, 71–2,
    113–14, 125
  in TPK 32, 54–5, 73, 140
  in Sarraute 50, 52
  in Levé 60, 69
  in Woolf 97, 101, 149
Spirit 42, 68, 104
  Holy 23, 132 n.12
Stein, Gertrude 49, 85–6

The Pale King (characters):
  Claude Sylvanshine 124
  IRS (*the*) 7, 7 n.12, 29, 55, 59, 128, 130,
    133–6, 140–3, 145, 150
  Lane Dean 59, 140–1, 143
  Rand-Drinion 133, 143–5
  Toni Ware 95, 97, 128–9, 133, 153
  David [F.] Wallace 33, 127 n.10, 133,
    134, 143
Tillich, Paul 'Being-itself' 24, 29, 50 n.5,
    105
Truth 1, 11, 23, 30, 41, 57, 72, 80, 121, 125,
    127, 139, 149, 151
  in Wallace 18, 71, 124–5, 151
  in TPK 34, 56, 74, 75 n.8, 76, 123–4,
    128–31, 135, 143
  in Woolf 68, 98–9, 102–3, 107
  in D&G 54, 151–2
  in Nelson 116
  see also factoid

Umbilical (cord) 6 n.10, 29, 43
  in Bakhtin 30, 34
  in Wallace 31, 33, 34
  in Woolf 37
Unfinished 10, 45, 52, 61, 63–4, 75, 78
  TPK 7, 9, 33, 55, 62–3, 128, 131, 139,
    149
  in BtA 63–4, 101, 101 n.6
Unfinishedness 2, 6, 45, 58, 62, 62 n.11,
    78, 80, 151
  in TPK 5, 32–4, 46, 56, 62–3, 70 n.6,
    74–6, 124, 126, 134, 138, 143,
    149, 150
  in BtA 63–4

Vonnegut, Kurt
  Foma 127, 127 n.8
  Bokonism 127, 127 n.8
Vocational memoir 81, 130

Walwicz, Ania 114
Wittgenstein, Ludwig 8 n.14, 56, 105
  see also Family Resemblance
  in Wallace 55, 56, 65, 66
The Word 37, 39, 42
  see also Flesh (and The Word)
Woolf, Virginia (Works and characters)
  see also Atom (saturated)
  A Writer's Diary 1918–1941 8 n.16, 25,
    35–7, 68, 91, 99, 103
  Between the Acts (and BtA) 35–7, 63–4,
    101, 101 n.6, 102, 102 n.8, 103,
    106, 153
  Craftsmanship 102–3, 104 n.10
  Jacob's Room 61, 91, 93, 98 n.5
  Mrs Dalloway 36, 51–2, 59, 68–9, 92,
    95–100
    Clarissa 35, 51, 59, 69, 92–3,
      96–100
    Septimus 35, 52, 59, 93, 97–100
    human nature 98
  Orlando 35
  Modern Fiction 102–3
  The Waves (and TW) 36–7, 51, 53–4,
    93, 96–7, 103–4, 106–7, 149
  To the Lighthouse (and TtL) 9, 35, 94–5
    Lily 9, 94–5
    Mrs Ramsay 9, 52, 94–5

www.ingramcontent.com/pod-product-compliance
Lightning Source LLC
Chambersburg PA
CBHW052048300426
44117CB00012B/2031